IMAGES
of America
HARDIN COUNTY

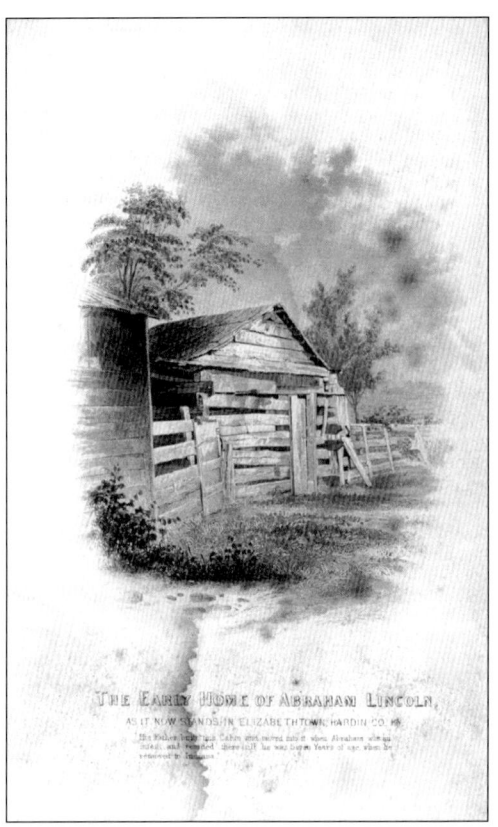

This original lithograph of Abraham Lincoln's birthplace in 1809 was used to print postcards in celebration of his 100th birthday. However, the description of Lincoln's birthplace is inaccurate. According to the Day Book from 1804 to 1806 of Bleakley and Montgomery, a merchandising store in Elizabethtown, Thomas Lincoln purchased many items while he resided in Elizabethtown, including materials for his marriage on June 12, 1806, in Washington County to Nancy Hanks. Prior to the wedding, the store employed Isaac Bush (the brother of Abraham Lincoln's stepmother, Sarah Bush Johnston) to construct a barge to carry cargo to New Orleans, and the store paid Thomas Lincoln and Isaac Bush to deliver the cargo in early 1806. After the delivery of the cargo, the partners returned to Hardin County by horseback on the Old Natchez Trace. Sarah, the sister of Abraham Lincoln, was born in 1807 to Thomas Lincoln and Nancy Hanks in Elizabethtown. The young president was born near Hodgenville, Hardin County, in 1809. Today the proposed cabin of Lincoln's birthplace is a national park near Hodgenville, Larue County. (Courtesy of Brown-Pusey House.)

ON THE COVER: Today's population of 90,000 in Hardin County has steadily increased since 1880. The county is a central location in Kentucky to meet others. The cover photograph of this book is of Ralston's Café in Elizabethtown, located across from the new Justice Center. This building was razed and is now part of the city parking lot. In the café, Annie Oldham Lawler's 54 birthday, on September 22, 1954, was well received by her family. Pictured in front, from left to right, are Marvin Hilton, Betty and Blond Gaddie, and Tom Vance. Sitting around the table are, from left to right, Pauline Hilton, holding Caroline Hilton; Hazel Lawler, holding Bonnie Greenwell; Tom Oldham; Richard Greenwell; John and Angie Oldham; Annie Oldham Lawler; Lyndell Oldham, son of John and Angie; Ruth Lawler Vance, holding Billy Jo Vance; Nellie Oldham Lodgson; and Mavona Oldham, Lyndell's wife, holding baby Oldham. Homer Lawler, Annie's husband, died in 1951. Homer lived for years in and around Millerstown and Upton. He played professional baseball in Japan. (Courtesy of Steve Gaddie and Michelle Walters.)

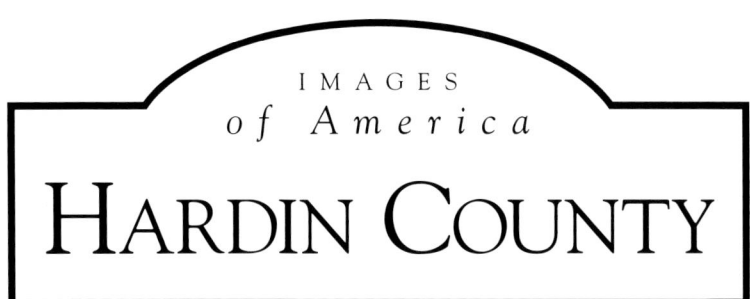

IMAGES of America
HARDIN COUNTY

Meranda L. Caswell

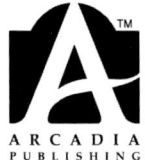

Copyright © 2006 by Meranda L. Caswell
ISBN 0-7385-4256-3

Published by Arcadia Publishing
Charleston SC, Chicago IL, Portsmouth NH, San Francisco CA

Printed in the United States of America

Library of Congress Catalog Card Number: 2005939112

For all general information contact Arcadia Publishing at:
Telephone 843-853-2070
Fax 843-853-0044
E-mail sales@arcadiapublishing.com
For customer service and orders:
Toll-Free 1-888-313-2665

Visit us on the Internet at www.arcadiapublishing.com

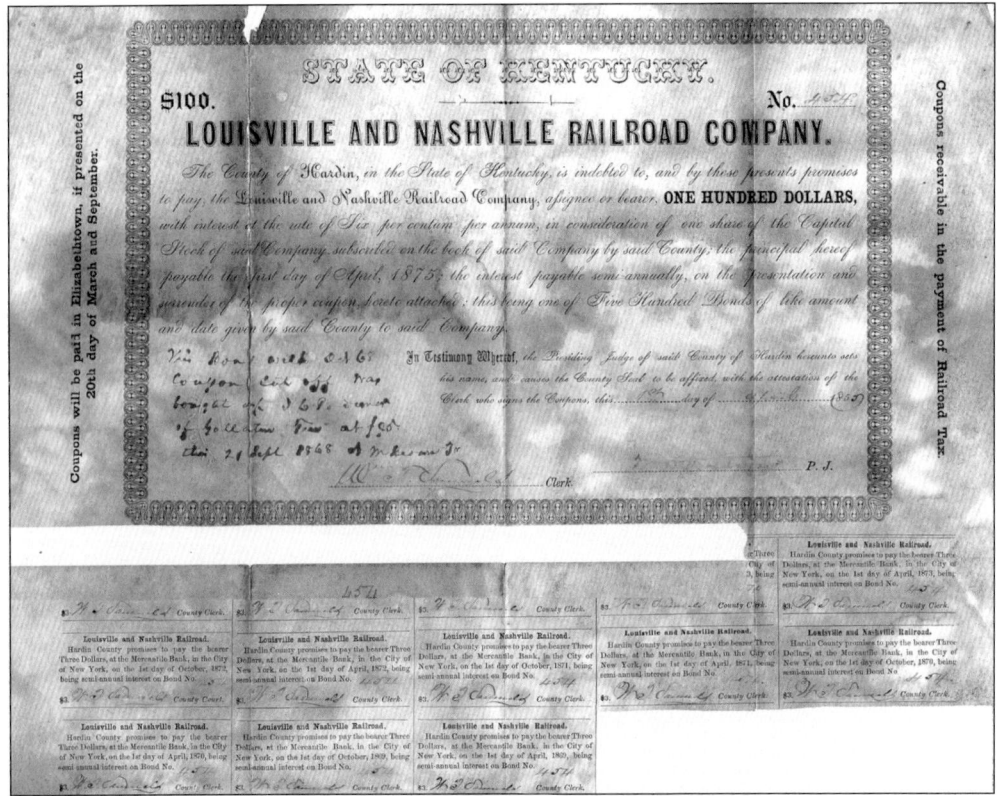

Construction of the Louisville and Nashville Railroad (L&N) developed towns along the tracks. Many of these railroad towns exist today but with smaller populations and fewer businesses. Hardin County bought stock in the L&N in 1855, which was redeemable in April 1875. Elizabethtown, the county seat, is the only progressive L&N railroad town that still exists today. Alfred Mackenzie Brown cut the coupons from this certificate in 1868 to be sold to someone in Gallatin, Tennessee. (Courtesy of Brown-Pusey House.)

CONTENTS

Acknowledgments	6
Introduction	7
1. Towns along U.S. 31 West	11
2. Lincoln Heritage	33
3. Glendale and White Mills	43
4. West of U.S. 31 West	55
5. Wars	67
6. East of U.S. 31 West	75
7. Hill's Hotel	83
8. 19th Century Scenery and People	101

Acknowledgments

The contributed photographs for this project by the Brown-Pusey House Corporation and the following individuals are greatly appreciated: Michelle Walters and Steve Gaddie, Elvin Smith Jr., Helen Glasgow, Carolyn Wimp, Millie Robinson, Pat Sadler, Dr. R. T. Clagett, Bruce Reeves, Ray Baird, Kenny Tabb, Matthew Rector, Carmel Powell, and Billie Ray Alvey.

    This book is dedicated to my brother, David, and his family; my mother; and my daughter. An affectionate dedication is to Alan Vance for his support, love, and objectivity. This special dedication is to my friend, Twylane Van Lahr, who has greatly supported me in all efforts. The overwhelming support from Carolyn Ritchie; R. R. Thomas; Kenny Tabb; Mary Jo and Jim Jones; the Garden Club of Elizabethtown; the Daughters of the American Revolution; the guests, staff, and board of the Brown-Pusey House; the members of the Hardin County Historical Society; the City of Elizabethtown; the Hardin County government; and many others, like Barbara and Harry Lee, Donna Dailey, Debbie Donnelly, and my editor, Lauren Bobier, has been warmly received. Thank you.

Knob

The small rounded knoll descends into a creek
Where the leaves and animals meet.
My brother comes jumping rock to rock
Until the entrance of a cave has him to stop.
The water streams around the rim and
Empties by the way of a linn.
Jump into the cool water and
Look inside. Fishes with one fin?
The rocks in the creek have large feet
Holes here and there.
I bet they were for grinding corn and nuts
Large limestone rocks with deep cuts.

—Meranda L. Caswell

INTRODUCTION

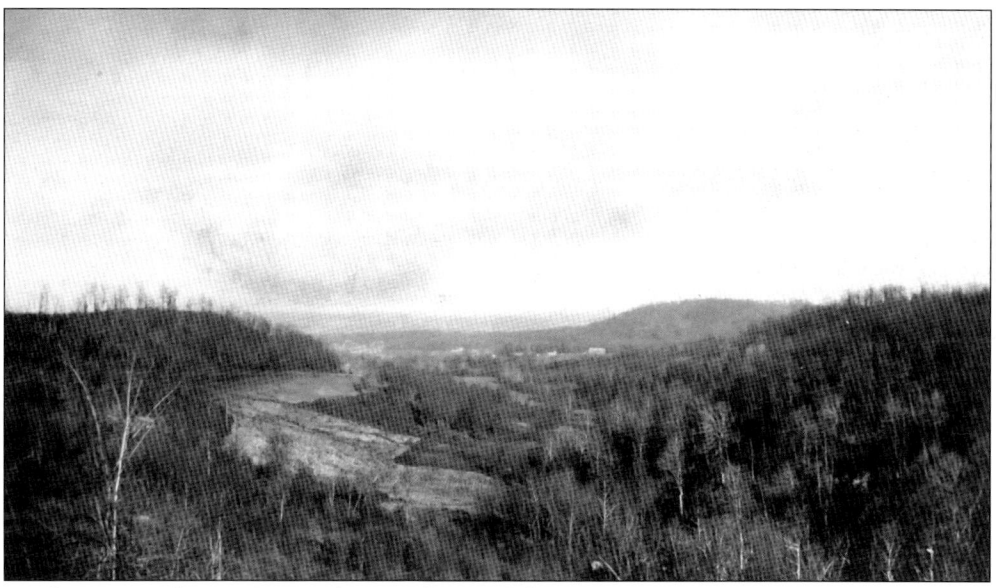

Hardin County lies in the north-central part of the Commonwealth of Kentucky. This early-20th-century view of Muldraugh's Hill, another name for the upper part of Hardin County, was similar to the view in the 18th and 19th century. The county's was created in 1792 from Nelson County and was named in honor of Col. John Hardin, who arrived in 1780 and located a considerable amount of land. The oral history passed from the early settlers of Hardin County to each generation contains information about attacks from Native Americans as well as the integration of Native Americans with the settlers. In the Elizabethtown City Cemetery is a grave site dedicated to the Native Americans of this area. However there are no official accounts in the Hardin County records about marriages to Native Americans, nor are there census, deed, tax, militia, or court records of Native Americans.

In 1923, evidence of Native Americans in Hardin County, specifically the sites in Howe's Valley and Vine Grove, was retrieved by an extensive survey of this region by Professors A. M. Miller, G. B. Roberts, W. D. Funkhouser, and W. S. Webb. Rock houses, bone awls, ground stones, arrowheads, burials, and other items were excavated during the investigations. Native Americans in this region made specialized tools for milling with distinctive individualism, probably serving a whole village living under the cliffs. Even though Willard Rouse Jillson wrote about these Native American findings of Hardin County in 1928, no reports or artifacts collected from these sites can be found today. The archival center of Elizabethtown, the Brown-Pusey House Corporation, has no artifacts collected from Hardin County in its current collection. George W. Pirtle and Raymond Miller drew a map of Hardin County for oil and gas development in December 1, 1924. This map (not included in this edition) was done for the Kentucky Geological Survey and is the first complete map of Hardin County.

The towns of Hardin County are diversified by their surroundings. Nature reserves, such as White Mills, Hardin Springs, Freeman Lake Park, the Greenbelt Trails, and Tioga Falls, offer the tourist a chance to view the natural beauty of the county. Nolin River is the waterway mentioned in the early records as Knoll Linn Creek. This misnomer, Nolin, had been carried in the records even as early as 1800. Knoll means a small hill or mound; today the word is knob. Linn means a waterfall or ravine. Usage of Nolin in early records includes George Clous in 1794, who lived on 216 acres on the south fork of Knoll Linn Creek, where his father lived in consideration of his operating gristmill and whiskey still. Josiah E. Best, of No Lynn from 1823 to 1825, gave his son, Samuel C. Best, the patent rights and profits on a Columbian steam still. Some of the original Hardin County towns are presently in other counties. Elizabethtown was laid out in 1793, and three of the original towns were Vienna, at the falls of Green River; Hardin's Station, now Hardinsburg in Breckinridge County; and Hartford, the county seat of the present county of Ohio. Hartford was established as a town in Hardin County in 1796 to 1797. Gabriel Madison and Harrison Taylor made deeds to lots to be sold in the town of Hartford.

A list of Revolutionary War soldiers and/or officers or their wives in 1840 in Hardin County includes Anthony Ament (83), Samuel Aubrey (82), Warren Cash (80), Michael Hargan (85), Thenas Hoskins (82), Patrick Marvin (82), Alex McDougle (101), John Scott (99), Joseph Smith Sr. (78), John Smoot (89), Richard Winchester (86), Susan Hardin (79), Margaret Haycraft (80), and Rebecca Vanmeter (63). Gen. Lafayette, a hero who assisted George Washington during the Revolutionary War, traveled the United States in 1824–1825 and received an invitation from the governor to visit the state of Kentucky. In May 1825, he visited Louisville and was greeted by a large celebration by Revolutionary War officers and soldiers, including the ones from Hardin County; by the local citizens; and by the city authorities. Pres. George Washington sold his land in Hardin County, presently Grayson County, for a horse. George Washington was not known to have traveled to his property prior to the transaction.

Bullitt, Breckinridge, Daviess, Edmonson, Grayson, Hart, Larue, Ohio, and Meade Counties were formed from Hardin County prior to 1843. Larue, the last to break from Hardin County in 1843, recorded its inhabitants in the 1840 Hardin County census, the 1843 to 1850 Larue County Tax Records, and the 1850 Larue County Census. Researchers travel to Hardin County every year in search of their ancestors, only to find that some of their records are actually listed in the Larue County records. The *1859–1860 Kentucky State Gazetteer* lists only the following post offices and post villages of Hardin County: Elizabethtown, Yagersville, Howell's Springs, Stephensburg, Red Hill, Otter Creek, Nolin, Cofer, Howe's Valley, and West Point. Upton is located in Hardin County, but in 1859, Upton was called Uptonville, and its post office was located in Hart County. Uptonville was a station on the L&N with T. J. Upton as postmaster and operator of a dry goods and clothing store in the 1880s. The post offices in Hardin County in 1874 are Cecilia, Dorrett's Run, East View, Elizabethtown, Franklin Cross Roads, Grand View, High Up, Howe's Valley, Nolin, Red Hill, Robertsonville, Sonora, Stephensburg, Uptonville, Vine Grove, West Point, and White Mills. By the census of 1880, Hardin County had a population of 22,500, and Elizabethtown had a population of 2,500.

The Paducah and Elizabethtown Railroad (P&E), developed in 1869, had a station at Elizabethtown with Robert Meek as the general manager in the 1880s. Samuel Thomas was the first president of this line, which was the shortest and best line to Paducah and all points in Western Kentucky and Missouri. Cecilia, six miles west of Elizabethtown, is at the junction of the P&E with the L&N and had a population of 200 in the 1880s. John Heller was a shoemaker and later a hotelkeeper in Cecilia. Another station on the P&E, East View, shipped large quantities of livestock and had a population of 50 in the 1880s. Long Grove, nine miles southwest of Elizabethtown, was on the P&E. The postmaster of this village was M. M. Kerfoot, who also operated a general store.

Gov. John L. Helm was the first president of the L&N, which was developed in 1852. During construction, many villages, towns, and stations erupted alongside the tracks. Records of the 1880s show information on the following stations. Boothe's Station had only a farmhouse, post office, and a station on the railroad 10 miles north of Elizabethtown. P. Booth was the postmaster, railroad agent, and hay dealer, and Silas French was a distiller. Nolin, a station on the railroad 10 miles south of Elizabethtown, had a flour mill that ran by water power from the Nolin River. Shipments were comprised of flour and hogs, and the village had a population of 175. J. J. Swan was the postmaster. Otter Creek had a country post office and shipped hogs, cattle, and wheat. The population was 25. V. S. Long was the postmaster and station agent. Mrs. A. F. Long was the operator of a hotel. St. John, also called Bethlehem, had a village with 50 residents in the western part of Hardin County. Its principal shipments were tobacco, wheat, and cattle. Rev. H. Mertens was the Catholic priest at Bethlehem Academy, and H. Simpson was the railroad agent and mail express agent, and he operated a general store. Stephensburg was on the Memphis branch of the L&N. Luthor Chenault was the postmaster and the liquor dealer. A. J. Ament and Company operated a general store, and the church had Rev. Fount Cundiff. Tip Top was 18 miles from Elizabethtown. W. A. McMoron was the postmaster. W. A. Melbourne was the railroad and express agent and telegraph operator, and he operated a general store. Meeting Creek had a livestock dealer, John S. Cralle and Brother, in the 1880s.

Many people know of the Emancipation Proclamation in 1863 announced by Abraham Lincoln. However, since the early 1790s, landowners of Hardin County had emancipated some of their slaves. A few men—Armistead Smith, Patrick Brown, James Edlin, John Vertrees, and Benjamin Wright—had given a deed of emancipation to their slaves. General Braddock, a former slave of Jacob Vanmeter, earned his freedom in the early 1780s. Today about seven percent of the population of Hardin County are African American.

When one researches the early history of Hardin County in the county records, one must remember that the records focus heavily on the county seat, Elizabethtown. The outlying communities were residences as well as trading facilities on the way to the market at the county seat and other meeting places. The Market House was built in the center of the Public Square, where the old courthouse is now. In the late 1830s, the Market House was 40 feet long, 16 feet wide, and built by John S. Cully. Commerce was the main reason for traveling between communities and states.

Today commerce and tourism are the main reasons to travel to Elizabethtown and Hardin County. In the early 19th century, the road people took was the Louisville and Nashville Turnpike, used primarily by stagecoaches and horses. After World War II, U.S. Highway 31 West was created, bypassing the original road or using parts of the original road. When one travels to Elizabethtown, one may bypass the historic downtown area by turning onto the newly developed Ring Road to exit onto Interstate 65. When travelling I-65, exits to towns in Hardin County are few, but they are apparent: Radcliff, Vine Grove, Elizabethtown (one exit for the historic downtown and one for Ring Road), Glendale, Sonora, and Upton. When travelling U.S. 31 West, the towns listed above are seen, as well as several others throughout this book.

The resources used for this book are primarily from the Brown-Pusey House Corporation, an archival center as well as a community center. The vision of the donors of the Brown-Pusey House Corporation included the ideas of education, recreation, and a meeting place to develop one's curiosity, human fellowship, and culture. The building itself contained the first private yet public library in Hardin County in 1923. The library was filled with magazines that ranged from educational journals, parenting guides, and gardening guides, to various types of non-fiction and fiction books until 1960. Then the library was moved to the Morris Building, adjacent to the Brown-Pusey House, until 1967. The library that is located in one room of the Brown-Pusey House Corporation developed, with the assistance of the Hardin County Historical Society and the Daughters of the American Revolution, into a genealogy library and continues today as a genealogy and history library.

The photographs for this book are primarily from the archives in the Pusey Room Museum of the Brown-Pusey House Corporation. These archives are located in a fireproof room adjacent to the genealogy library room. The gathering of these archives began with Dr. William Allen Pusey, an educated and prolific author who was clearly ahead of his time. After he died in 1940, his wife, Sallie Warfield Cunningham Pusey, continued his gathering of materials until her death in 1950. Lena Johnson, the secretary of the Brown-Pusey House Corporation and Sallie's second cousin, continued the legacy until 1959, when she retired. Two organizations—the Hardin County Historical Society Incorporated and the local Jacob Vanmeter chapter of the Daughters of the Confederacy—continued the archival legacy of the Pusey brothers. The archives in this room range from the 1780s to the present, but mostly cover the 1780s to 1940. The Hardin County clerk's office and other organizations and individuals donated microfilm of Hardin County records to the Brown-Pusey House Corporation. The original tax record books from 1795 to 1875 have been misplaced and not found; however, microfilm copies exist at the Brown-Pusey House Corporation and the Elizabethtown Community Technical College. These tax records from 1803 to 1816 contain the proof that Thomas Lincoln, the father of Pres. Abraham Lincoln, was over 21 years of age and a citizen with 200 to 238 acres of land in the Mill Creek Community of Hardin County. The Hardin County Deed Book B, page 253, records the proof of this purchase as well. In the Hardin County marriage book, Thomas Lincoln married Sarah Bush Johnston in Elizabethtown in 1819. Another vital primary source of Thomas Lincoln is the Bleakley and Montgomery store records from 1804 to 1809, on microfilm at the Brown-Pusey House Corporation.

One may ask, "Why should I be concerned with the Brown-Pusey House Corporation? What does it offer to the community, the public, and the world?" The early local history (1780–1850) of the central region of Kentucky is housed in this building. The Brown-Pusey House Corporation is an excellent reserve for archives on local history and genealogy material. Much of the archives had belonged to the Brown, Pusey, and Cunningham families. Many individuals and a few organizations had donated their original records, photographs, genealogy files, magazines, books, local historical items, and insight to the Brown-Pusey House Corporation to be preserved for later generations. This building is recognized in the community as a community center. The main purpose of this building was to educate and inspire the community as well as the tourists to advance their education, curiosity, fellowship, and talents. Do not dismiss this building as *only* a recreation facility; this building provides more than a place to meet and socialize with your fellow man. The Brown-Pusey House Corporation is an outstanding archival facility and genealogy library that needs financial support from the community and the nation. Please send monetary donations as well as Hardin County documents and family information to Brown-Pusey House Corporation, 128 North Main Street, Elizabethtown, Kentucky, 42701, or call (270) 765-2515 for more information about the Brown-Pusey House Corporation.

The compiled history of Hardin County can be purchased from the Hardin County Historical Society. A growing facility of local historical items is the Hardin County History Museum. The actual documents of Hardin County may be viewed at the Brown-Pusey House Corporation and the Hardin County Clerk's Office. One may contact Meranda L. Caswell for a fee-based research on genealogy and history of Hardin County (1780–present) at P. O. Box 452, Elizabethtown, Kentucky, 42702.

Enjoy the never-before-seen photographs of Hardin County and much unpublished archival information gathered in this book. Minor mistakes may occur in this edition; however, research is an ongoing search for knowledge and to prove or disprove theories.

One
Towns along U.S. 31 West

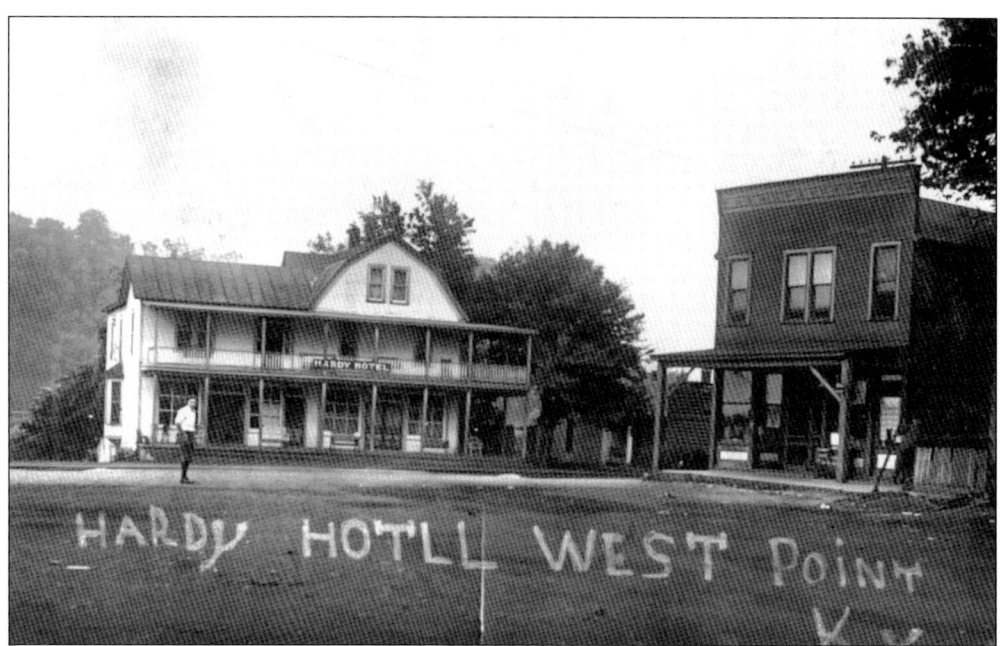

Hardy Hotel, pictured, was located in West Point. John Shields, the blacksmith on the Lewis and Clark expedition in 1802, built the first cabin in West Point in 1798 at the mouth of the Ohio and Salt Rivers. James Young used slave labor to build several buildings in West Point. The Guthrie brothers operated the Ditto House as a boardinghouse and bank in 1850. (Courtesy of Carolyn Wimp.)

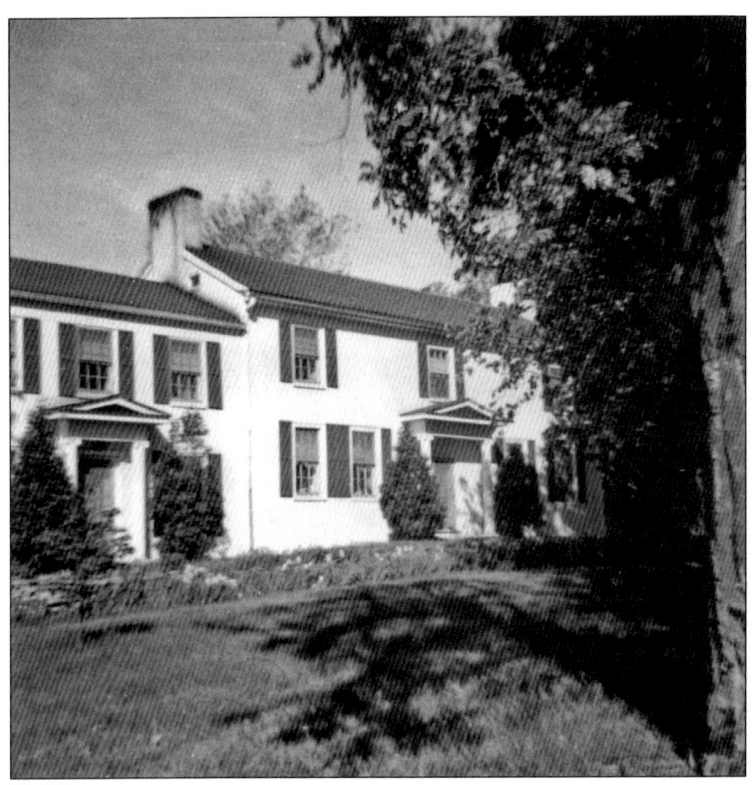

Haycraft Inn, pictured, was built about 1814 and is located nine miles north of Elizabethtown in Radcliff on Old U.S. 31 West, now Kentucky 447. Owned by D. C. Haycraft, it served as a hotel and stagecoach stop. Radcliff, organized as a town in the 1950s after the Fort Knox establishment, has a current population of about 21,000, the second largest town in Hardin County. (Courtesy of Brown-Pusey House.)

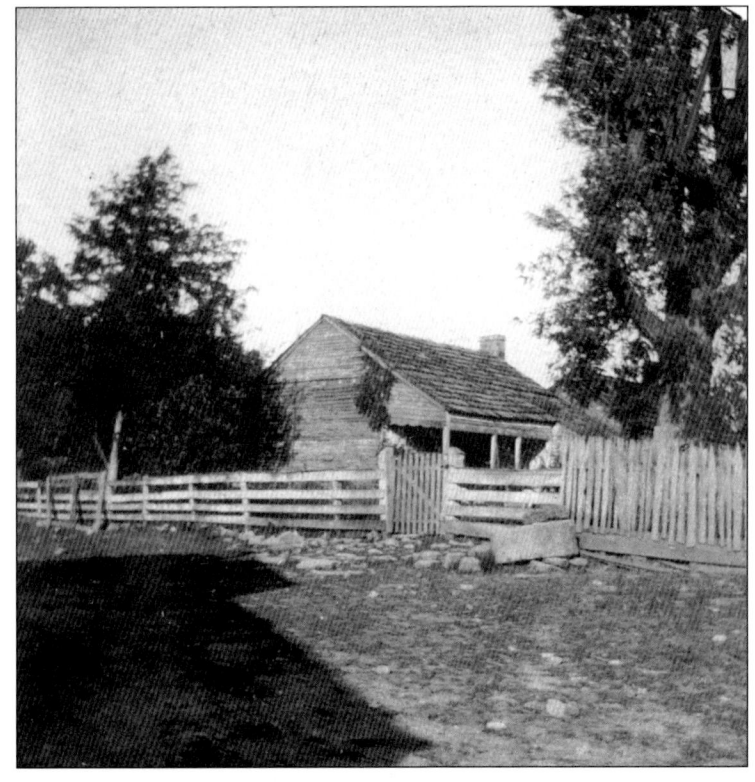

Meade County separated from Hardin County in 1824. Garnettsville is a town of Meade County. Pictured is a house that once belonged to Joel and Anne Roup Pusey after their emigration from Maryland to Garnettsville, Hardin County, Kentucky, in 1822. Joel and Anne, whose ancestors were originally Quakers from Pennsylvania, had 10 children. This area has belonged to the Fort Knox Reservation since 1943. (Courtesy of Brown-Pusey House.)

Dr. Henry Kinger Pusey, the son of Joel and Anne Pusey, had studied and practiced medicine in Garnettsville in the 1880s and was later the superintendent of the Central Asylum at Anchorage. His son, Dr. Henry M. Pusey, pictured, practiced medicine in Louisville, Kentucky. (Courtesy of Brown-Pusey House.)

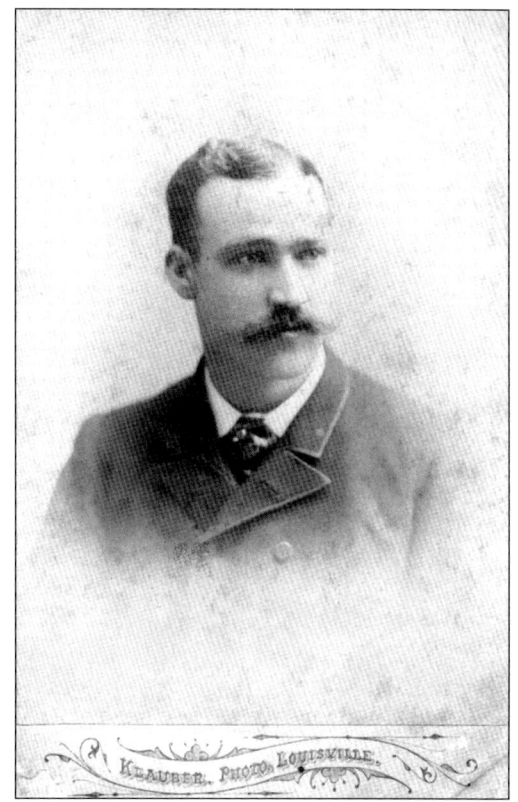

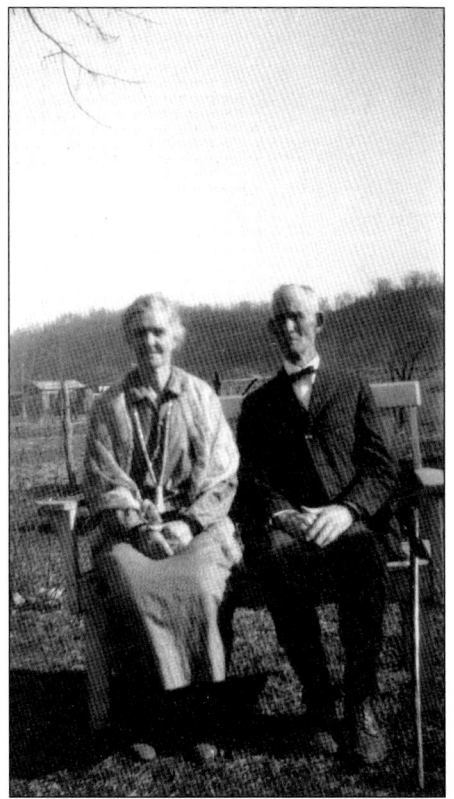

George H. Pusey is pictured with Annie, his wife. George was the son of William Pusey, who was one of the three sons of Joel and Anne Pusey, who immigrated to Kentucky. The Puseys were Quakers who came to America with William Penn. A picture of the Pusey watering horn from the 17th century is located at the Brown-Pusey House in Elizabethtown. (Courtesy of Brown-Pusey House.)

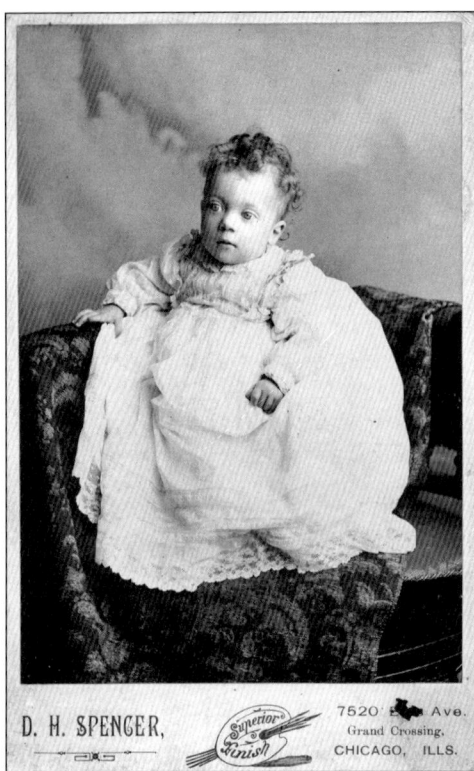

Pictured is Dr. Frank G. Pusey, who practiced in Vine Grove in the 1880s and died early. He was the brother of Charles M. Pusey, who practiced in Chicago, Illinois. These were the sons of Evan Pusey. When the Pusey family immigrated to Kentucky, Joel and Anne brought their three sons, Evan, William, and George. (Courtesy of Brown-Pusey House.)

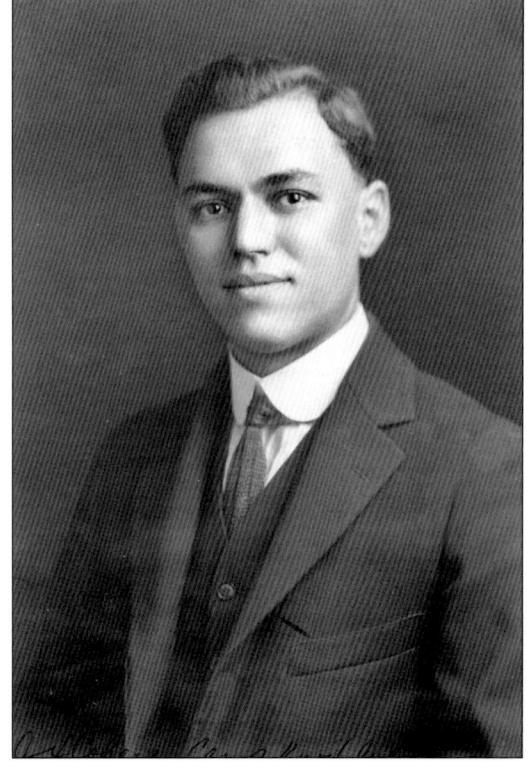

Pictured is J. H. Cohen, who was at Camp Knox, Kentucky, on July 2, 1919. There were two locations called Camp Knox, Kentucky. One was located in Hardin County, where the town of Stithton was until 1917. It was called Camp Henry Knox National Forest until the 1930s. It is currently the Fort Knox Military Reservation. A monument unveiled by Gov. Keen Johnson on September 27, 1942, marks the location of the other Camp Knox, which was settled in 1770 by Col. James Knox on the county line between Greensburg and Columbia. (Courtesy of Brown-Pusey House.)

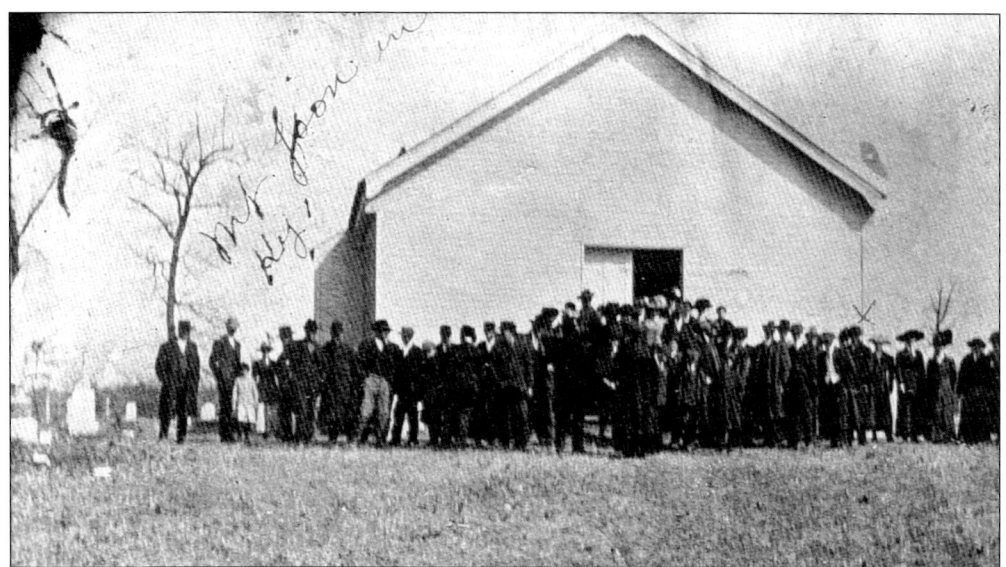

Mount Zion Baptist Church, pictured in 1838, is located in Elizabethtown south of Radcliff and Long View off of U.S. 31 West. Mill Creek runs behind the church. The X is either Josiah or Margaret Berry. In the 1880s, James A. McKenzie, from Long View, was a member of Congress. A. L. Carter and M. Radford were two livestock dealers in Long View. The former town currently has three businesses and several residents, but the postal address is Elizabethtown. (Courtesy of Brown-Pusey House.)

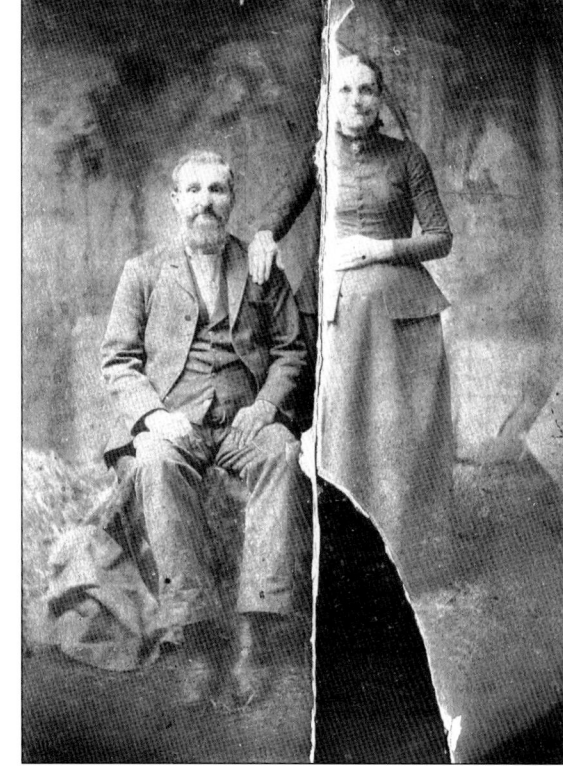

Josiah and Margaret Burchman Berry of Elizabethtown attended Mount Zion Baptist Church in the 19th century. The grandparents of Pres. Abraham Lincoln were Abraham and Bathsheba Lincoln; their youngest child, Nancy Ann Lincoln, married William Brumfield. The Brumfields owned the Mill Creek farm at one time. The Brumfields are related to the Berry family. (Courtesy of Brown-Pusey House.)

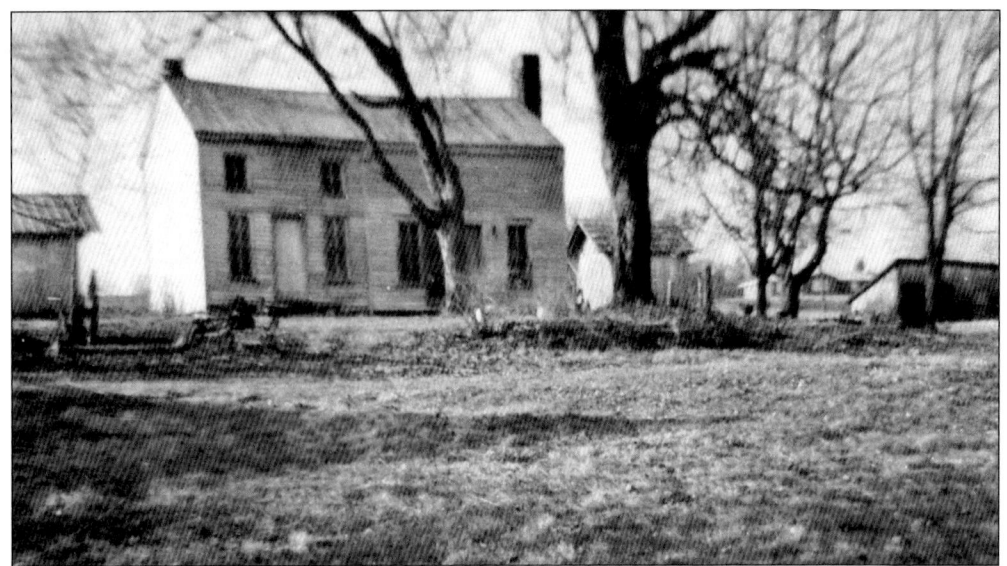

Pictured is the Cofer House, which was once located three miles north of Elizabethtown and a half-mile west of Old U.S. 31 West. Martin Hardin Cofer was the son of Thomas Cofer and Mary Hardin, a daughter of Martin Hardin, who was the brother of Col. John Hardin, for whom Hardin County was named. From 1859 to 1881, Hardin County had a post office located in the village Cofer, which was located 72 miles southwest of Frankfort. (Courtesy of Brown-Pusey House.)

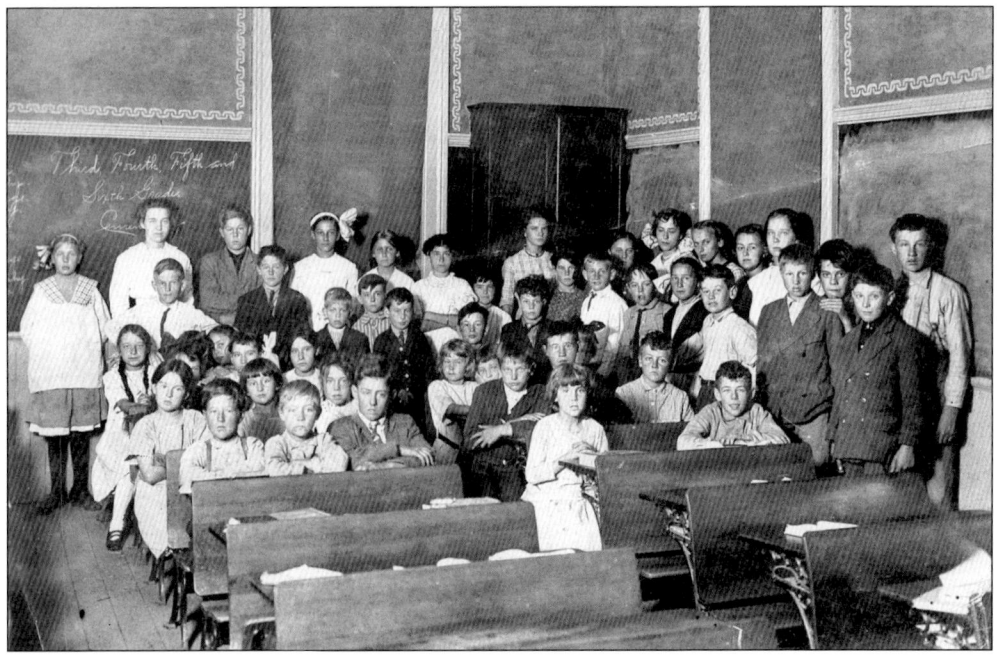

One-room schoolhouses were numerous in Hardin County until World War I. Pictured are unidentified children inside a one-room schoolhouse during the late 19th century or early 20th century in Elizabethtown. The restored 1892 one-room Summit schoolhouse is located in Freeman Lake Park of Elizabethtown. Public education was implemented in the county about 1840, and Alfred Mackenzie Brown was the first superintendent of public education. (Courtesy of Carolyn Wimp.)

Pictured is the First Presbyterian Church, located in Elizabethtown during the early 20th century. Helping Hand operates from this location today. To the left of the First Presbyterian Church, from the late 19th century until the 1950s, was the Elizabethtown Public School. To the right of the church was once the Ethan Allen Gallery furniture store owned by the Brandenburg family. This building burned to the ground on May 15, 1991. (Courtesy of Elvin Smith Jr.)

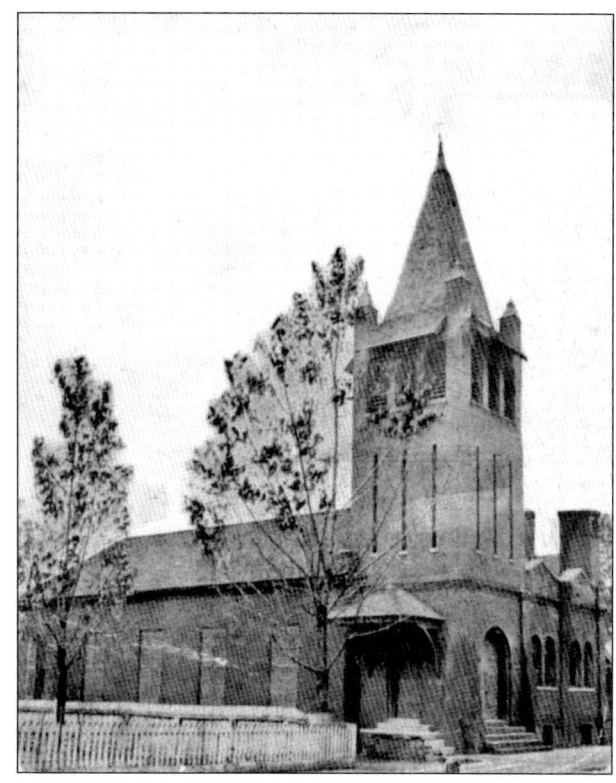

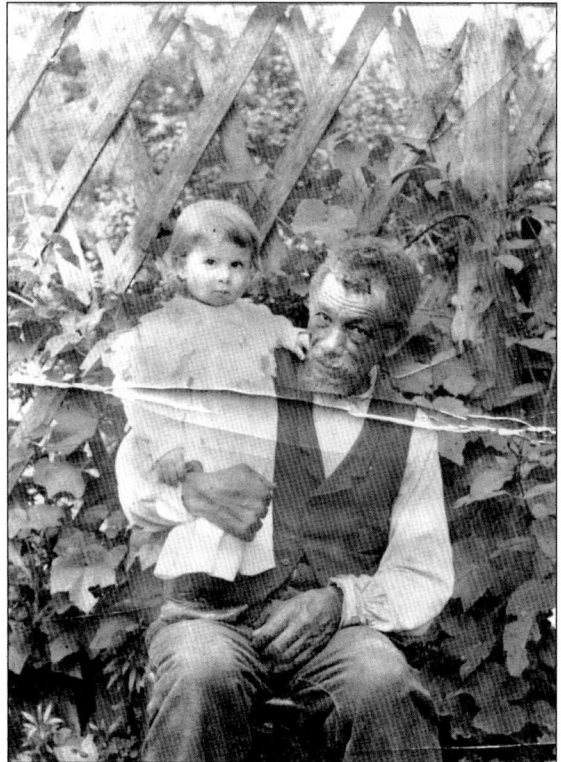

Henry Taylor, a former slave, was the gardener for Dr. Elisha Warfield. Henry, beloved by the children who visited the garden, is sitting with Charles Young, a son of Henry Young, in the Warfield Vineyard in 1896. The Middleton family built a house on the east side of Maple Street in 1869, opposite of Dr. Warfield's grape arbor. The Middletons attended the First Presbyterian Church. (Courtesy of Brown-Pusey House.)

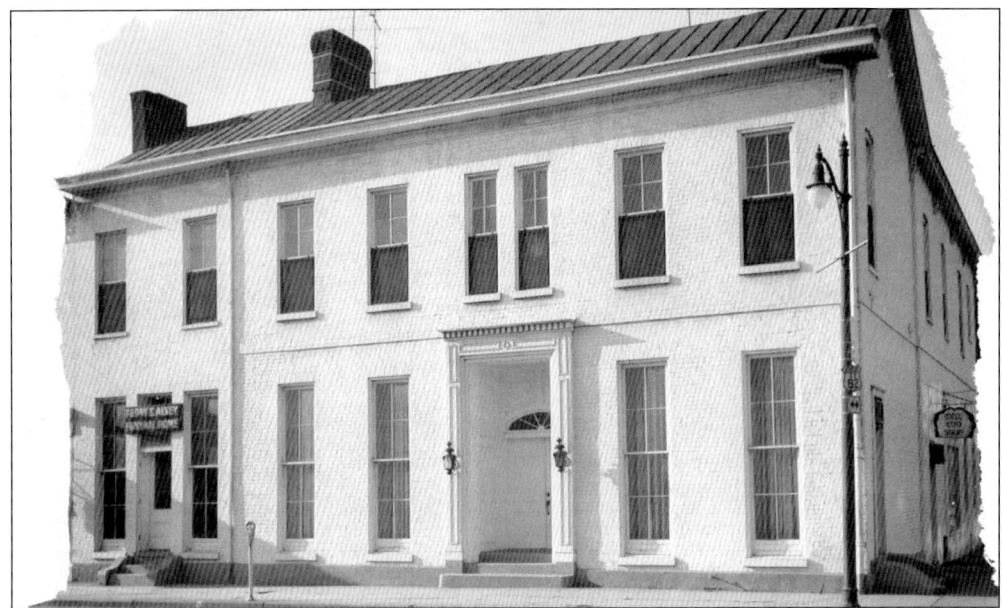

Pictured is the Perry and Alvey Funeral Home building, located on the corner of U.S. 31 West and South Mulberry Street in Elizabethtown. In the 1920s, this site was J. R. Wilson Restaurant, which sold regular meals, ice cream, and tobacco products. Prior to 1963, the Mill End Shop and the Alvey-Hays Youth Store were located on the side facing Mulberry Street. Fritz Raubold's candy shop, a fairyland for children, was located adjacent to this building on U.S. 31 West. The windows were filled with fish- and heart-shaped candy, small sets of dishes, and tiny doll buggies. (Courtesy of Bruce Reeves.)

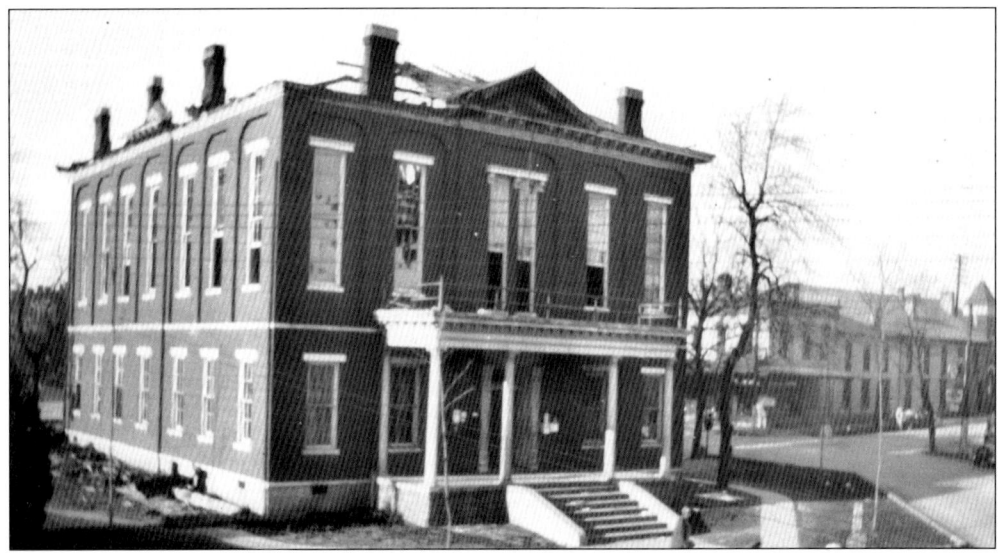

Hardin County has one courthouse, located in Elizabethtown, the county seat. The courthouse pictured was built in 1872 and burned in 1932. The courthouse from the early 19th century to 1872 was located to the side of the Public Square in front of the Old Vault Deli, and the center of the square contained a market house and a throughway for the roads. A current example of this 19th-century layout is in Greensburg, where the oldest courthouse in Kentucky is located. (Courtesy of Brown-Pusey House.)

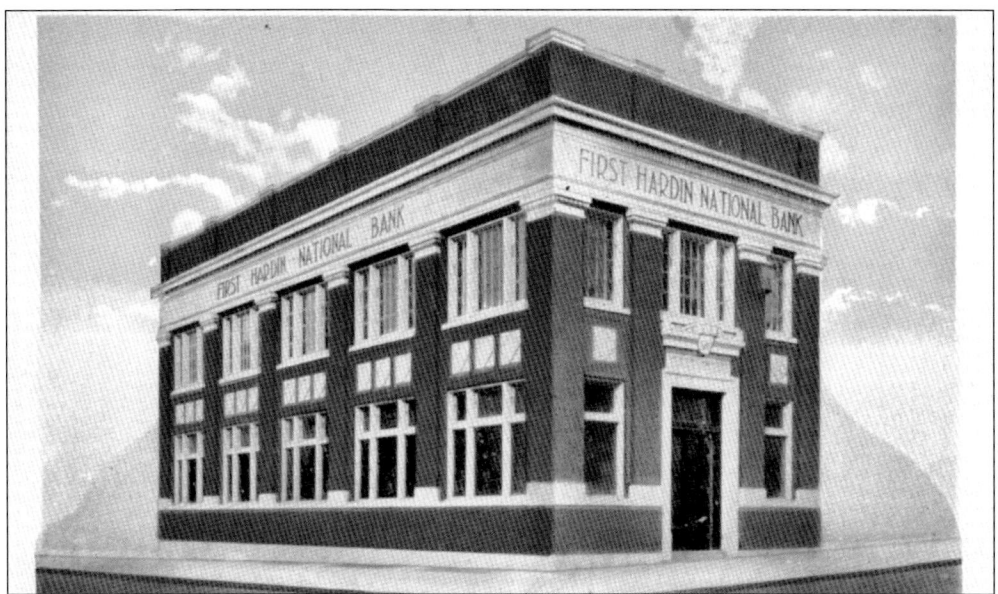

On July 1, 1911, Hardin National Bank and First National Bank consolidated to become First Hardin National Bank, pictured. This building, constructed in 1922, is located in Elizabethtown at 102 West Dixie Avenue, at the corner of West Dixie Avenue and Public Square. The president of the bank was W. C. Montgomery; Horace Hays was the head cashier, and Starling Wells, W. H. Robertson, and G. E. Taber were assistant cashiers. The bank has been called PNC Bank since 1994–1995. (Courtesy of Meranda Caswell.)

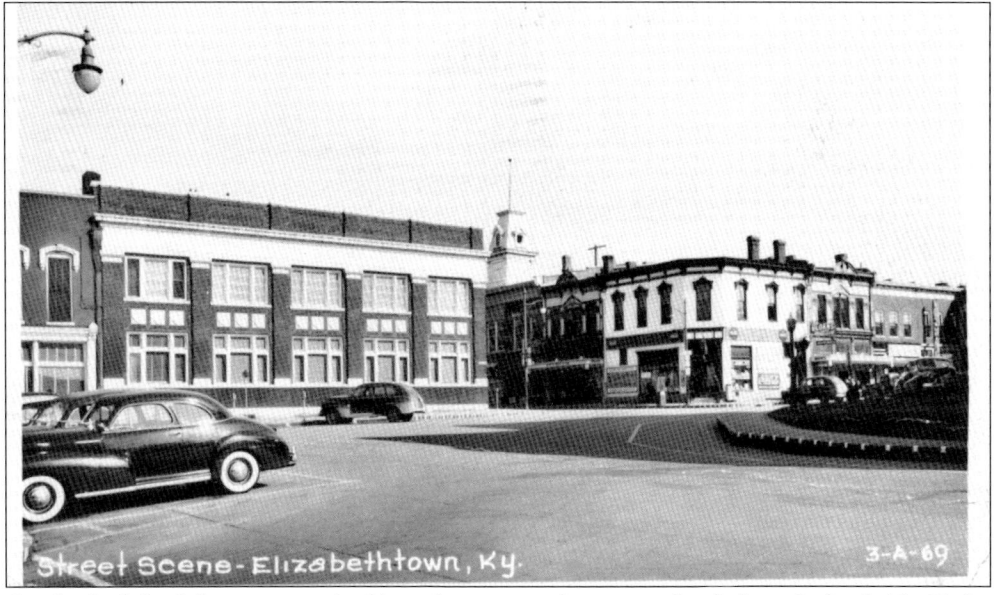

On the far left of the street is a building that was used once as a bank, heavily funded by Philip Arnold prior to 1872. Today this building retains the vault from the bank and is the Old Vault Deli. Adjacent to this building on the corner is the First Hardin National Bank building. Across the street on the right is the Marshall Jewelers building, an L-shaped building that wraps around the corner, which is First Hardin National Bank's former site. Ernest Kelly and J. M. Smith had opened the Model Drug Store in this building. (Courtesy of Carolyn Wimp.)

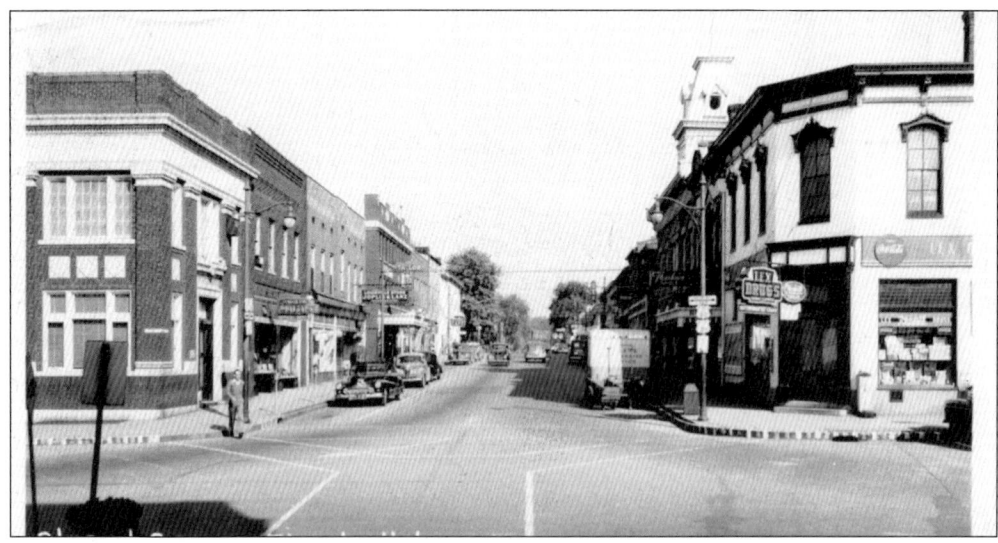

This street scene of U.S. 31 West includes the Taylor Hotel, previously the Watkins and Company site, and the State Theater. On the corner of U.S. 31 West and North Mulberry Street is the post office building built in the 1930s. A. Heady Jenkins was postmaster from 1942 to 1965 and had been actively associated with the Elizabethtown Post Office for more than 50 years. Reba Mae Richardson Terry succeeded Jenkins as postmaster in 1965. This building was the Hardin County Free Public Library from 1967 until 2001 and today is the Hardin County History Museum. (Courtesy of Carolyn Wimp.)

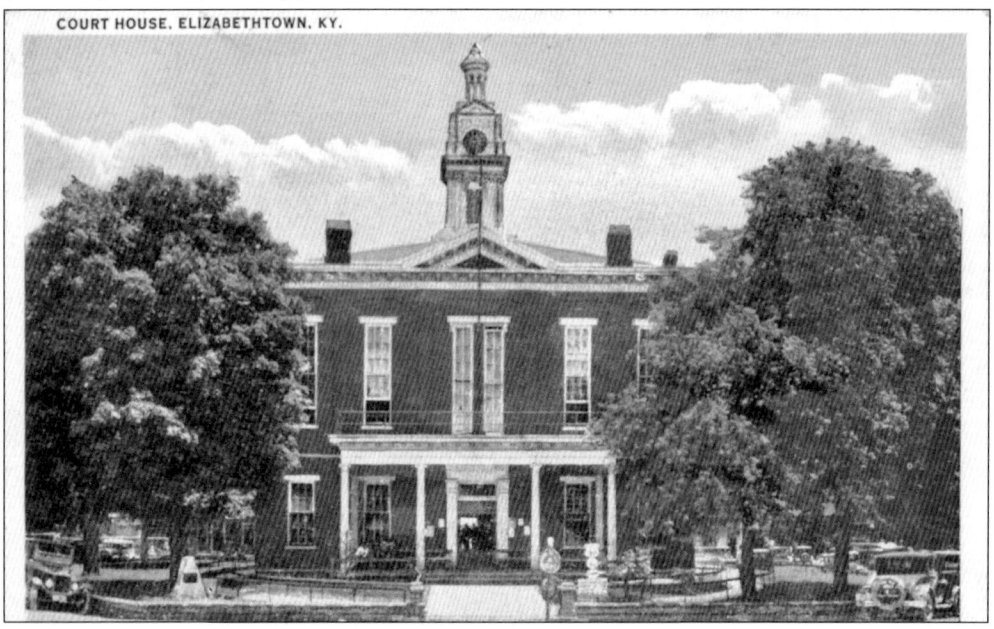

This postcard view of the courthouse in Elizabethtown is from between 1922 and 1932. Notice the limestone obelisk commemorating the family heritage of Pres. Abraham Lincoln. Bleakley and Montgomery, a merchandising store since 1801, was located on the Public Square. Thomas Lincoln purchased the following items from the store in 1804 and 1805: casteel saw, plane bit, file, auger, foot adze, hat, one pair of suspenders, and materials for groom attire to marry Nancy Hanks. (Courtesy of Elvin Smith Jr.)

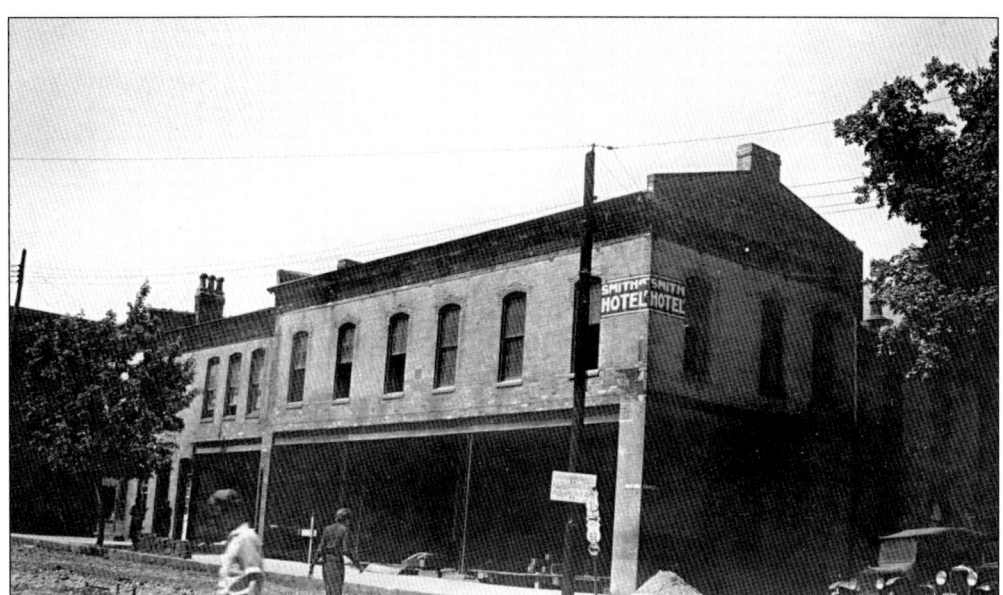

Doctors William Allen Pusey and Alfred Brown Pusey bought the Smith Hotel, pictured, and remodeled it. Jenny Lind spent the night in the Eagle Hotel (later called Smith Hotel) in 1851. At that time, the courthouse was not in the center of the Public Square; in front of this hotel was situated the area for market day, which could accommodate hundreds of people. When the townspeople asked Jenny Lind to sing, she sang on the front steps of the Hill's Hotel on North Main Street, one block from the Eagle Hotel. (Courtesy of Brown-Pusey House.)

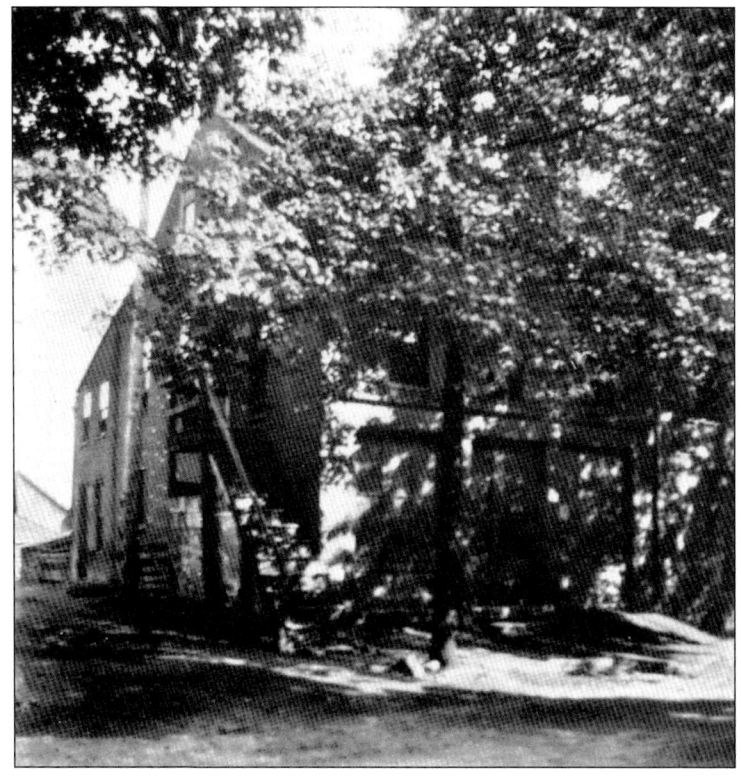

This building was near the corner of North Main Street and the Public Square, across from the Smith Hotel. In 1871, Mr. Middleton operated a grocery store in this building; the lower floor of the house was being used as a butcher shop and the upper floor for the law offices of Murray and Brown. Additions were made to the front of this building, and today it is the Hardin County Clerk's office. (Courtesy of Brown-Pusey House.)

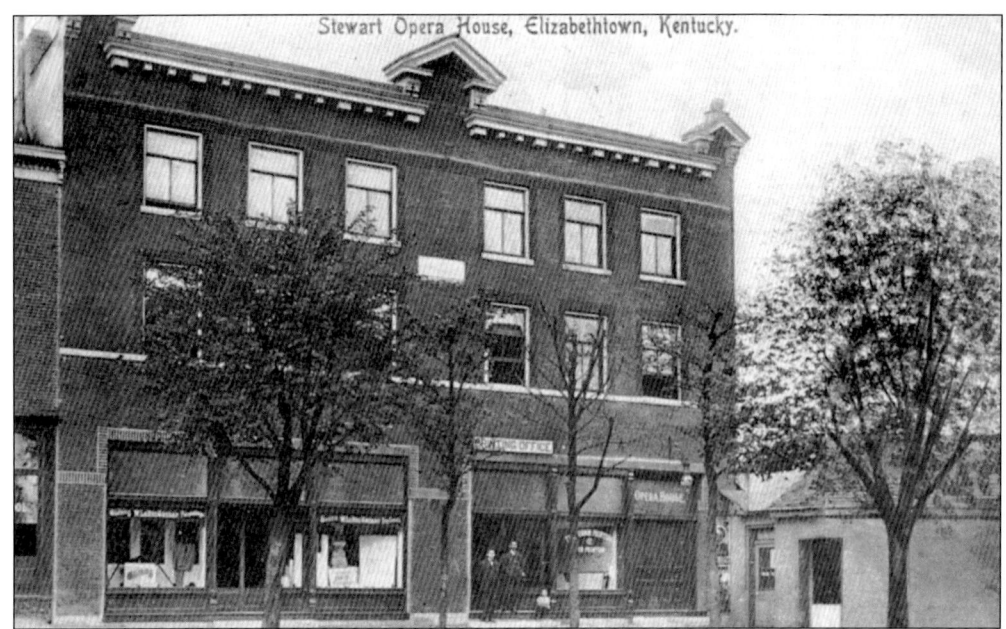

J. W. Stewart operated the Stewart Opera House in Elizabethtown about 1908. Today this building is attached to the old Middleton grocery store as part of the Hardin County Clerk's office. This building had been renamed the R. R. Thomas Government Building. Thomas had been the county clerk of Hardin County for about 15 years before he became the Hardin County judge executive. (Courtesy of Elvin Smith Jr.)

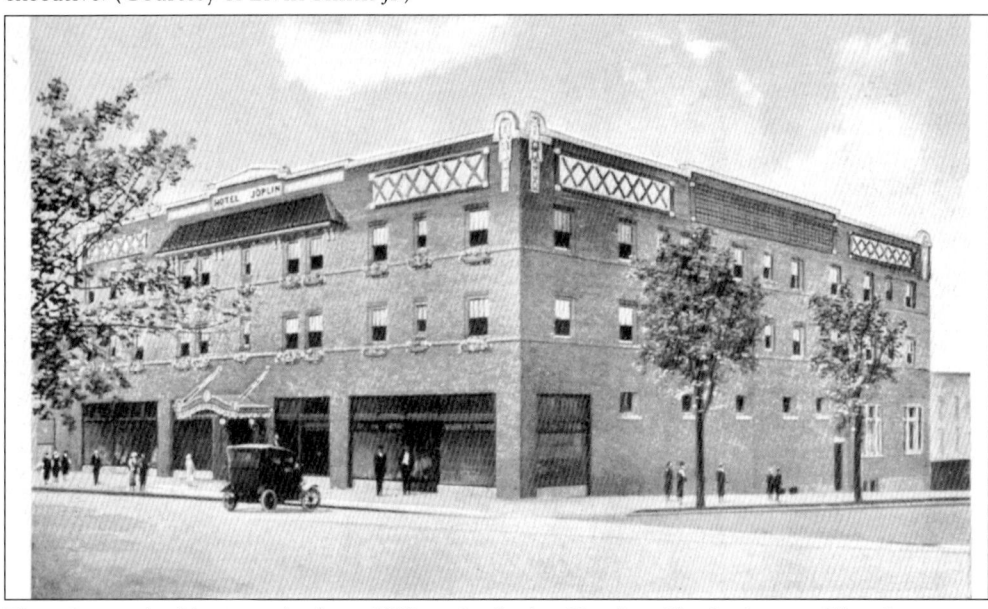

This massive building was built in 1922 as the Joplin Hotel in Elizabethtown. The three-story hotel was built of pressed brick. The Jenkins-Essex Planing Mill supplied all the millwork for this hotel, erected at a cost of $75,000. The mill, which became the Jenkins-Essex Company in the 1920s, maintained a lumberyard in Elizabethtown and two hardware stores, one in Glendale and one in Vine Grove, in the 1920s. This building can be seen today in the movie *Elizabethtown*, by Cameron Crowe. (Courtesy of Meranda Caswell.)

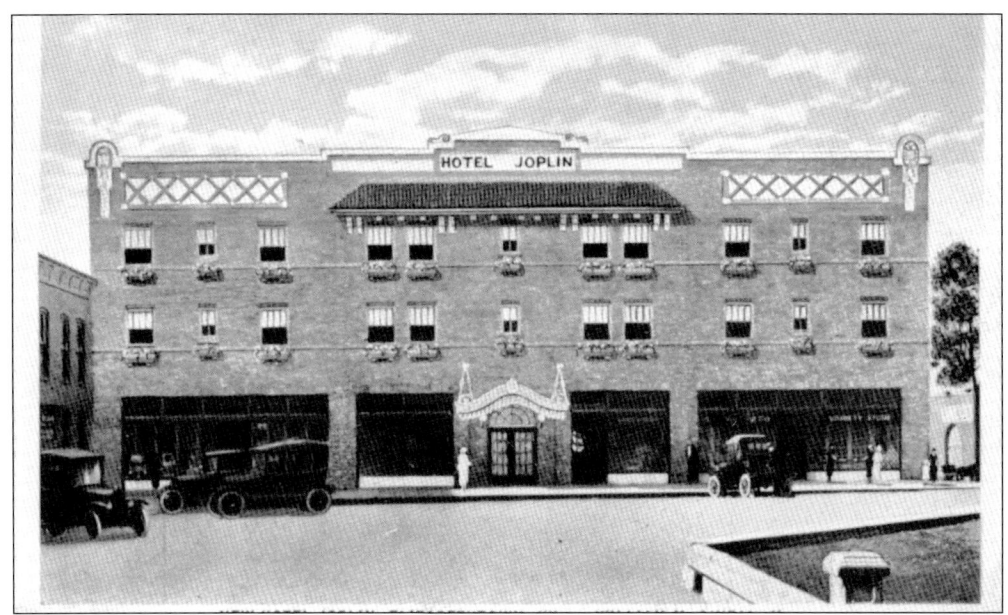

From the 1880s to the late 1920s, election day was full of excitement. Farmers would back their wagonloads of watermelons against the courthouse curb, and melon lovers would swarm around the wagons until the day was over, throwing the rinds in the gutter, where the hogs could finish them. The guests of the Joplin Hotel would witness events such as these after 1922. (Courtesy of Elvin Smith Jr.)

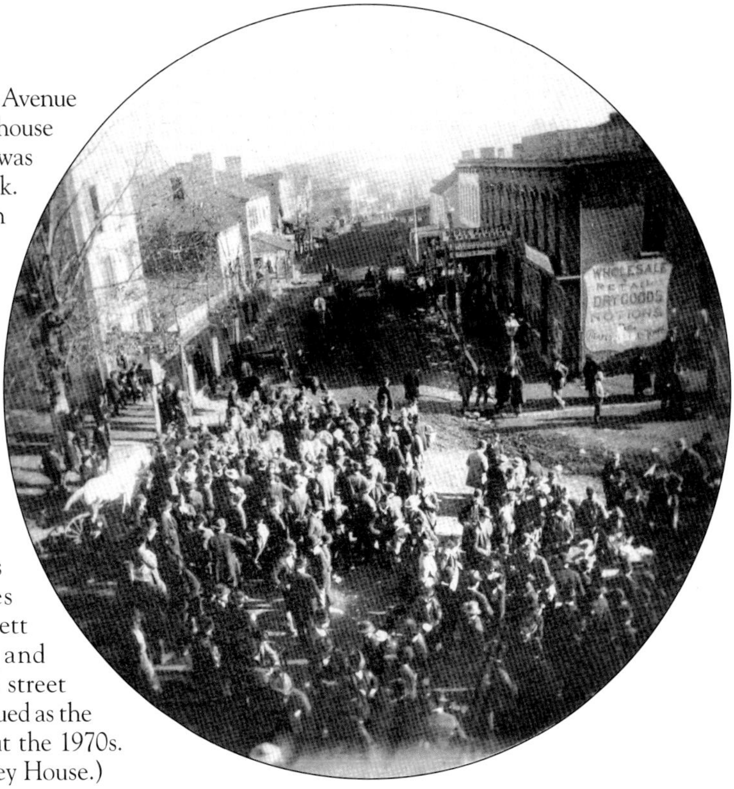

Elizabethtown's East Dixie Avenue is pictured from the courthouse in the 1880s. The bridge was over Severns Valley Creek. Most of the buildings on this street up to the bridge were built after 1900. In the 1930s, the following businesses were on this street: Shower and Hayes Drug Store, Larue Cofer Coal Company, Elizabethtown Feed and Coal Company, R. M. Phillips Jewelers, Rogers Meat Market, Walters Coal Company, Hayes Coffee Company, Corbett Hardware Company, and more. This commercial street and Public Square continued as the shopping hub until about the 1970s. (Courtesy of Brown-Pusey House.)

In the 1880s and 1890s, the corner of the Public Square that faces East Dixie Avenue in Elizabethtown accommodated hundreds of people as a marketplace and a place to deliver speeches. The Elizabethtown Canning Company was located across from the Elizabethtown City Cemetery from 1869 to 1893, when canning prices dropped and the company went out of business. George Lemmon was the first supervisor, and in 1889, C. L. Barnes was the next supervisor. (Courtesy of Brown-Pusey House.)

Pictured is the view from East Dixie Avenue looking at the Hardin County Courthouse in the 1880s. Two children, Margaret and Emma Middleton, who were sleeping in their room overlooking the courthouse yard on a moonlit night, witnessed a mob take an African American man from the county jail to the north side of the courthouse, where they lifted him onto horseback. He was driven out of town and hung. (Courtesy of Brown-Pusey House.)

Pictured is the Hardin County Courthouse in Elizabethtown about 1906. A clock with four dials faced four different streets. It was installed in the tower of the courthouse in 1907. Electric lights were strung behind the faces to make the eight-inch numerals more prominent. The courthouse burned about noon on December 5, 1932. All records were saved except some stored upstairs. The fire caught in the attic, and the first flames were seen from the clock. Mary Lasley's house and the two houses opposite the Goldnamers' residence caught on fire too. (Courtesy of Brown-Pusey House.)

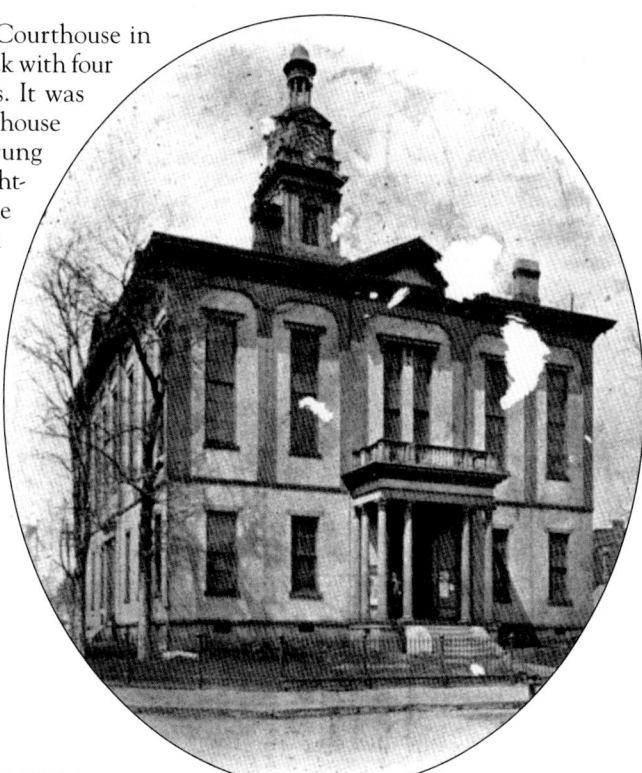

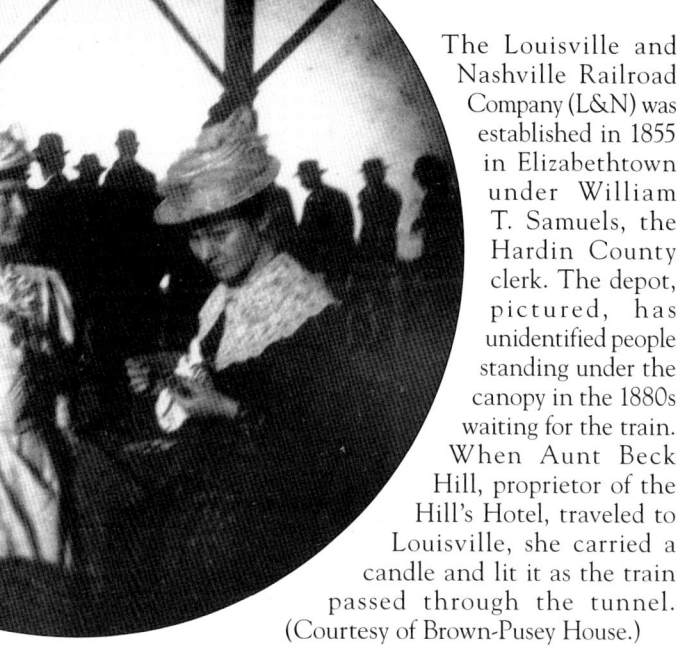

The Louisville and Nashville Railroad Company (L&N) was established in 1855 in Elizabethtown under William T. Samuels, the Hardin County clerk. The depot, pictured, has unidentified people standing under the canopy in the 1880s waiting for the train. When Aunt Beck Hill, proprietor of the Hill's Hotel, traveled to Louisville, she carried a candle and lit it as the train passed through the tunnel. (Courtesy of Brown-Pusey House.)

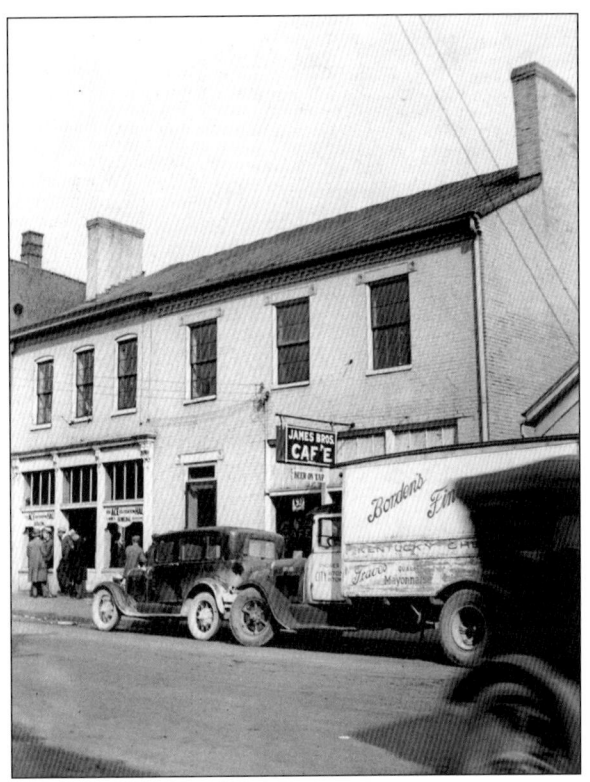

The businesses of James Brothers Café and Ace Recreation Hall were located at 117 and 123 East Dixie Avenue about 1933. Pictured is the Bordens Fine Food delivery truck in front of the café. J. R. Mock had a photography gallery on East Dixie Avenue next door to Henrich Goranflo's Shoe Shop and over S. H. Bush's law office in the 1860s and 1870s. (Courtesy of Brown-Pusey House.)

Pictured from left to right are Ace Recreation Hall, James Brothers Café, a doctor's office, and Corley's Billiards in the 1930s. The building next to Corley's Billiards is the former Herb Jones Auto Sales building. In the 1920s, it was the Keith Monument Works and the Woodard and Brown Garage. (Courtesy of Brown-Pusey House.)

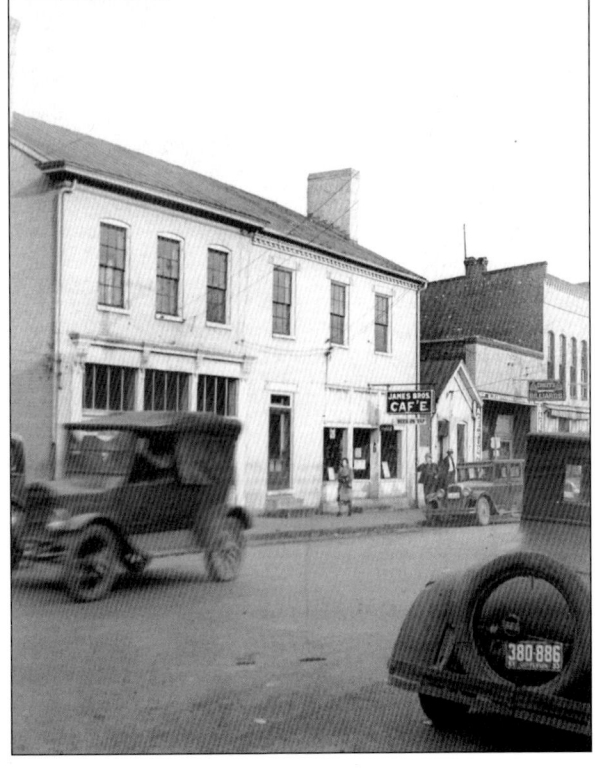

The horse and buggy is in front of the middle building, Dr. Pusey's office, with the Stith House to the left and Henrich Goranflo's Shoe Shop on the right side during the 1880s. This photograph was taken with the first Kodak camera purchased by Dr. William Allen Pusey. William, the son of Dr. Robert Burns Pusey, practiced medicine in his father's office for one year, from 1889 to 1890, after the death of his father. (Courtesy of Brown-Pusey House.)

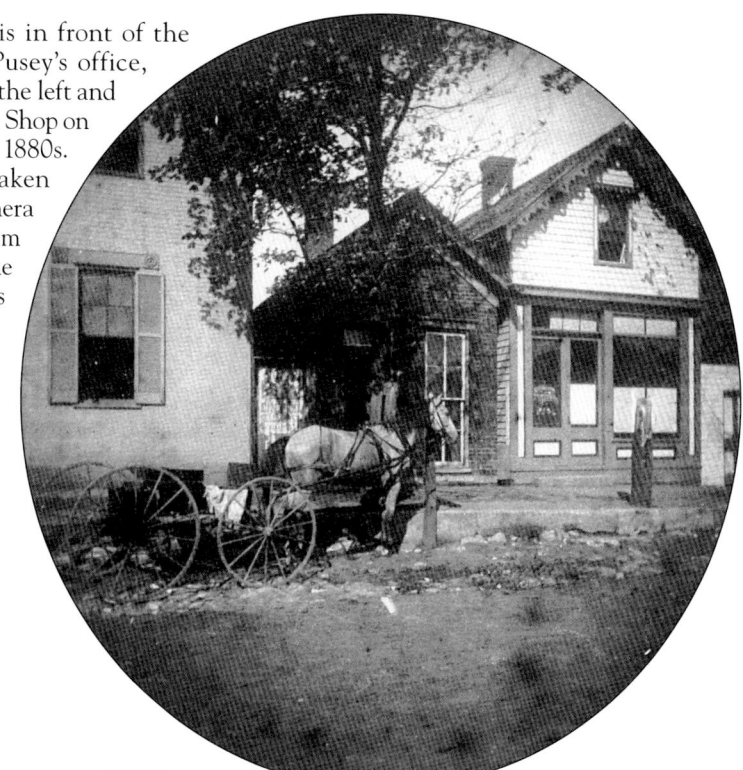

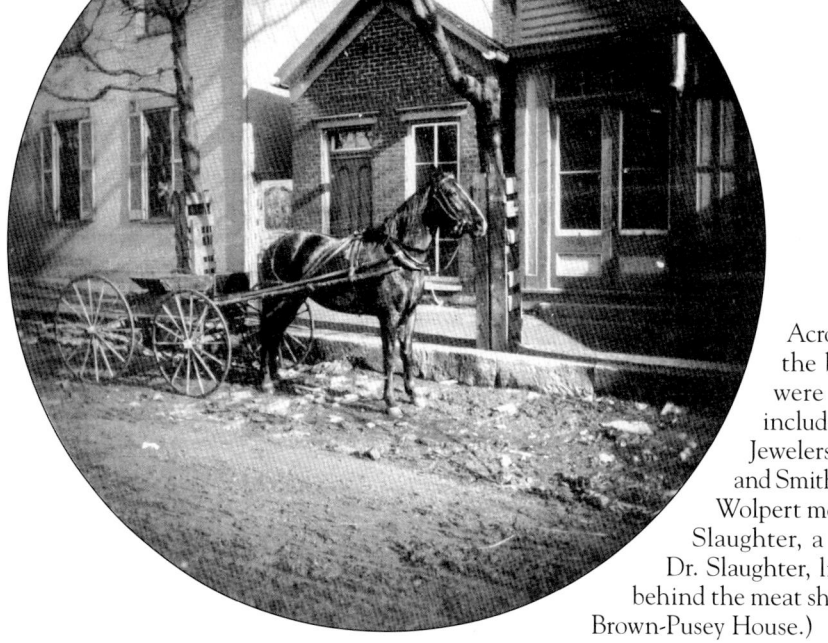

Across the street from the buildings shown were businesses that included R. M. Phillips Jewelers, the McCubbin and Smith Restaurant, and Wolpert meat shop. Clarisa Slaughter, a former slave of Dr. Slaughter, lived in the alley behind the meat shop. (Courtesy of Brown-Pusey House.)

Pictured are a man and a child in front of Dr. Robert Burns Pusey's office in the 1880s. An advertisement for the traveling circus hangs on the wall of the Stith House. The Jennie Holman Company, a theatrical company, came annually for several years to play a week during the fair at the Bryan's Hall. Among the players was Francis Kingdon, a brother of Mrs. George Gould. Kingdon was member, if not the leader, of New York's 400. He was the dressmaker for the company and spent most of his time during the day sewing. (Courtesy of Brown-Pusey House.)

Robert Burns Pusey earned his doctoral degree from a university in Philadelphia, Pennsylvania, in 1860 and practiced in Elizabethtown. His office, pictured in the 1880s, was used to store his surgical tools and to attend to his books. Pusey was a country doctor who traveled by horse or by rail to see his patients. (Courtesy of Brown-Pusey House.)

Robert Burns Pusey and Frank Strickler purchased this partial lot from Samuel Haycraft Jr. in 1878 and built this physician's office in Elizabethtown, pictured with the door closed. Dr. Strickler sold his interest to Dr. Pusey soon afterwards. After Dr. Pusey died in 1889, Dr. Strickler bought the building from the Pusey family. This photograph was taken in 1889 or 1890 with the first Kodak camera model available to the public. Today this building is Cobbler's Café. The façade was remodeled in the early 20th century. (Courtesy of Brown-Pusey House.)

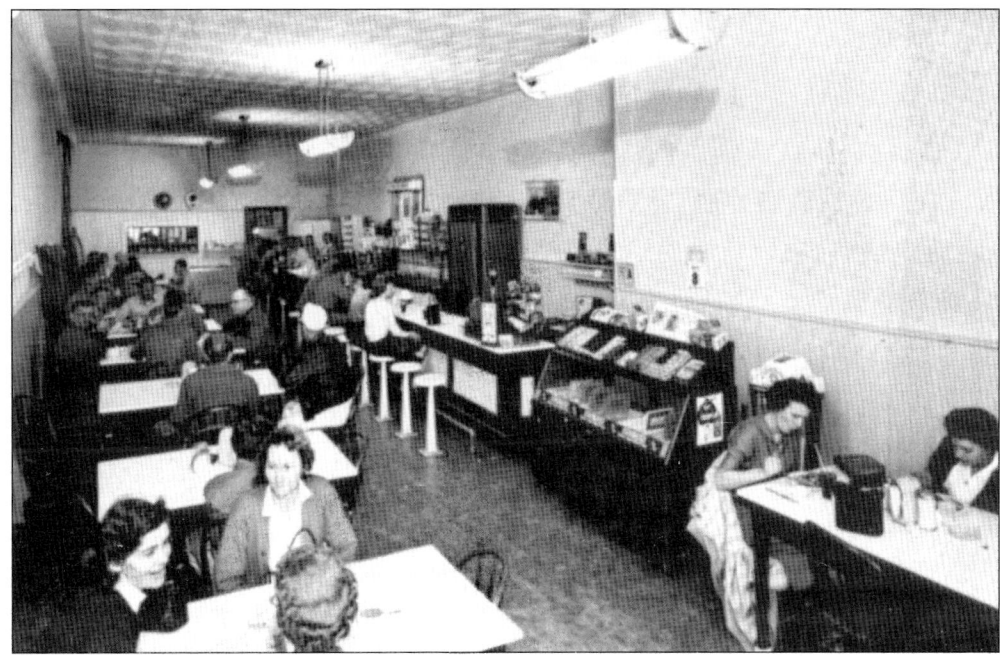

Dixie Café, once located at 129 East Dixie Avenue and owned by Melvin and Grace Braddock, has been razed and is a parking lot. South Mulberry Street, South Main Street, East Dixie Avenue, and the side streets off of East Dixie Avenue were flooded from the rising of Valley Creek in Elizabethtown in 1967. This flood was larger than the flood in 1937. The Freeman's Creek Dam, constructed in the 1960s, saved parts of the city from extreme flooding. (Courtesy of Meranda Caswell.)

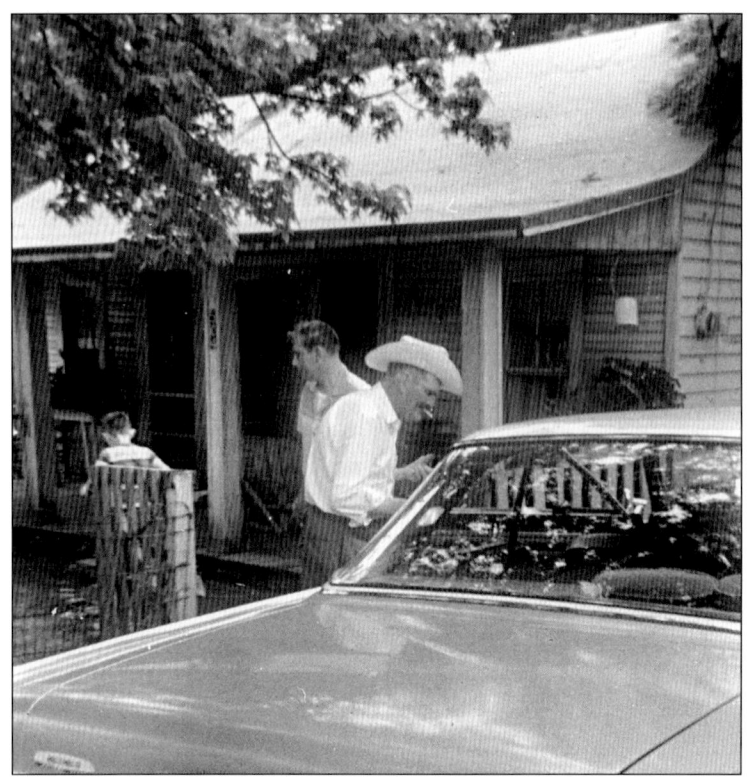

Bennie Musenchanko (left), Ronnie Musenchanko (center), and Ben Miller (wearing hat) are pictured in front of 504 Miller Street on Glendale Hill. Many residences, including this house on the highest point of Elizabethtown, have been razed. Glendale Hill has been under a redevelopment program by the City of Elizabethtown since 1983 in order to update the water and sewer systems, the roads, and the utilities. (Courtesy of Helen Glasgow.)

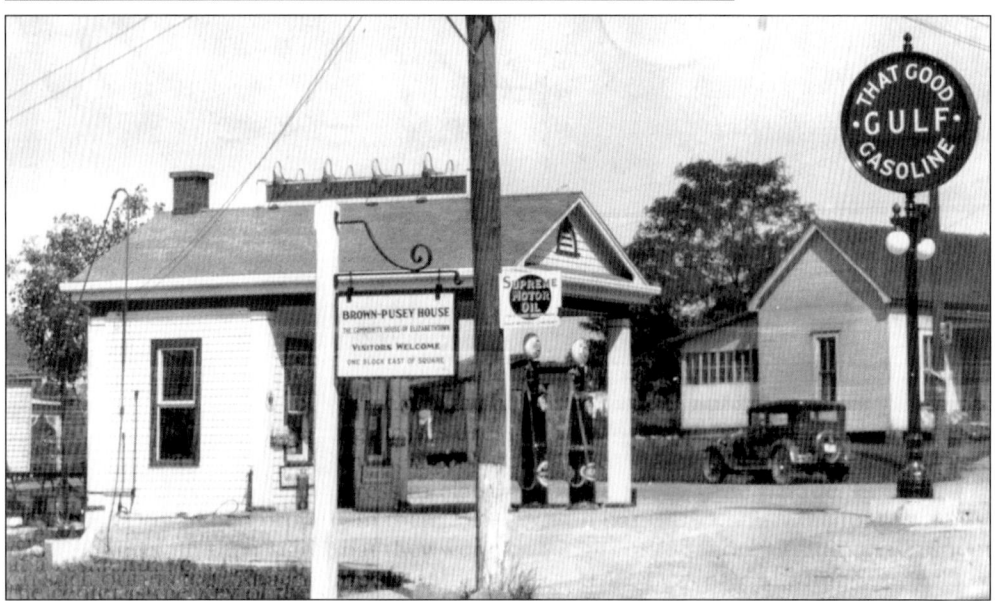

A Gulf Refining Company service station, pictured here in 1941, was located in Elizabethtown at 433 East Dixie Avenue on the corner of U.S. 31 West and Springfield Street. The office was located at 326 East Dixie. Across the street is the Glendale Hill subdivision, adjacent to the Elizabethtown City Cemetery. In 1845, Archibald Chalfin purchased land to make an addition to the graveyard. Lots 1 to 75 were sold, half lots 76 to 105 were used by the county for paupers, and lots 106 to 135 were for the African American population. (Courtesy of Brown-Pusey House.)

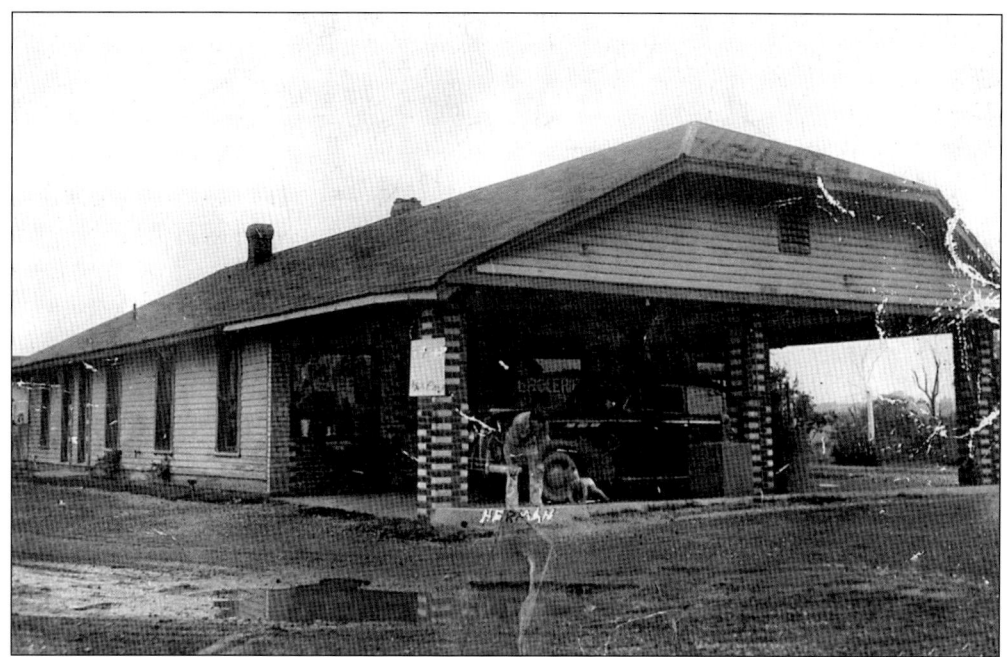

Ray's Market, a grocery store pictured in the 1940s, is still located on Hawkins Drive in Elizabethtown. The porch area was turned into the front of the store. To the right of the store was an RV camping ground that now is the Elizabethtown Trailer Park. Hawkins Drive and Sportsman Lake Road were part of the original U.S. 31 West highway. (Courtesy of Ray Baird.)

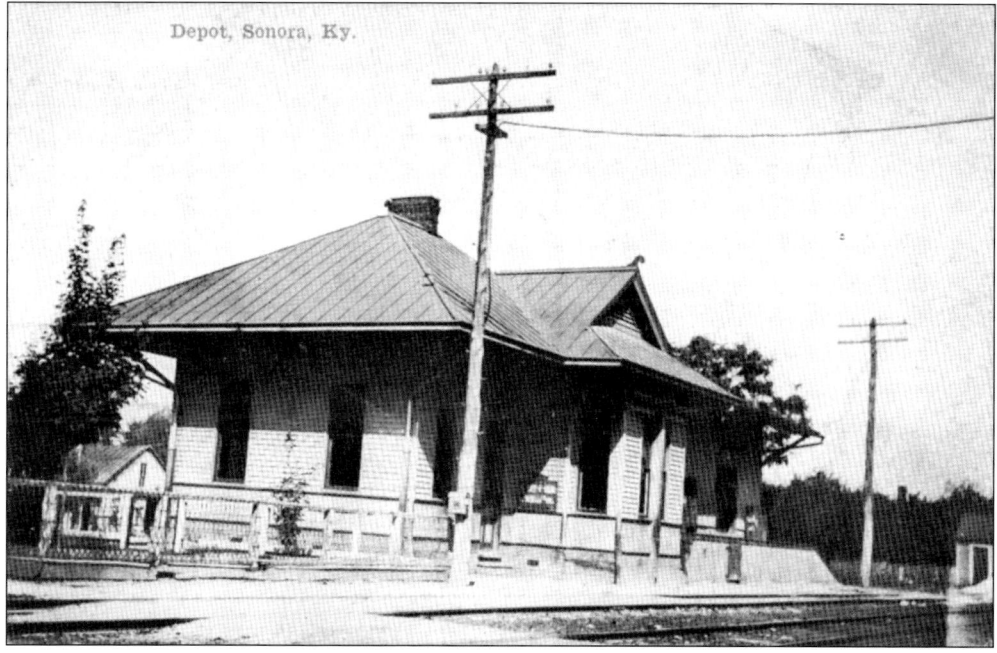

Pictured is the L&N depot in the town of Bucksnort or Sonora. The construction of the L&N lines in 1858 developed the area into a town. A post office called Sonora was established in 1859 with William Stuart as postmaster, and the town was incorporated in 1865. In 1881, Sonora had 300 inhabitants and exported wheat, hogs, and cattle on the railroad. (Courtesy of Carolyn Wimp.)

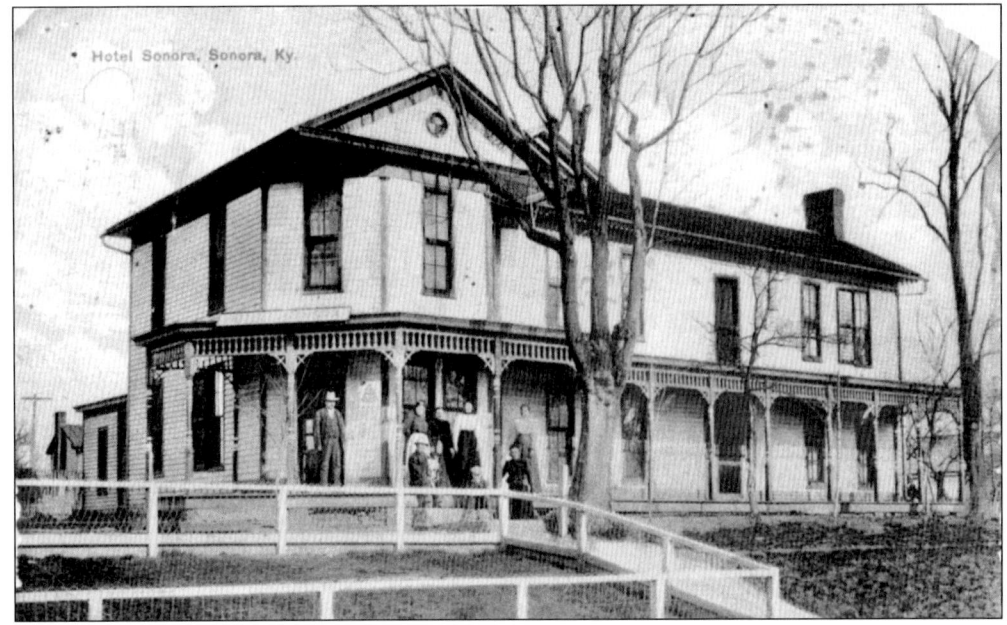

Mrs. Edward E. Perry had this postcard printed of the Hotel Sonora located in Sonora in the early 20th century. Another significant building in Sonora is the Thurman-Phillips home, built in 1897 by Josiah Phillips Jr., which was recently renovated by Charles and Claudia Thurman and open to the public as a bed and breakfast. (Courtesy of Elvin Smith Jr.)

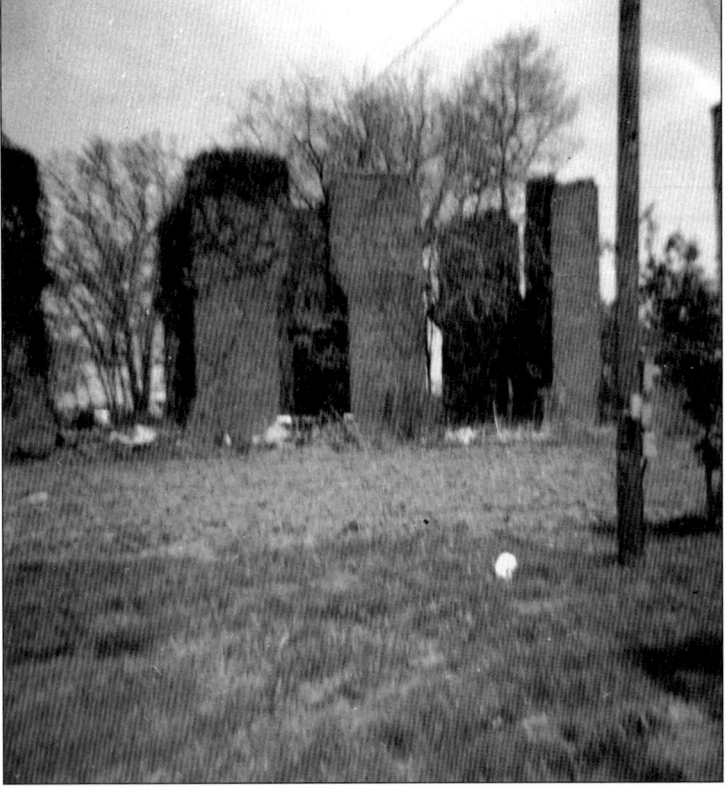

In the 1880s, Sonora had 300 residents and was a station on the L&N 13 miles from Elizabethtown. Lampton and Morrison had a business as harrow makers. The pictured ruins in Sonora are one of the many dilapidated or razed structures in the smaller communities along U.S. 31 West, such as Nolin, Upton, Flint Hill, Melrose, Seven Corners, Spurrier, and Red Mills. The only site that remains of the Red Mills community is the cemetery. (Courtesy of Brown-Pusey House.)

Two
LINCOLN HERITAGE

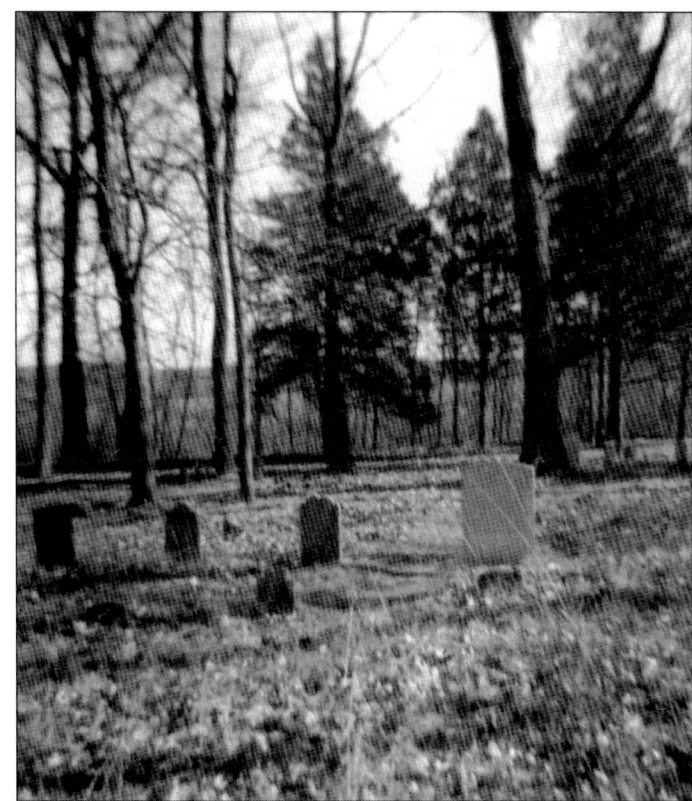

Mill Creek Cemetery, pictured, is located on Fort Knox property and can only be viewed on Memorial Day each year with a guide. This cemetery is the graveyard of Bathsheba Lincoln, the grandmother of Pres. Abraham Lincoln. About 1870, P. T. Barnum brought General and Mrs. Tom Thumb, Commodore Nutt, and Minnie Warren, who was a sister of Mrs. Thumb, to Kaufman's Hall. These little people had been presented to every court in Europe, to President and Mrs. Lincoln at the White House, and to the Senate of the United States, and they were being taken on a tour of the country. (Courtesy of Brown-Pusey House.)

Bathsheba married Abraham Lincoln, a Revolutionary soldier who died away from his Mill Creek home in Hardin County. Thomas, the son of Bathsheba and Abraham, purchased 238 acres of land in the Mill Creek community in 1803 from Dr. John F. Slator of Green County. Thomas Lincoln resided in Hardin County until about 1816, and then he moved to Indiana and into Illinois. On July 19, 1814, Thomas Lincoln bought one "Truckeles" wagon for eight and one-third shillings in Hardin County at the estate sale of Thomas Hill. (Courtesy of Millie Robinson.)

Christ Episcopal Church, built about 1840 on land donated by Armistead Churchill in Elizabethtown, had a huge willow tree in front of it in the 1880s and 1890s. In 1818, Holderman, Whiting, and Wilkins established Aetna Iron Furnace in Hardin (in Hart County as of 1819). This furnace made grease lamps, iron kettles, frying pans, dog-irons, and other iron utensils and implements. Jacob Holderman's son-in-law, Cadwallader Churchill (the son of Armistead), operated the furnace until about 1850. (Courtesy of Brown-Pusey House.)

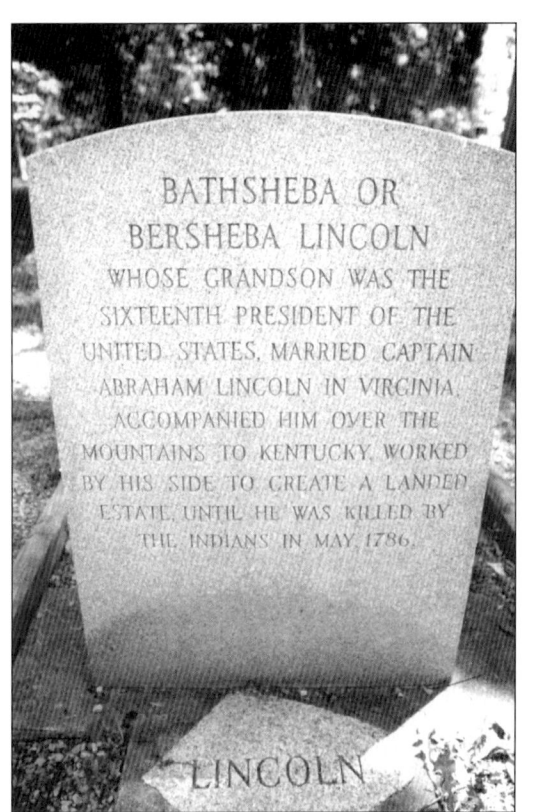

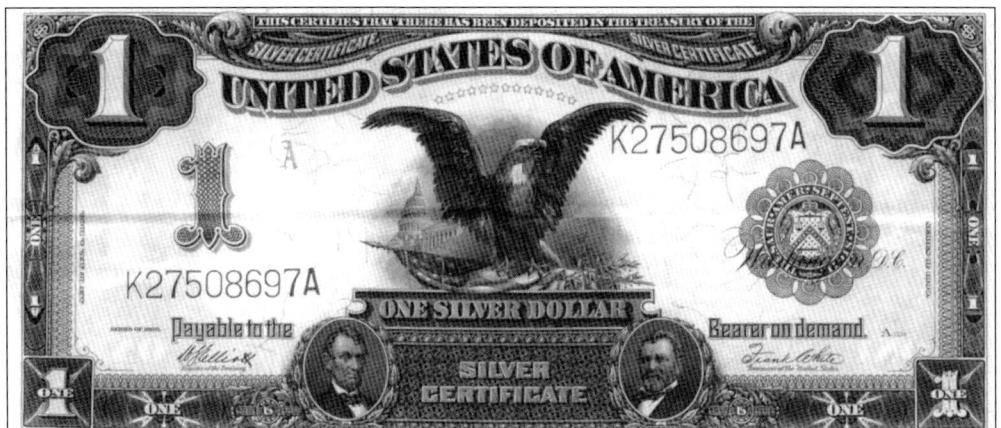

This silver certificate is dated 1899 with a photograph of Pres. Abraham Lincoln and a photograph of Pres. Ulysses S. Grant. In 1871, President Grant invited the Russian grand duke Alexis, fourth son of Tsar Alexander II, to travel the United States on a goodwill tour. Gen. Philip Sheridan, the grand duke, and Gen. George Armstrong Custer went on a buffalo hunt in the West led by Buffalo Bill Cody. The grand duke and Custer visited Hardin County in January 1872. (Courtesy of Brown-Pusey House.)

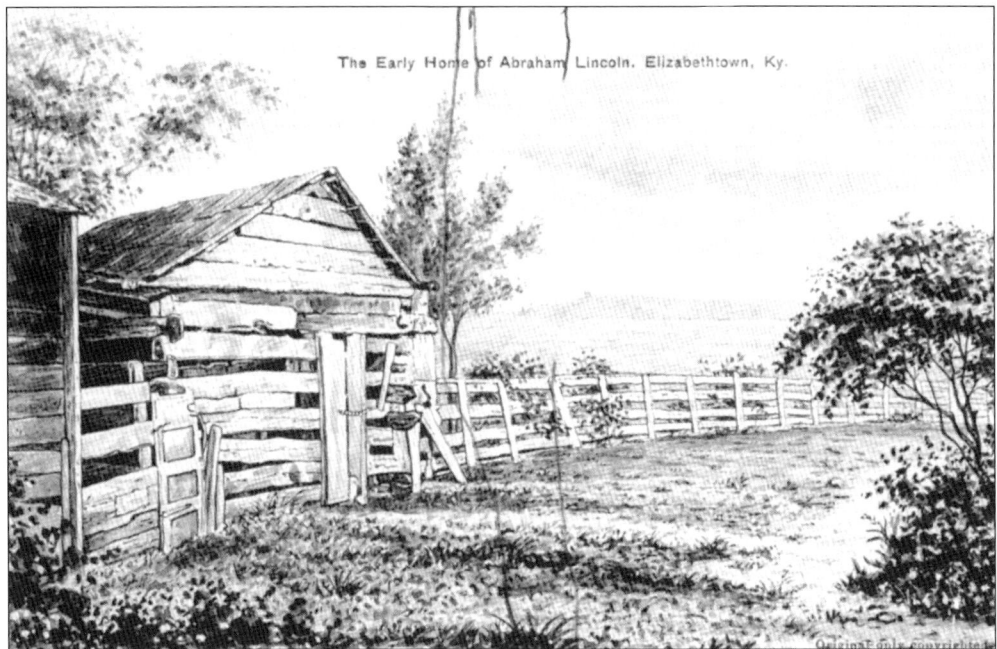

Prior to Sarah Lincoln's birth, Thomas Lincoln was involved in travel in 1806 from Hardin County to New Orleans, Louisiana. Thomas had a credit for the barge trip of 2,400 pounds of pork and 494 pounds of beef at the Bleakley and Montgomery store in February 1806 to be sold in New Orleans. Others stocked items like corn, potatoes, lard, hemp, and whiskey for the barge trip. Thomas Lincoln, a partner of Isaac Bush, was paid in gold for his venture. Prior to his marriage to Nancy Hanks, Thomas purchased material for his groom attire from this store. After his marriage, he purchased knives, forks, spoons, tobacco, and skeins of silk from the store. (Courtesy of Brown-Pusey House.)

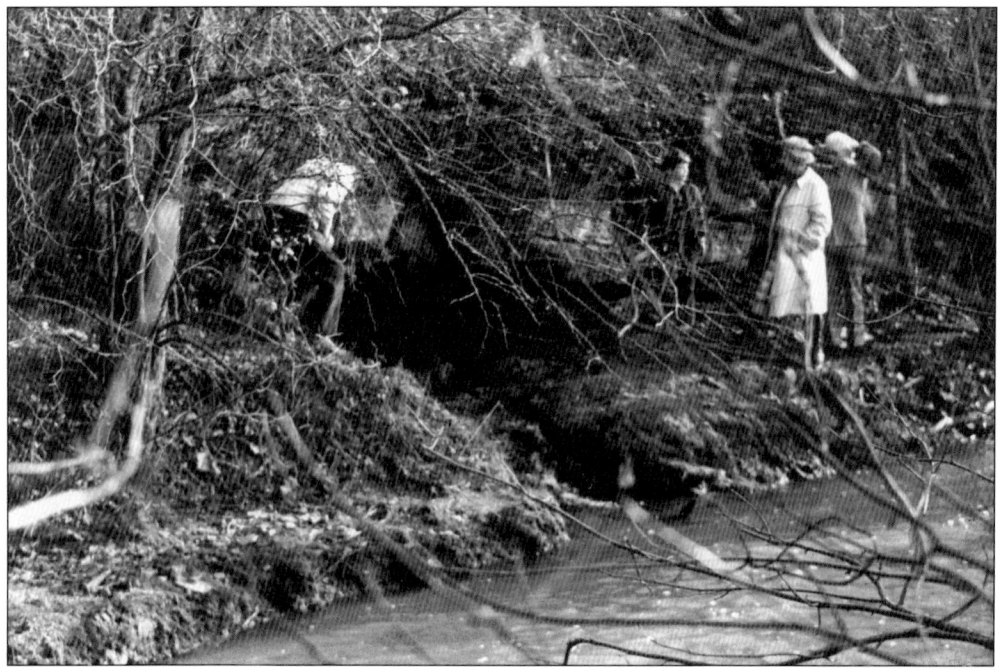

Pictured is Cave Spring in Elizabethtown. This is the area called Camp Haycraft, after a military post in the 1860s and 1870s. Capt. A. B. Cain, the leading officer of Company F of the 4th Infantry, and Lt. Col. George A. Custer, the leading officer of the Company A of the 7th Cavalry, had their headquarters on Mrs. Poston's land near Cave Spring from 1871 to 1873. These companies were stationed in Hardin County to pounce down upon the illicit distillers in Grayson and Larue Counties and to disband the Ku Klux Klan and carpetbaggers. (Courtesy of Dr. R. T. Clagett.)

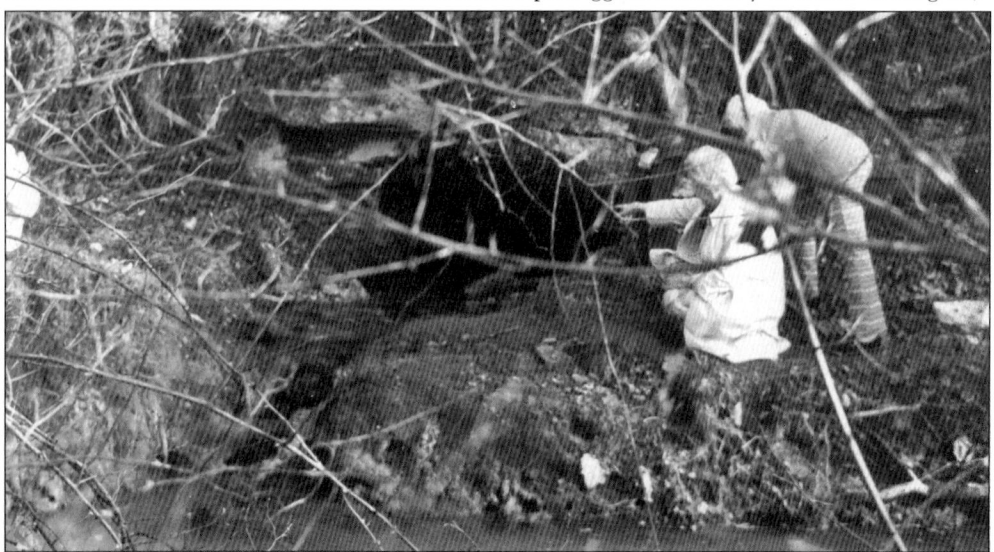

Another photograph of Cave Spring shows the spring that powered the Haycraft Mill in Elizabethtown. Thomas Lincoln was hired by Samuel Haycraft to build the mill about 1797. The only item left from the mill is the stream. A Greenspace walking trail leads behind the Hardin County Justice Center to the Valley Creek Bridge; across the bridge is the small Haycraft Mill historic park. (Courtesy of Dr. R. T. Clagett.)

Jacob Vanmeter, one of the first settlers, brought his family and about 30 other settlers including his nephew, Jacob Vanmeter, and the Haycraft family, to Fincastle County, Virginia, which today is Hardin County. There is nothing left of the Vanmeter Revolutionary fort on Highway 62. In error, many people refer to the fort on Cave Spring as a Revolutionary fort. Actually the Haycraft Fort is a Civil War fort and the military headquarters for Custer's troops during the 1870s. (Courtesy of Brown-Pusey House.)

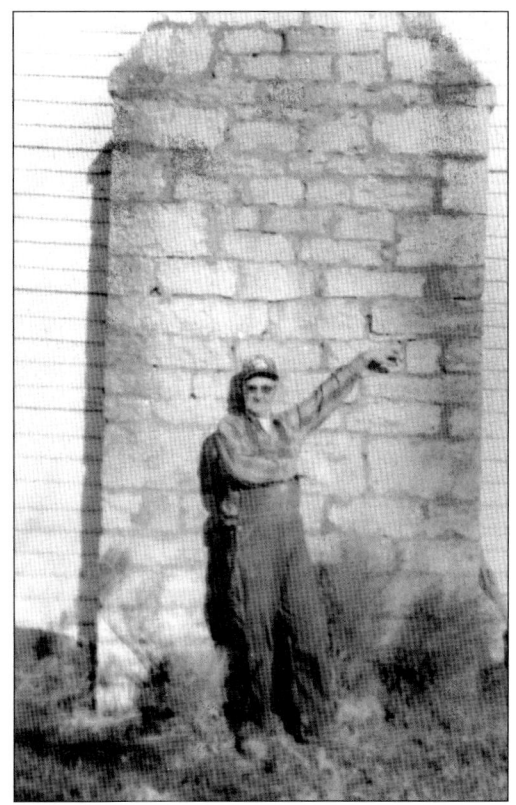

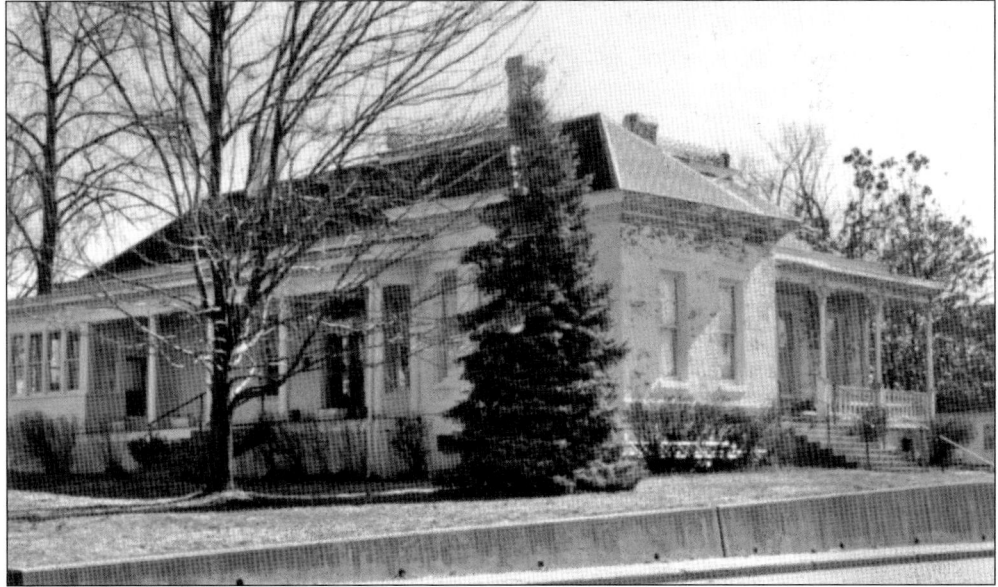

The first brick house in Hardin County was built in 1803 on this site, but it burned in 1882. Even though he did not live on the site, Joshua Barney purchased this property in Elizabethtown. Barney died on December 1, 1818, from a blood clot due to a leg wound from the War of 1812. However his family lived on the site. The building pictured was built around 1882. (Courtesy of Brown-Pusey House.)

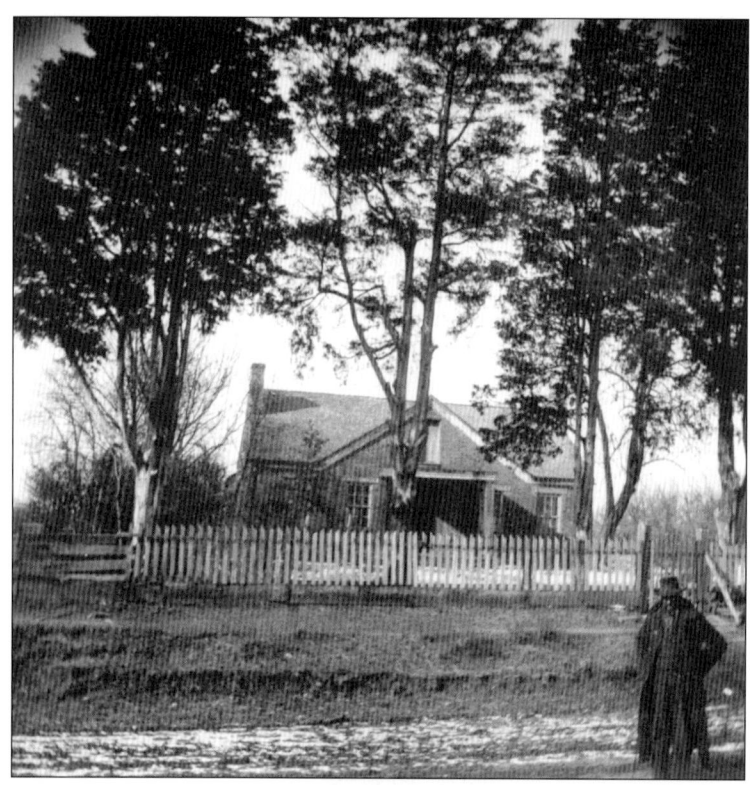

George Tobin visited the Roderick Warfield House on a hill called Mount Pleasant in Elizabethtown in the late 19th century. Roderick's wife, Ann S. Stockett, was the daughter of Dr. Thomas Noble Stockett, a surgeon at Valley Forge in the Revolutionary War. This family arrived in Hardin County about the time the Lincolns left Hardin County. (Courtesy of Brown-Pusey House.)

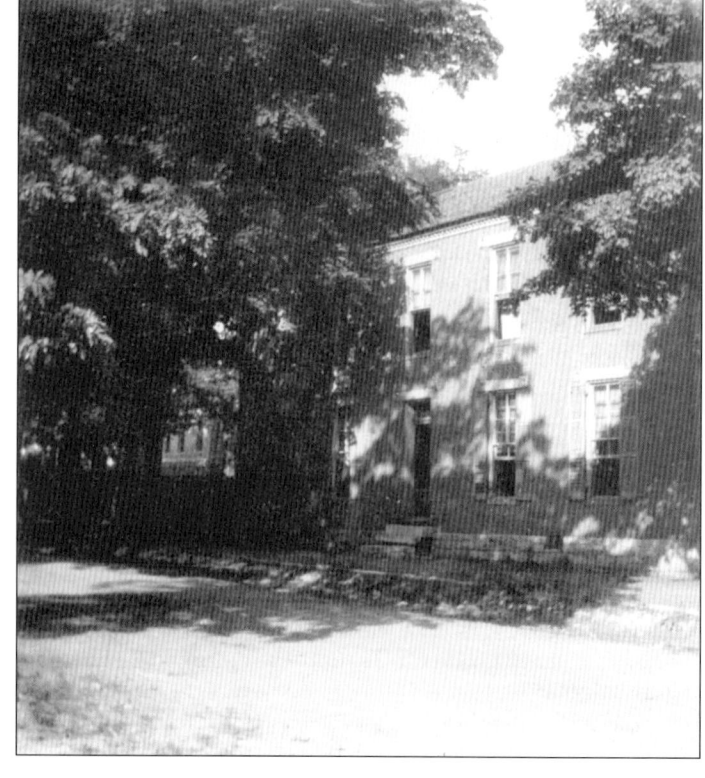

The clerk's office on North Main Street was a two-story Federal-style building razed in 1963. The Hardin County Circuit Court held in April and October during the 1880s included Sheriff Horace Branham, Circuit Clerk Christopher M. Fraize, and County Clerk John H. Wells. The building on the corner of North Main Street and East Poplar Street was built after 1891. This corner was an empty half lot from 1871 to 1891. Across the street was the Hill's Hotel. (Courtesy of Brown-Pusey House.)

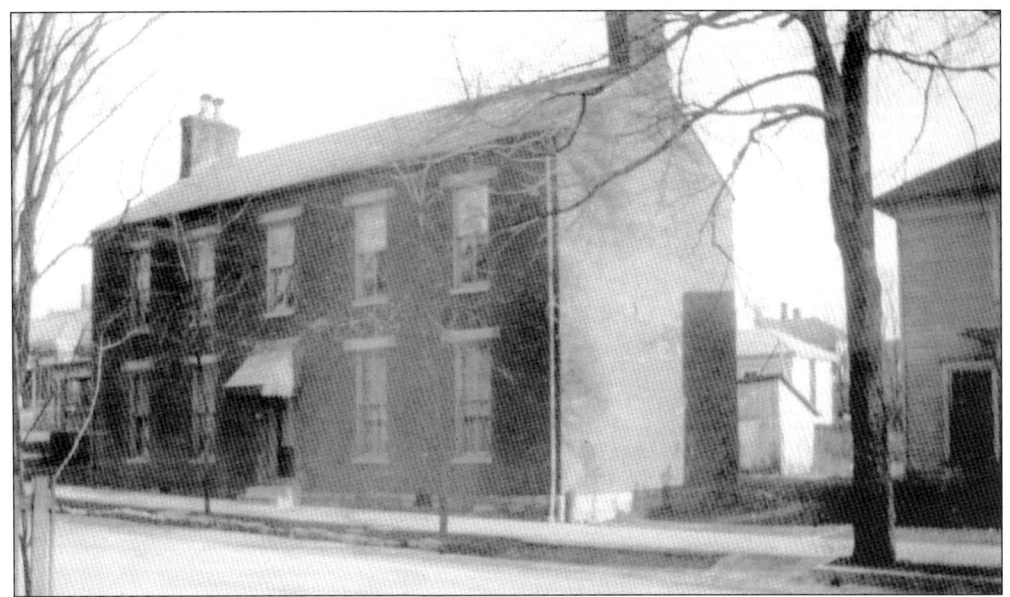

This building was a residence and then the county and circuit clerk's office in Elizabethtown from the 1790s to about 1900. Behind this building, somewhere near Race Street, was supposed to be the home of Thomas Lincoln and Nancy Hanks, where Sarah Lincoln was born in 1807. Also behind this building was Geoghegan's Row, where John Y. Hill and William Feaman had a tailor business in the early 19th century. (Courtesy of Brown-Pusey House.)

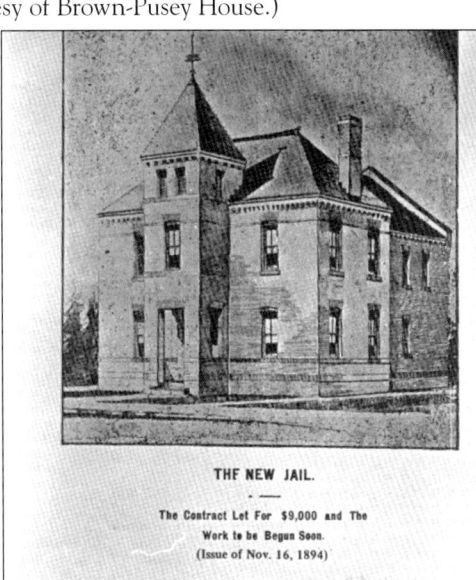

THE NEW JAIL.

The Contract Let For $9,000 and The Work Is to be Begun Soon.
(Issue of Nov. 16, 1894)

Pictured is a newspaper article from 1897 about the jail to be constructed on North Main Street. Isaac Hynes's distillery house in Elizabethtown was the first temporary jail in Hardin County. The first timber jail was built in 1794 on land donated by Andrew Hynes for the county to erect county buildings. Inmate Charles Sawyer, jailed for debt, burned the second timber jail, built in 1797. Afterwards, Sawyer was released to build the first brick jail in Elizabethtown. (Courtesy of Brown-Pusey House.)

The contract for a new jail for Hardin county was let by the jail committee last Thursday to the Pawly Jail Building Co., of St. Louis, for $9,000 and if the weather permits the work is to be begun this fall and pushed to an early completion. The committee bought the lot of Jas Montgomery on Main Street just above Cresap's store for $900 and sold the old jail lot to Joe Sweets for $600. The jail is to be a handsome two-story brick building built entirely of pressed brick with the Jailer's residence in the front part and the prison in the rear.

The residence part is to have four rooms, two below and two above 15x16 feet, a hall, an office and a kitchen. The principal prison is to be in the second story of the rear of the building and the cells are also to be built of case hardened steel with corridors between the cells and a corridor all around the outside. Prison cells are also to be built on the lower floor for those committed for misdemeanors and other minor offences. The prison is to be built with all the latest improvements for safety and will be one of the best in the State.

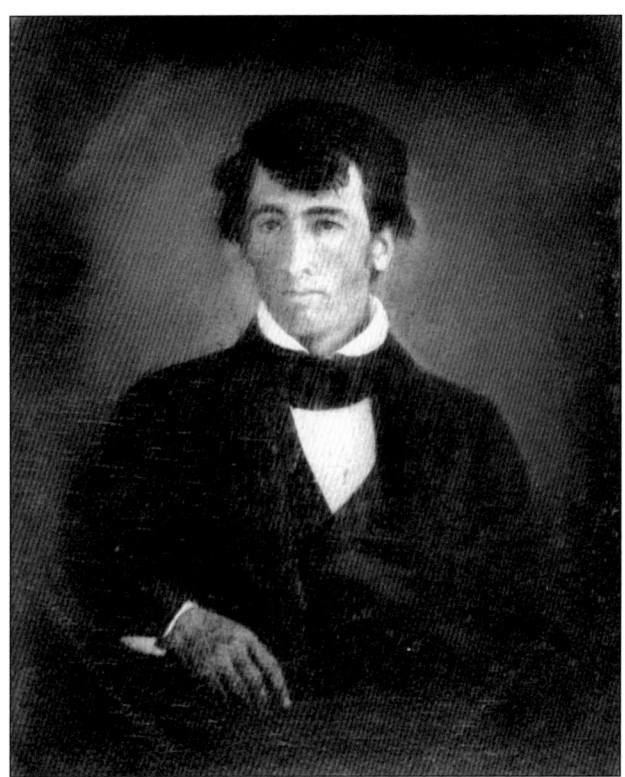

Alfred Mackenzie Brown, pictured about 1840, was the son of William Brown, one of the first Kentucky pioneers. William had several children, including John Thompson Street Brown Sr. J. T. S. Brown Sr. was the father of J. T. S. Brown Jr., who went into partnership of a wholesale liquor business in 1870 with his half-brother, George Garvin Brown. This business today is the Brown-Forman Company. (Courtesy of Brown-Pusey House.)

Elizabeth Wathen, pictured, was the daughter of Mehettable (Hettie) Cunningham and Richard Wathen and the niece of Sallie Cunningham Pusey. Hettie was the daughter of Anthony Hundley Cunningham and his second wife, Sallie Wathen. Anthony was a prisoner in Louisville during the Civil War due to his Confederate sympathies. Lydia Ann Cunningham, Anthony's sister, married Dr. Ambrose Geoghegan, whose father, Denton Geoghegan, was the high sheriff who kept Thomas Lincoln in litigation over the hewing of timber for a mill. (Courtesy of Brown-Pusey House.)

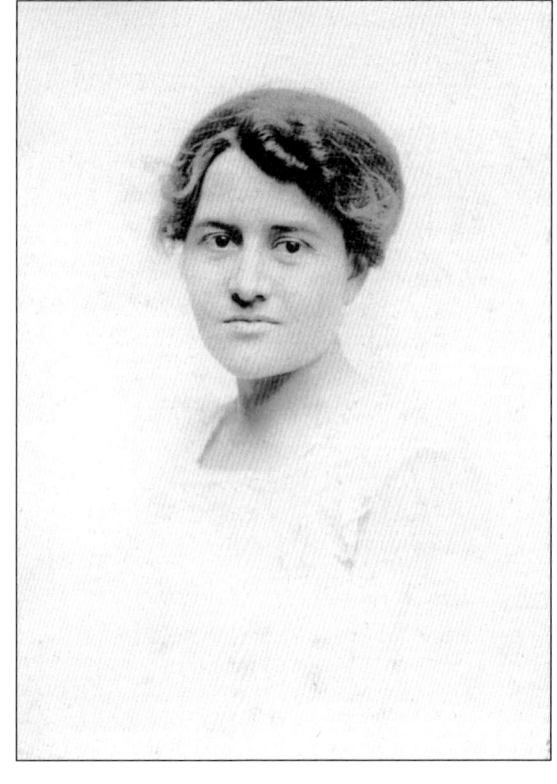

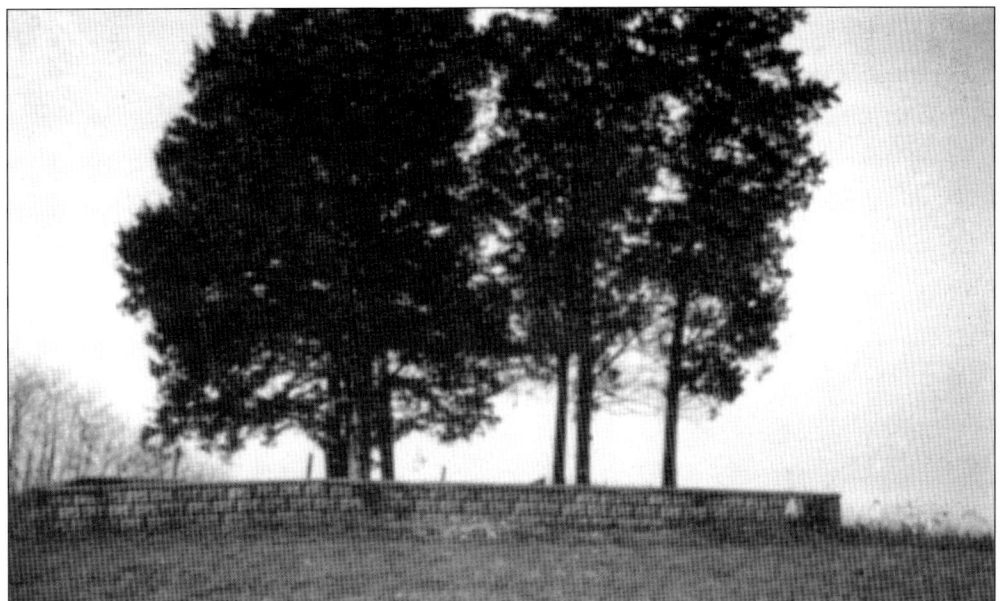

Hannah Street and William Brown, from Hanover County, Virginia, were buried on the farm patented to William about 1784 on the north fork of Nolin River, four miles north of Hodgenville. William's powder horn, books, and other items are on display at the Pusey Room Museum of the Brown-Pusey House in Elizabethtown. One of Brown's ancestors, John Boog, was killed in Glasgow, Scotland, for heresy. (Courtesy of Brown-Pusey House.)

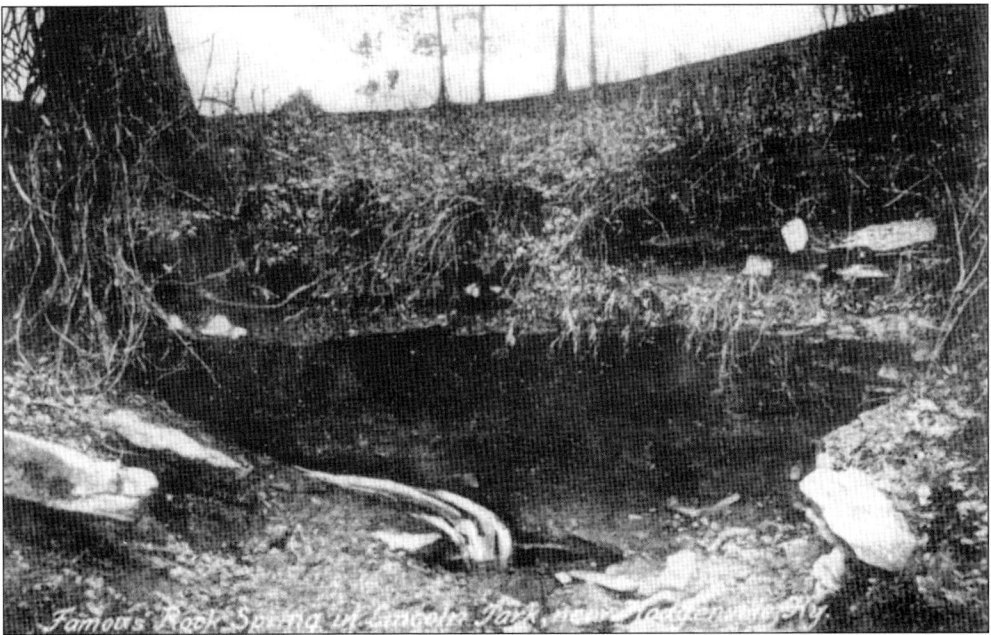

Sinking Spring, near Hodgenville, is part of the Lincoln's Birthplace National Park. This is one of the Hardin County properties that Thomas Lincoln was in court for because of a failure to secure a clear title. William Brown, one of Kentucky's first pioneers, lived near this property with his children, who were born during the time that the Lincolns were in Hardin County. (Courtesy of Brown-Pusey House.)

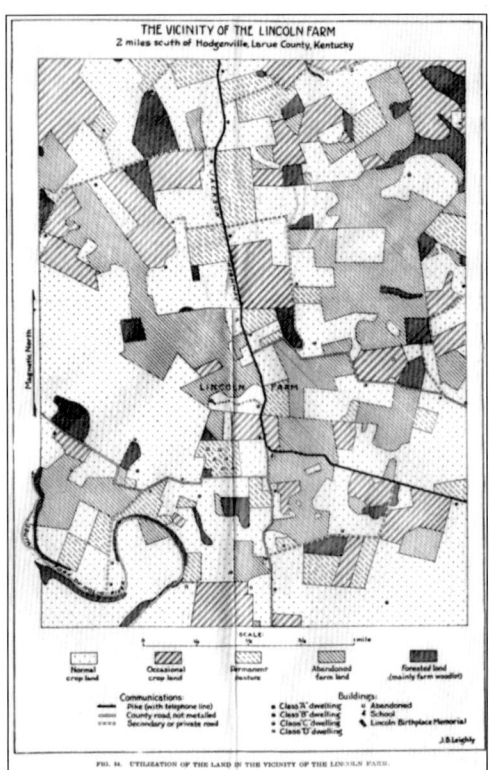

The Lincoln farm is part of the Lincoln's Birthplace National Park. Richard Mather actually owned the land and retained the property through procedural law. The Mather family still owns part of this land that retains a family cemetery. (Courtesy of Brown-Pusey House.)

This map of the Lincoln farm shows the site of the birthplace of Abraham Lincoln. Through the farm is Jackson Highway or U.S. 31 East, which can still be traveled today. The road that veers off to the right from the Lincoln farm leads to Greensburg. To the southwest of the farm is the south fork of Nolin River. (Courtesy of Brown-Pusey House.)

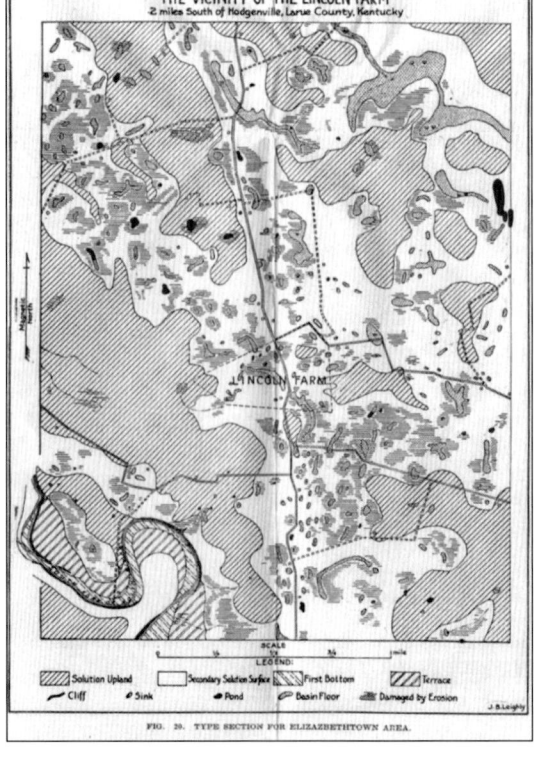

Three
GLENDALE AND WHITE MILLS

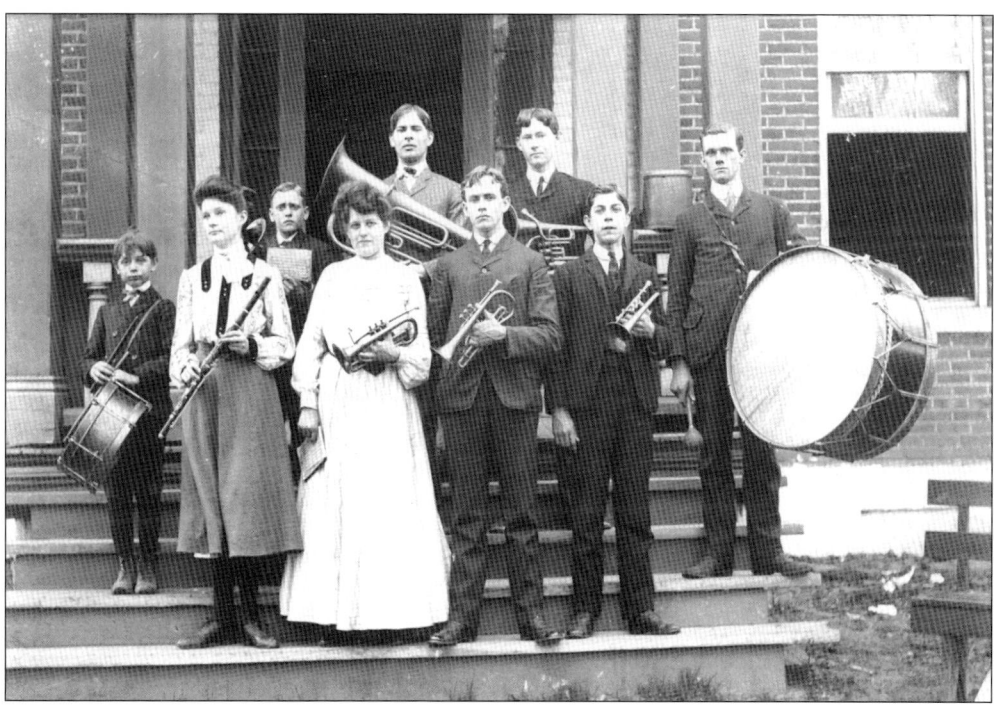

The pictured school was opened in 1867 as the Lynnland Female Institute. Hiram Overall deeded 16 acres in 1866 to Samuel, William, and Henry Sprigg; John R. Gaither; and Samuel Hansborough in exchange for 33 acres elsewhere in Hardin County. The land is located on the L&N between Glendale and Nolin and near Gilead Baptist Church on the Nolin River. The people are unidentified. (Courtesy of Brown-Pusey House.)

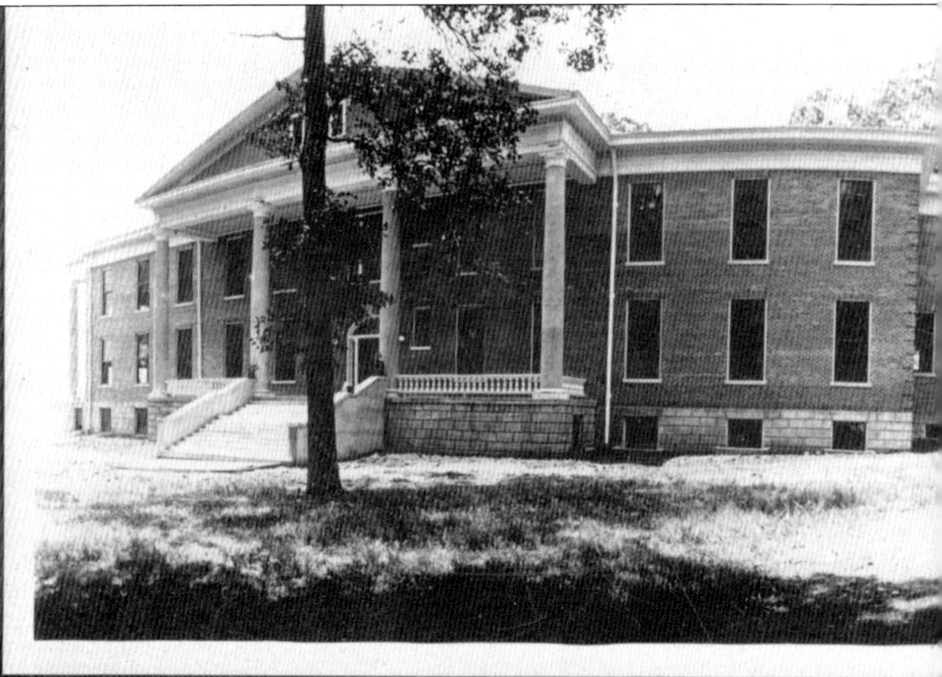

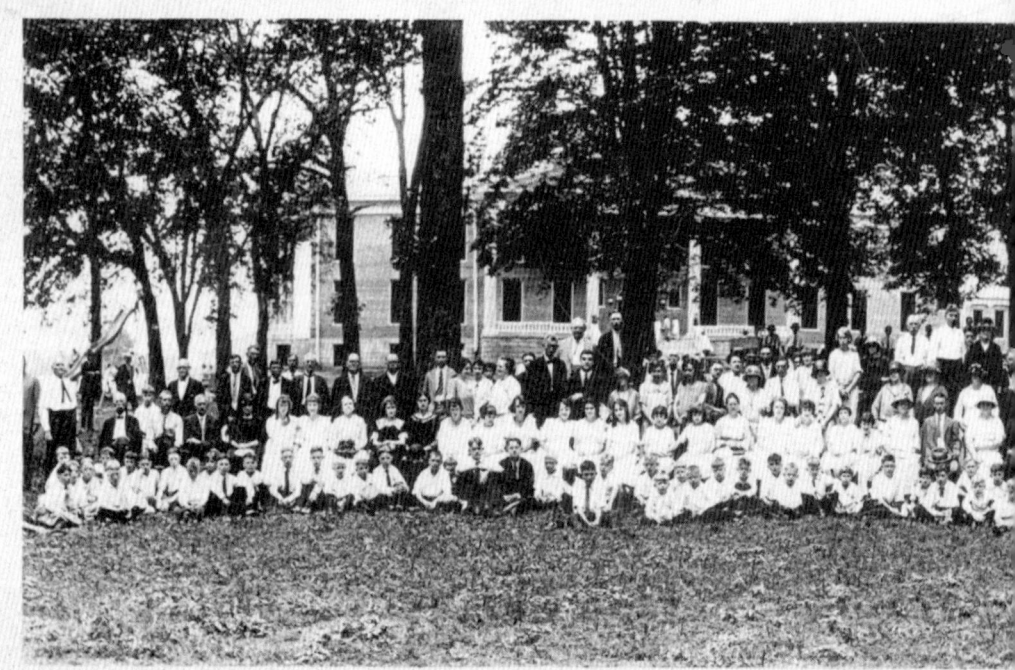

Samuel Sprigg bought the building in 1879, and his family lived in it until 1888. E. W. Elroe and E. W. White operated the school as a girl's school called Lynnland College until 1895. Rev. W. B. Gwynn opened it as a coeducational school under the name of Lynnland Academy. In 1907, it was sold to the Baptist Educational Society of Kentucky. In 1915, the Kentucky Baptist Children's Home purchased about 300 acres of fertile land near the old college. Rev. A. B. Gardner was

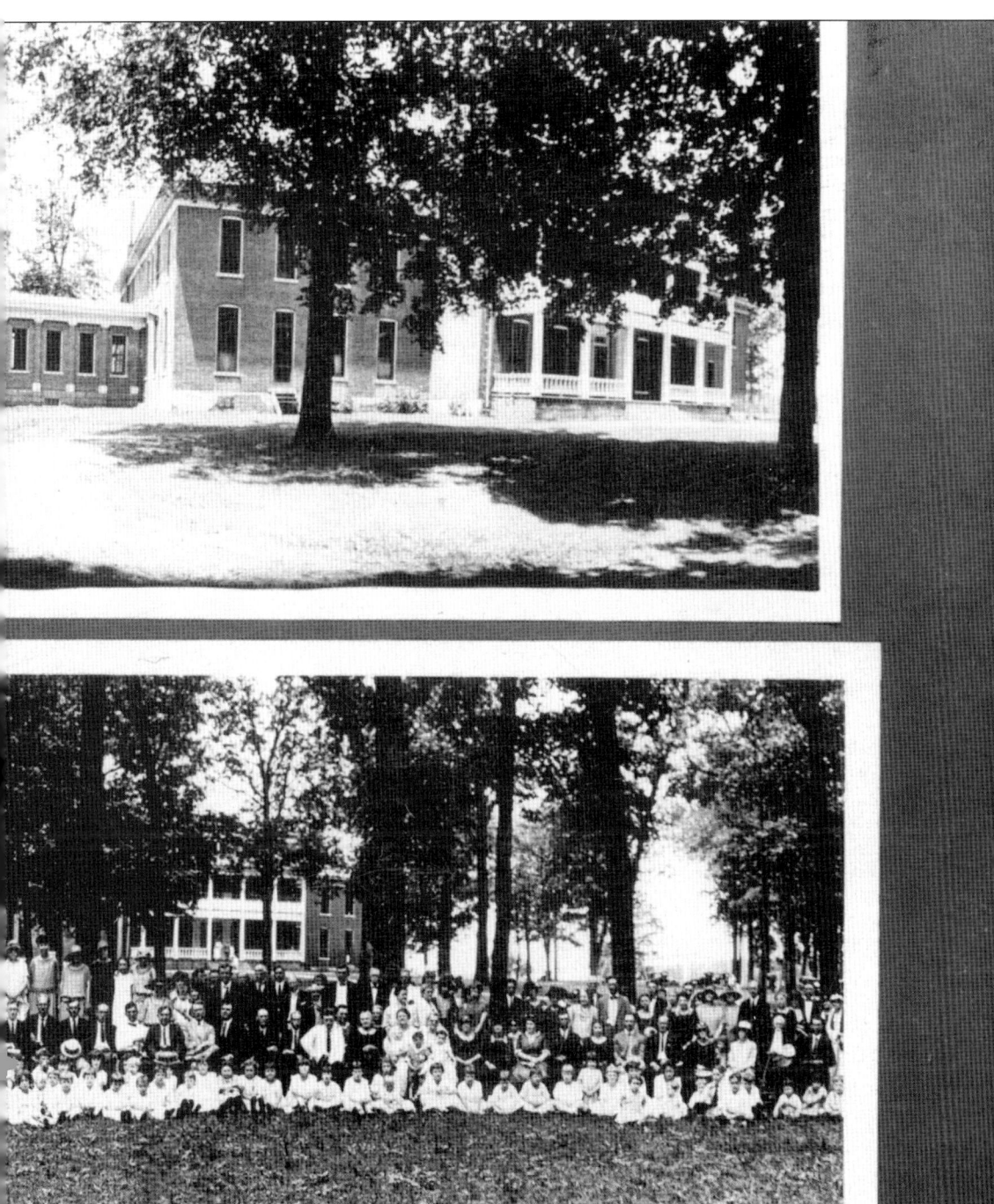

elected first superintendent, and the home was opened in 1915 for homeless, destitute children. The superintendents that succeeded Gardner were Rev. J. W. Vallandingham, George Moore, W. M. Stallings, H. C. Compton, C. K. Hoagland, and J. G. Barbe. In the 1940s, the school changed its name from Lynnland to Homeland. (Courtesy of Carolyn Wimp.)

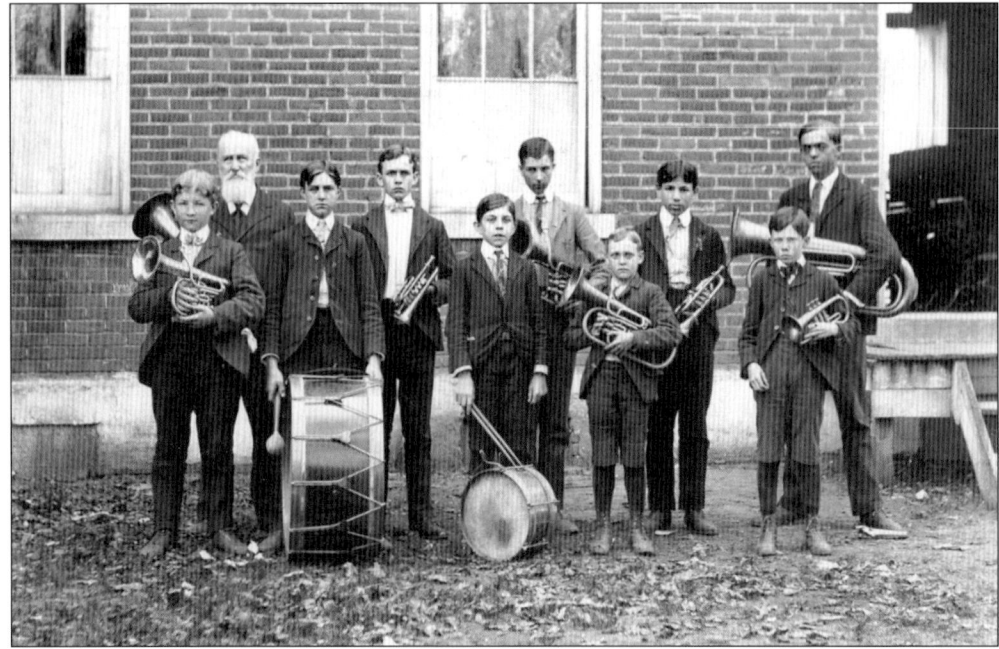

J. H. Davis, who had an art studio in Elizabethtown, took this photograph. The band students are unidentified. His studio was close to Dr. Robert Burns Pusey's office. John Peyton Hobson settled in Elizabethtown and practiced law with Alfred M. Brown. Hobson married Ella Nourse, and one of their six children was named Robert Burns Pusey Hobson after the country doctor. (Courtesy of Brown-Pusey House.)

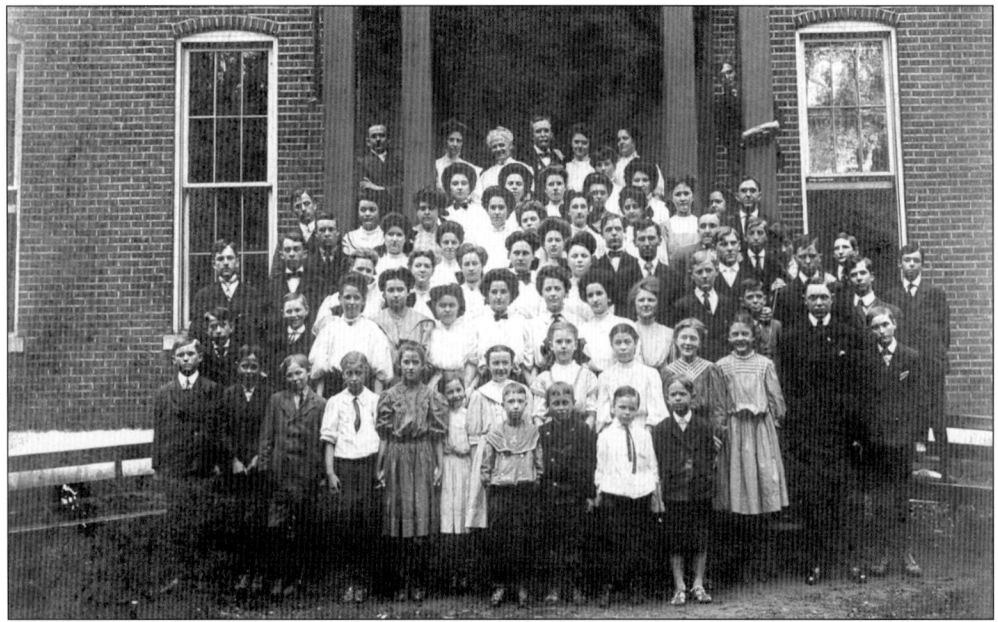

Lynnland Academy had Rev. G. A. Coulson, a Baptist minister, as the first superintendent. In 1868, the name was changed to Lynnland Institute. The people are unidentified. Near Lynnland College in Glendale, John W. Woodring had a hotel in the 1880s. W. C. Neighbor operated a saloon. (Courtesy of Brown-Pusey House.)

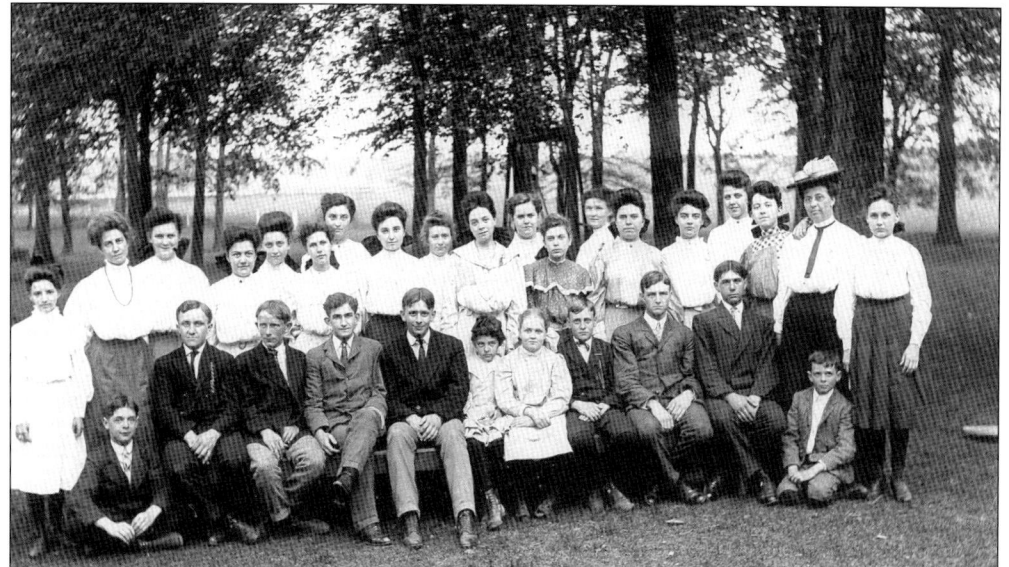

Gen. William F. Perry, who served in the Confederate army, operated the school from 1870 to 1879. Perry and Maj. Peter Epes Harris purchased the school and changed it to Lynnland Military Institute, where females were also allowed to attend and graduate. Perry asked Gen. Robert E. Lee to recommend a well-qualified teacher—John Peyton Hobson. The people pictured are unidentified. (Courtesy of Brown-Pusey House.)

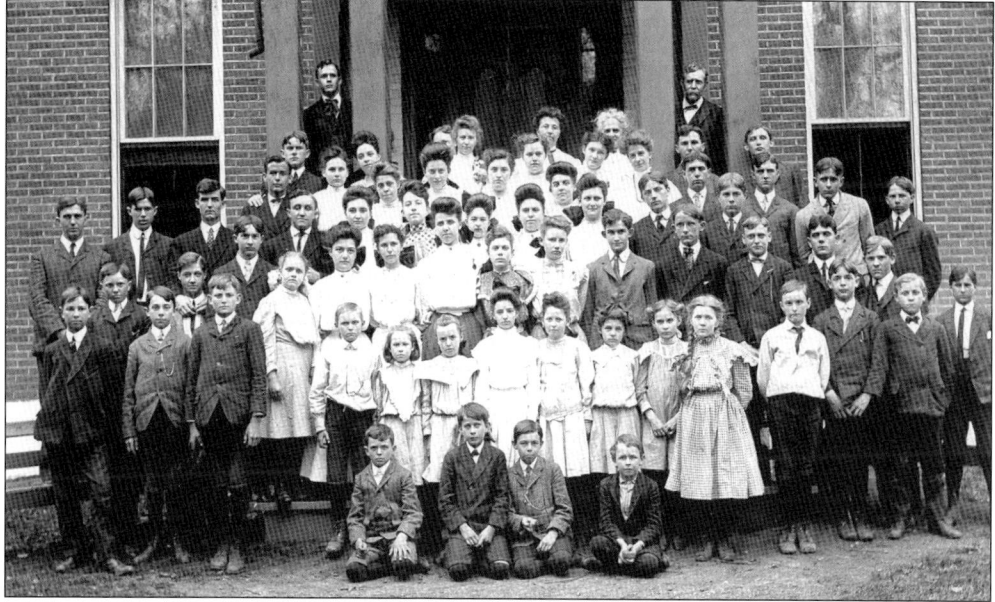

To the west of U.S. 31 West and Glendale are the communities of Stephensburg and Franklin Cross Roads. In 1854, Rev. Robertson Gannaway visited Judge William Love and his wife, who was a sister of Robertson. Judge Love was married to Elizabeth Gannaway in Wythe County, Virginia, in 1795, and she died in 1813. Then Judge Love married Elizabeth's cousin, Sarah Gannaway, in 1814. She was the daughter of Thomas and Sally Gannaway. Both Elizabeth and Sarah were buried with the Glasscocks (Love descendants) on an old farm on the road between these two towns. The pictured students are unidentified. (Courtesy of Brown-Pusey House.)

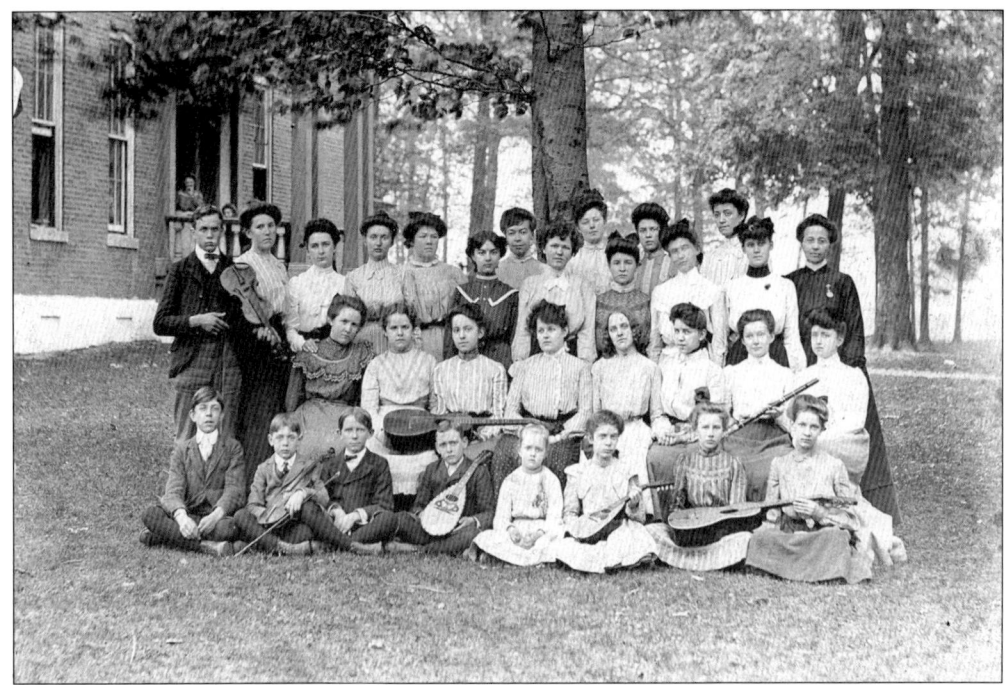

Bessie Patterson, Alma Means, Everett Smith, Maude Hardin, Katie Lee Slaughter, and Ursa Warren were graduates of Lynnland College, near Glendale, in 1900. The people in the photograph are unidentified. (Courtesy of Brown-Pusey House.)

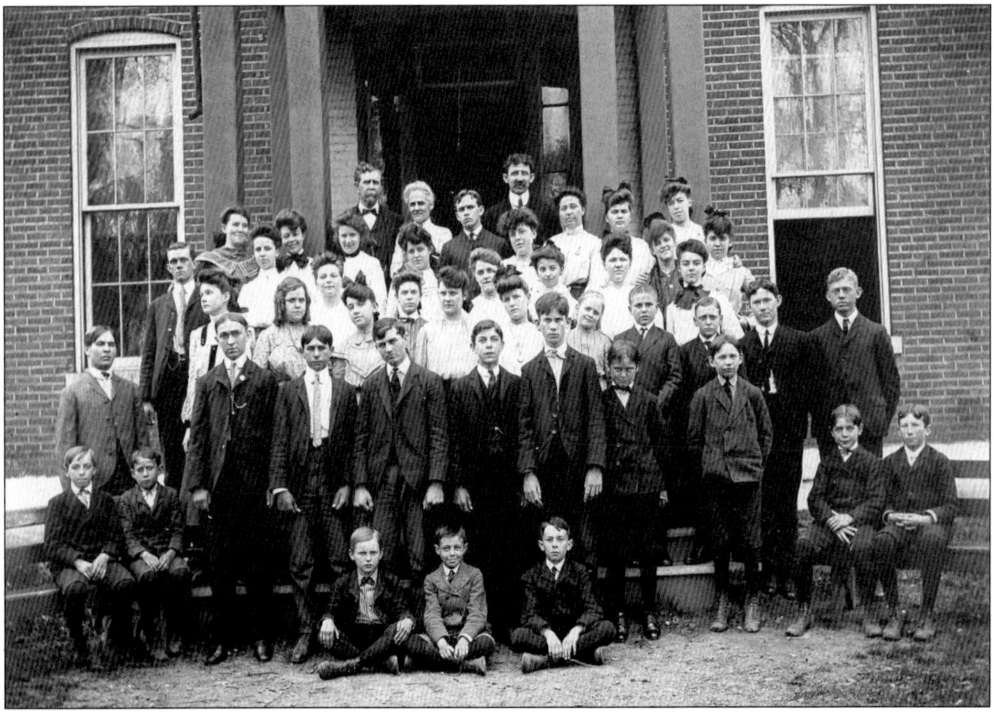

Pictured is Lynnland College in Glendale, and the people are unidentified. (Courtesy of Brown-Pusey House.)

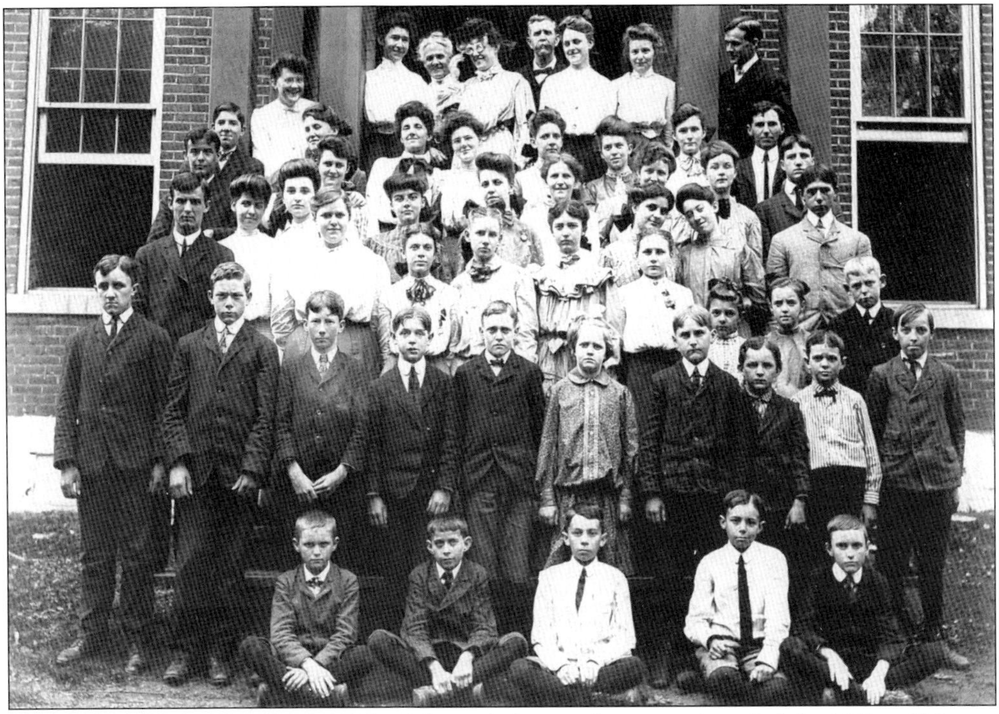

Pictured is Lynnland College in Glendale, and the people are unidentified. In 1931, a 69.2-acre airport was built at Glendale and leased to the U.S. government. Bethlehem Academy, another well-known school in Hardin County, was founded in St. John in 1830. (Courtesy of Brown-Pusey House.)

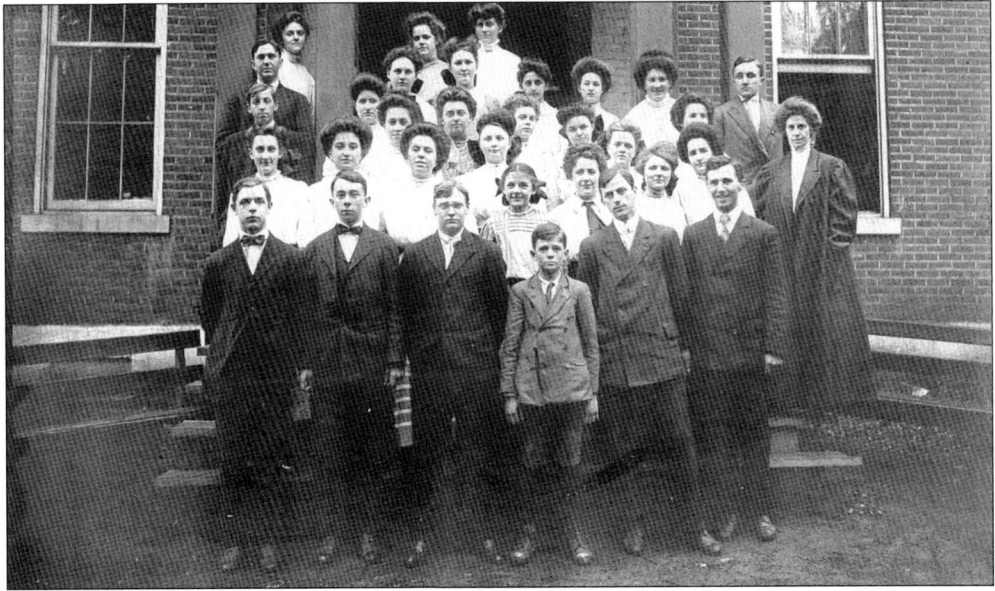

Pictured is Lynnland College in Glendale, and the people are unidentified. The school was variously known as Lynnland College, Lynnland Military Institute, Lynnland Female College, and Lynnland Male and Female Institute. Social activities in the early 20th century were held at Lynnland, Bethlehem, and Hardin County Fair. (Courtesy of Brown-Pusey House.)

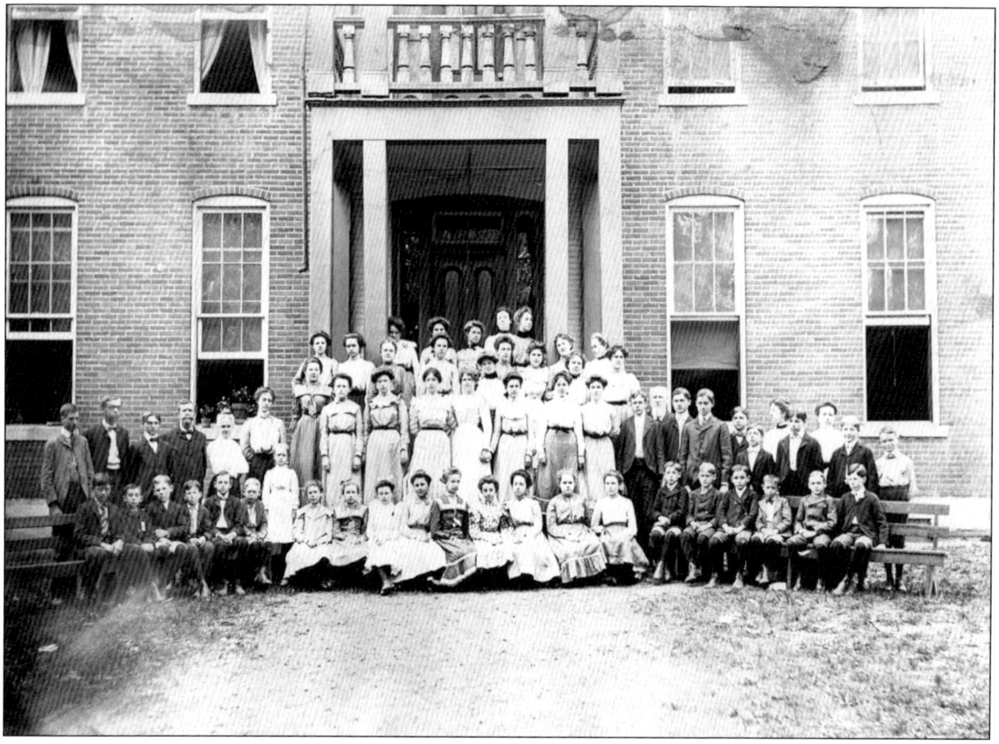

Pictured is Lynnland College in Glendale, and the people are unidentified. (Courtesy of Brown-Pusey House.)

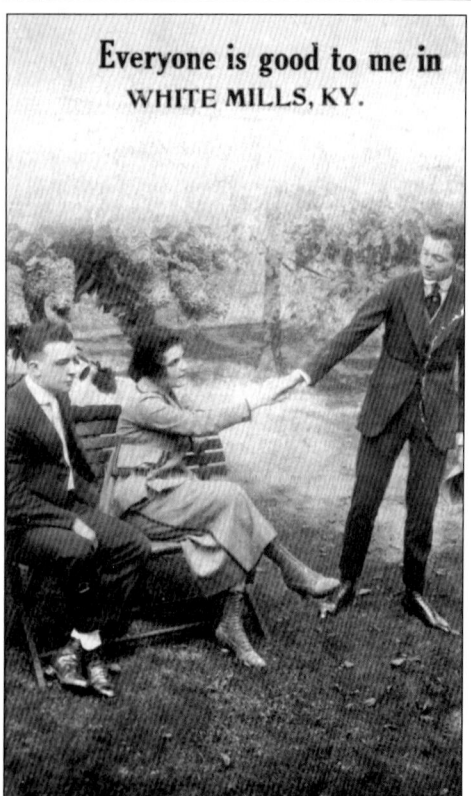

White Mills is located in the southwestern part of Hardin County, about two miles from East View on the Paducah and Elizabethtown Railroad (P&E). In 1879, the population was 127; F. M. Caswell was a wagon maker. Advertisements in the late 1880s invited manufacturing enterprises to White Mills because of the superior waterpower. (Courtesy of Meranda Caswell.)

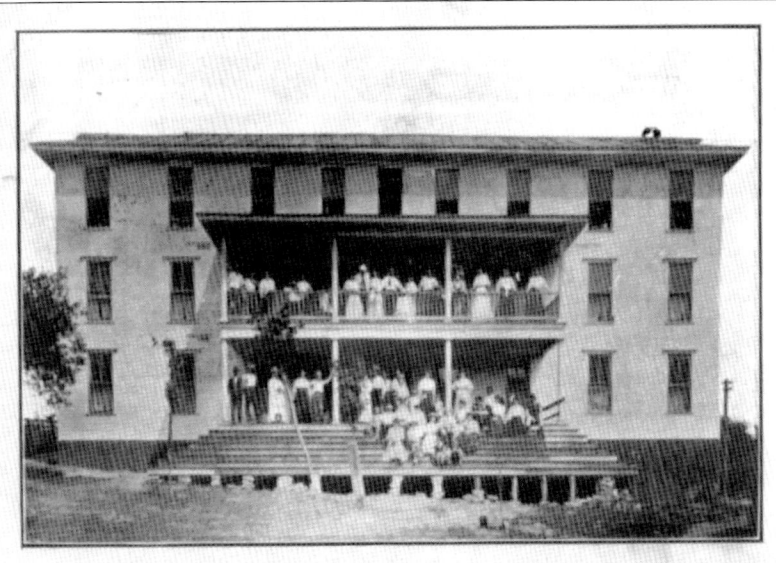

White Mills Hotel, White Mills, Ky.   Pub. by R. O. Morrison

This picture postcard shows the White Mills Hotel and is postmarked August 12, 1907. B. A. Hatfield had a boardinghouse in the 1880s. J. C. Percival was a manufacturer of grain cradles in the 1880s. The population of White Mills has been, at most, about 150 inhabitants. This area was good for fishing, swimming, and boating. (Courtesy of Meranda Caswell.)

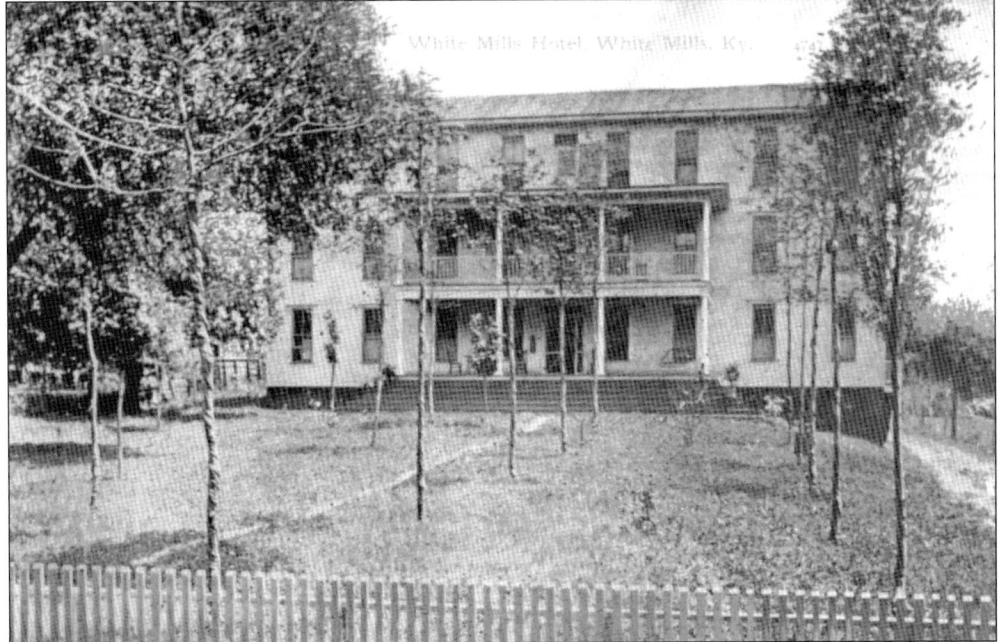

James Buchanan, the 15th U.S. president, arrived in Elizabethtown in 1813 to defend the title to the 5,900 acres of land that his father had purchased on Doe Run in Meade County (then Hardin County) and four miles south of the mouth of Valley Creek in White Mills in 1796. The title was in litigation from 1803 until it was cleared in 1822. The Buchanans were able to sell the land for a profit soon after. (Courtesy of Meranda Caswell.)

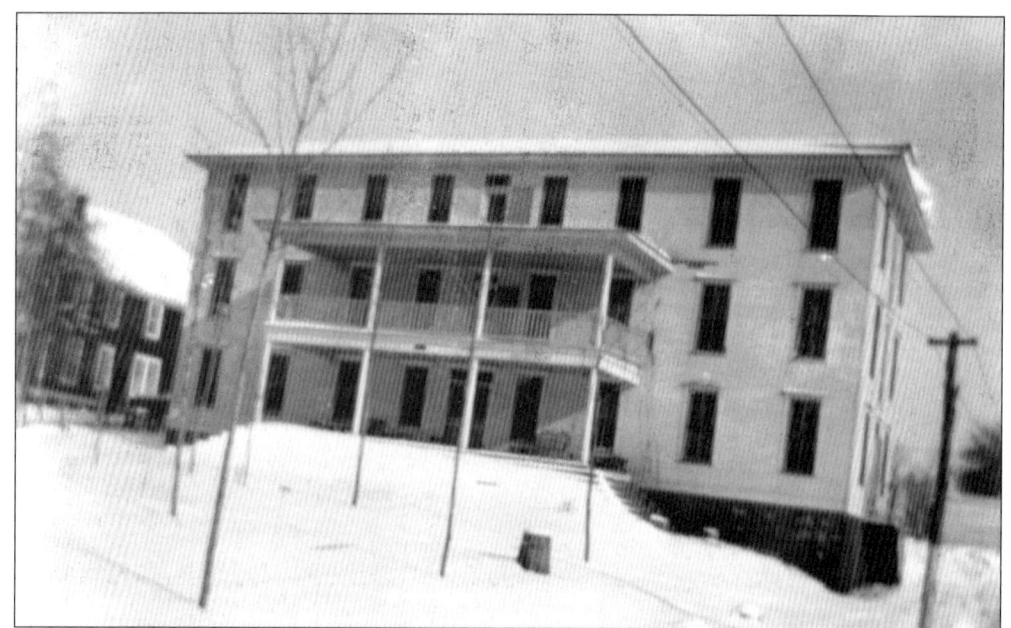

Richardson Hotel was a large, three-story, frame building with 50 rooms and a dining-room capacity of about 200 people. Dr. and Mrs. Hayward Richardson established it. Joe D. Richardson owned the mill rights. Guests arrived by train at East View. The hotel declined and closed about 1938. In 1943, Louis Songster reopened the Richardson Hotel and operated it for about 10 years. In 1948, White Mills Christian Assembly bought the hotel and started a summer camp for young people of all denominations. (Courtesy of Brown-Pusey House.)

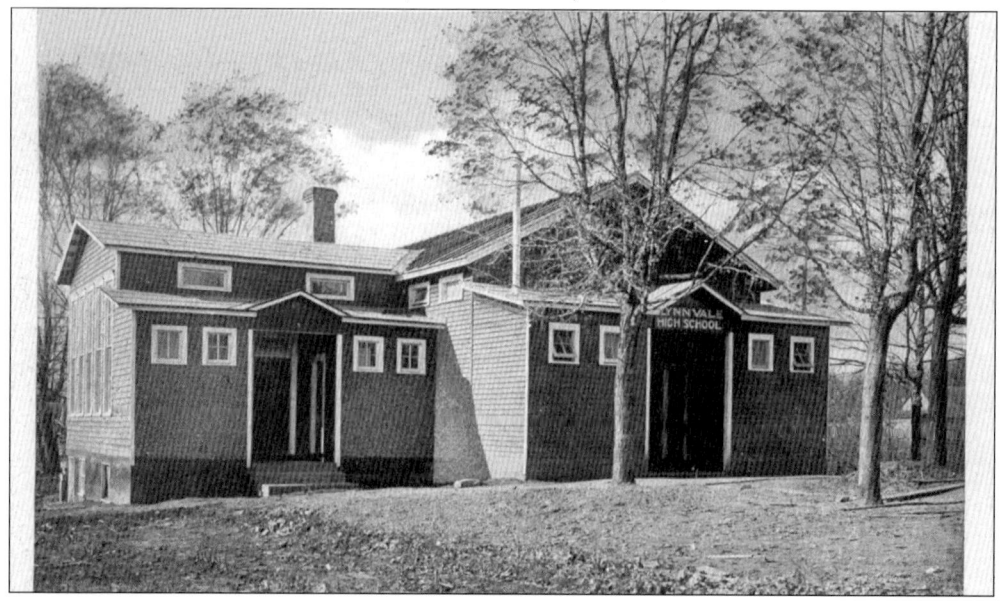

The first school at White Mills was the Lynnvale Academy, which was conducted from 1870 to 1910. Lynnvale High School, located in White Mills, was built in the early 1920s and was remodeled in 1943. In 1943–1944, Henry E. Pilkenton was the principal. Hardin County high schools were consolidated in 1962, and this school was closed. This postcard was published for Guy W. Jones on June 24, 1925. (Courtesy of Carolyn Wimp.)

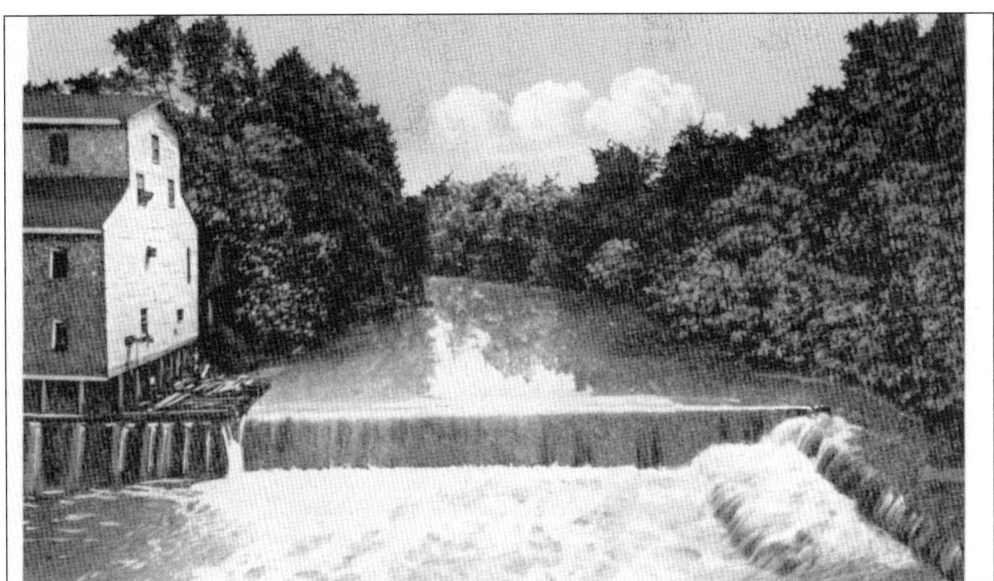

This postcard of the mill in White Mills was published for Guy W. Jones. Rev. J. D. Richardson was a miller at White Mills. He had a wool-carding machine and bought a great deal of wool all over the county. The wool was turned into cording material and was taken by ox-drawn wagons to East View, the nearest railroad station, for shipment. He was founder and the chief cornerstone of the White Mills Christian Church. His son, Marshall, succeeded him in business. (Courtesy of Meranda Caswell.)

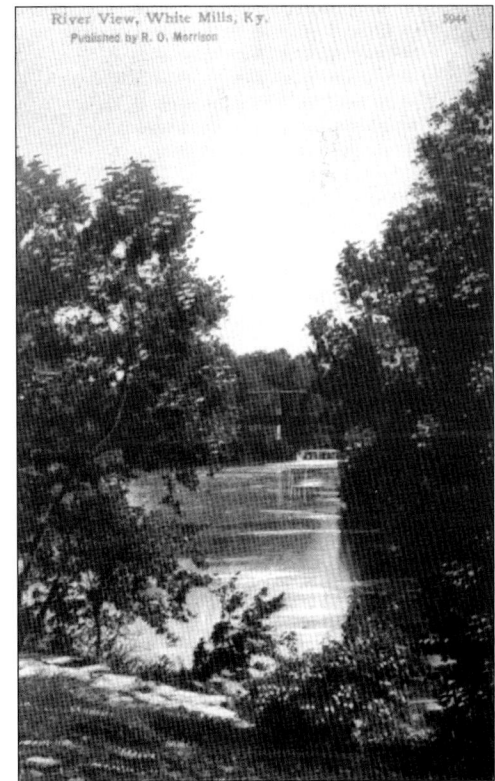

This river view in White Mills is postmarked on June 26, 1912. In 1901, J. D. Richardson and Sons had completed their new store dam at White Mills. Wortham and Richardson had a flour mill and wool-carding business in 1879. The Hatfields had several businesses here, such as a boardinghouse, funeral home, and a post office; later they were in the hotel business. (Courtesy of Meranda Caswell.)

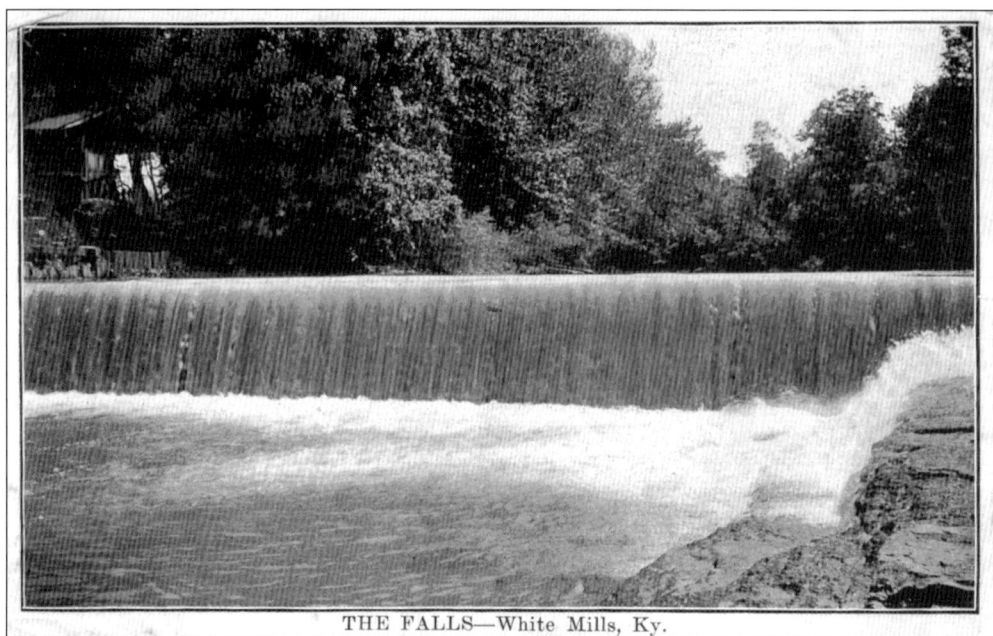

The falls at White Mills, seen in this postcard postmarked in August 1919, are located on land once owned by James Buchanan of Franklin County, Pennsylvania, father of Pres. James Buchanan. The high iron bridge spanning the river in the center of town was built in 1899. The White Mills post office was established June 19, 1866, and the first postmaster was Granville S. Hastings. (Courtesy of Elvin Smith Jr.)

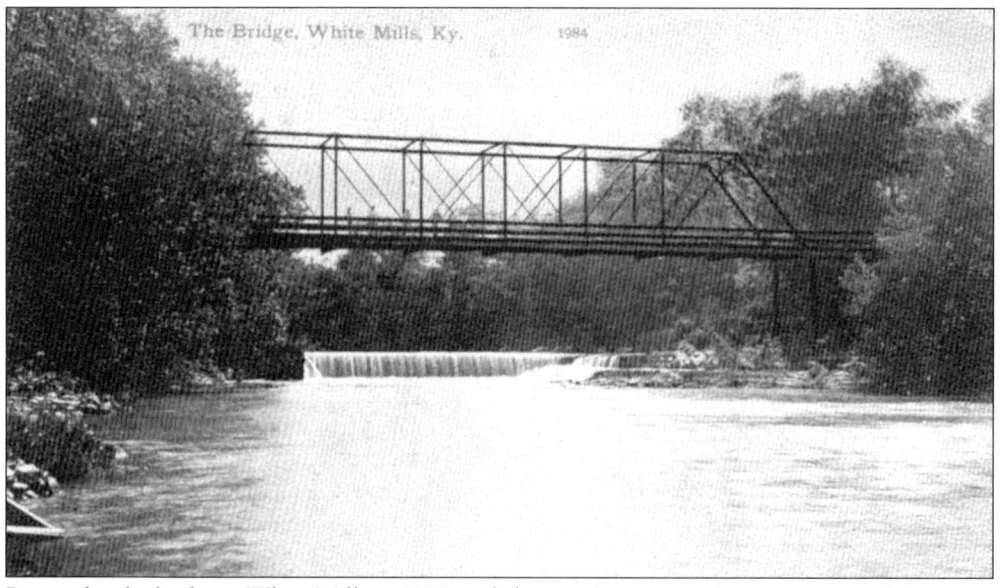

Pictured is the bridge at White Mills in 1909, and close to this town is the community of Harcourt, which saw the immigration of Catholics in the early 19th century. The church St. Ignatius was built in 1842 and was razed prior to the 1920s. In 1874, the Hardin County post offices were Cecilia, Dorrett's Run, East View, Elizabethtown, Franklin Cross Roads, Grand View, High Up, Howe's Valley, Nolin, Red Hill, Robertsonville, Sonora, Stephensburg, Uptonville, Vine Grove, West Point, and White Mills. (Courtesy of Meranda Caswell.)

Four
WEST OF U.S. 31 WEST

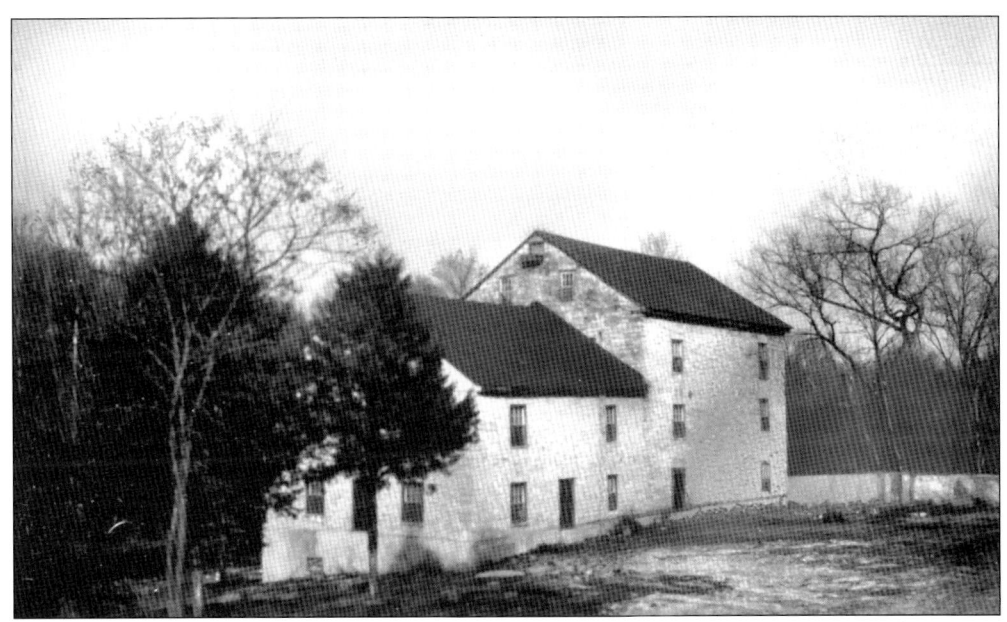

Doe Run Mill, pictured in the late 19th or early 20th century, is still in existence in Meade County. Meade County separated from Hardin County in 1824. To research Meade County records and families, one must research the records in its surrounding counties as well as Hardin County and Jefferson and Fincastle Counties, Virginia. Another example of an early-19th-century mill is located in Bardstown, Nelson County, next to the Civil War Museum. (Courtesy of Brown-Pusey House.)

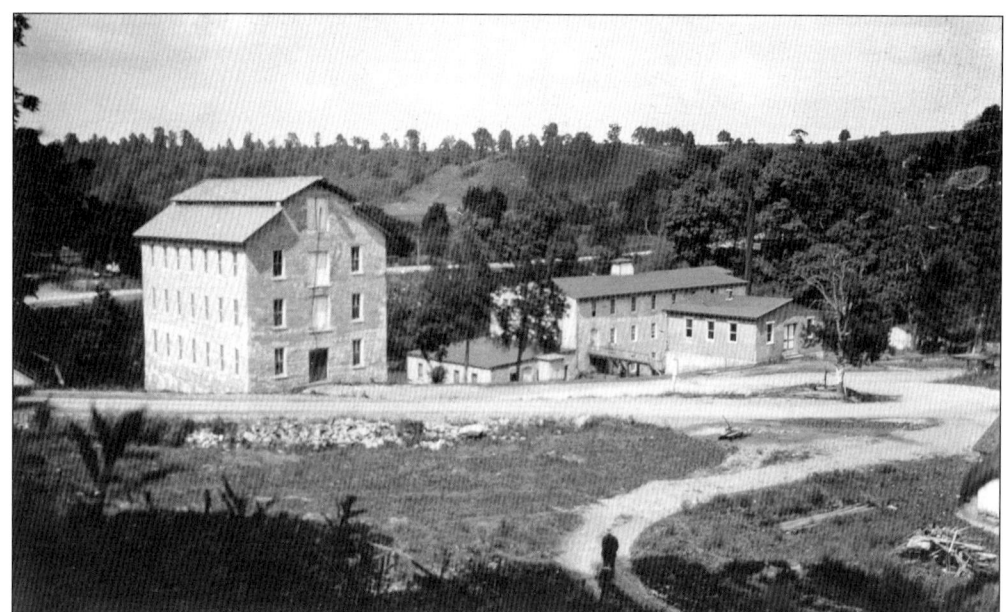

Grahampton Mill was a rock milldam about 150 feet long and 8 feet high. It had a large stone flour mill four stories high. A turnpike was partially built at Grahampton intended to run to Rock Haven but was not finished because building of the Louisville and Cecilia Railroad rendered it unnecessary. J. E. Brawner was a water boy during the construction and a rodman on the survey of the pike in 1868. Grahamton, the oldest textile mill in Kentucky, was closed on October 22, 1940, to make way for the expansion of Fort Knox. (Courtesy of Brown-Pusey House.)

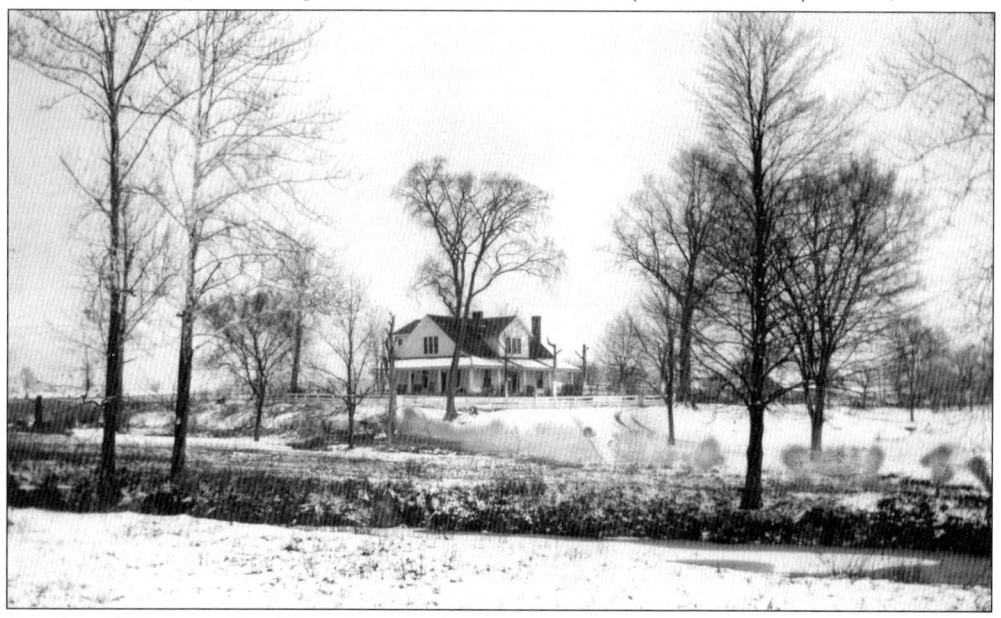

Comfortable homes and well-kept farmsteads were seen in Hardin County in the late 19th century. After the Great Depression in 1937, Pres. Franklin D. Roosevelt designated the last Thursday of November as a day of national thanksgiving. President Roosevelt passed through Elizabethtown on June 14, 1936. He visited the Lincoln farm at Hodgenville, then he returned to Elizabethtown, where he boarded a train for Louisville. (Courtesy of Brown-Pusey House.)

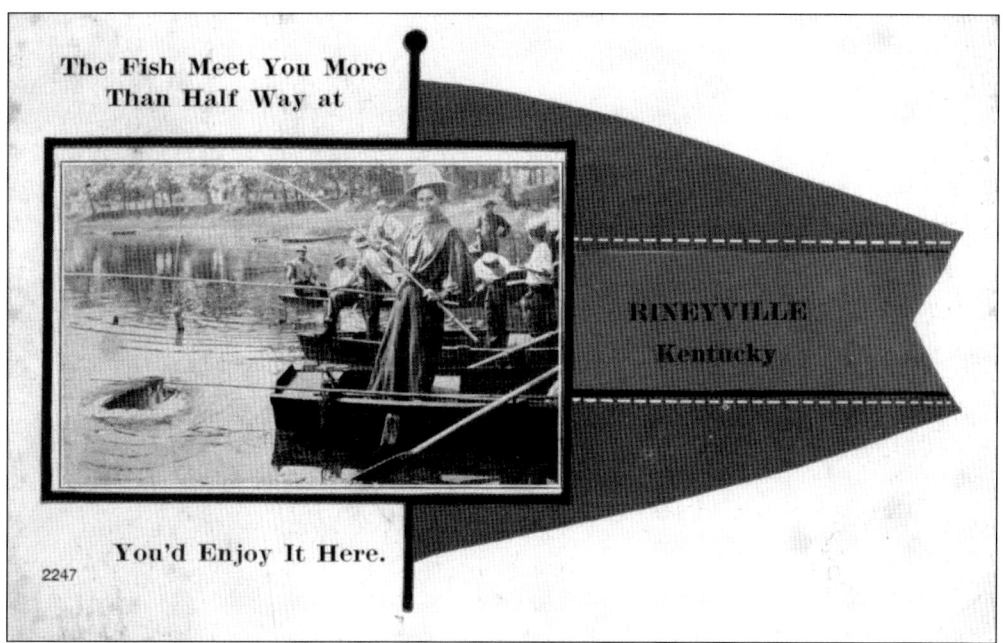

This postcard was postmarked in 1910. Rineyville was named after Zachariah Riney, the first schoolteacher of Pres. Abraham Lincoln. In the 1880s, this town had 75 inhabitants with John Miles as postmaster and operator of a general store. This station was on the Cecilia branch of the L&N. (Courtesy of Meranda Caswell.)

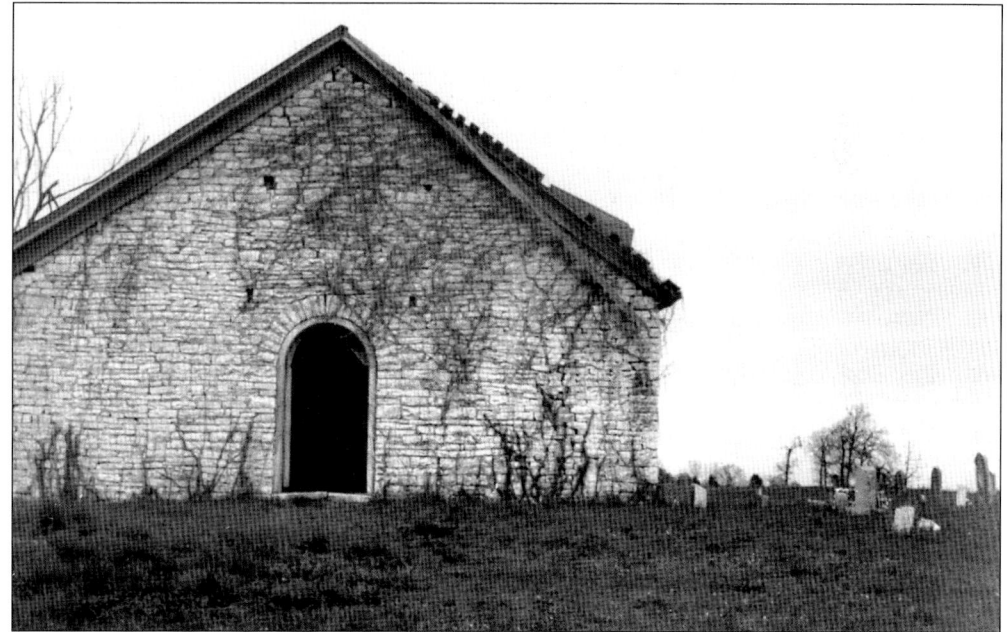

Old Stone Church, pictured with a cemetery, was located in the Star Mills area. This church was a meeting place for different denominations and burned down after the 1960s. James Marriott was the founder and operator of Star Mills in 1879. One mile from this site, John Morrison built a two-story home about 1835. The first story was made of the same type of stone used in the church. (Courtesy of Brown-Pusey House.)

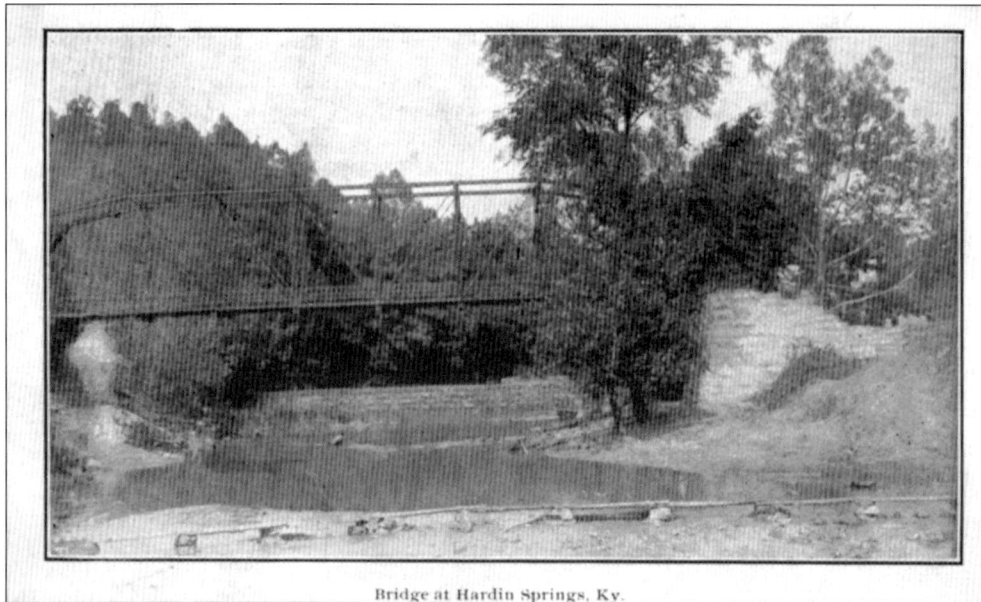

Bridge at Hardin Springs, Ky.

The Bridge at Hardin Springs was erected in 1911. Hardin Springs is located at the western edge of Hardin County just a few yards from both Grayson and Breckinridge Counties. This was a commercial center for the agriculture area. Hardin Springs is still a popular place for fishing. (Courtesy of Carolyn Wimp.)

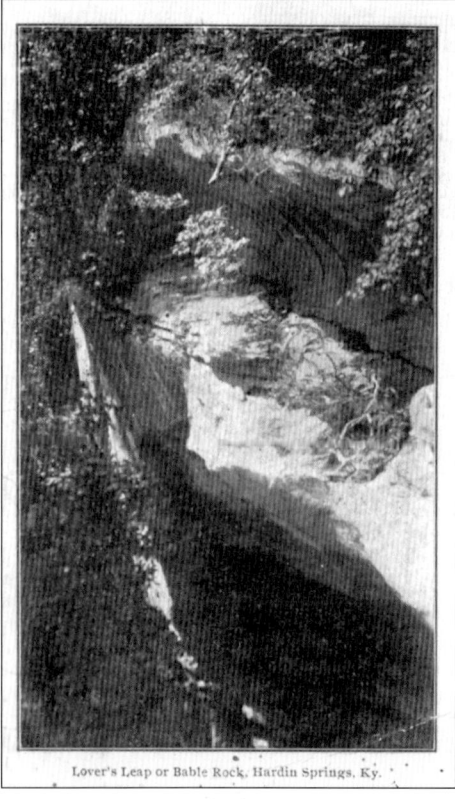

Lover's Leap or Bable Rock, Hardin Springs, Ky.

Lover's Leap or Bable Rock is located in Hardin Springs. From 1900 to 1903, Merry Makers, a club that met each year for two weeks, camped at Hardin Springs. Virgil Harris, Frank Warren, Hugh E. Bland, Claude Brown, Charlie Gray, and Henry Hardin organized this club. Residents of Hardin County and surrounding counties visited Hardin Springs, Grayson Springs, White Mills, Sulphur Springs, and many other water areas for medicinal waters and entertainment. (Courtesy of Carolyn Wimp.)

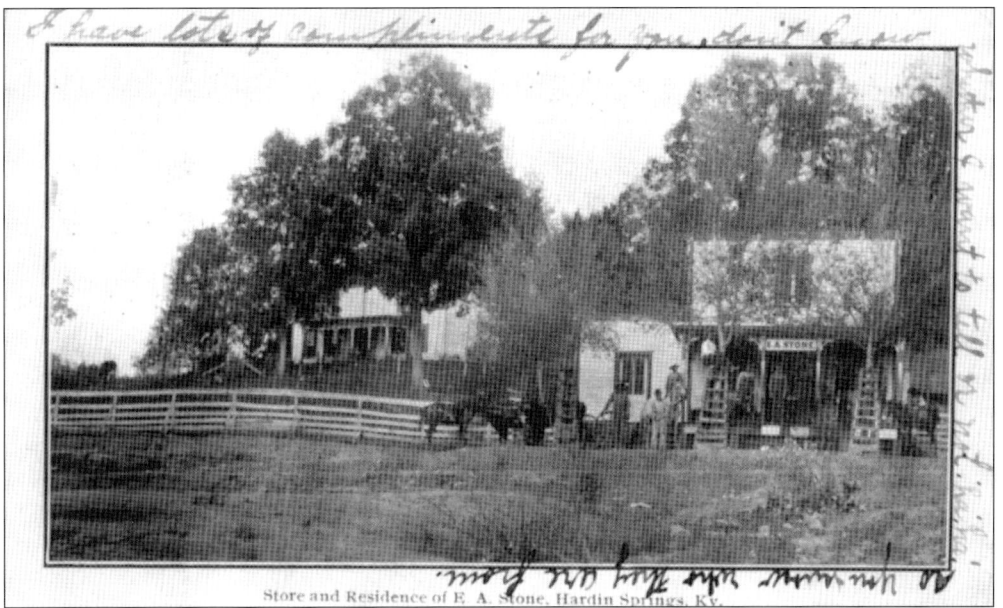

This early-20th-century general store located in Hardin Springs was also the residence of E. A. Stone. Stone sold caskets at his general store. Hardin Springs, the popular watering place, opened on June 15, 1895, with Allison and Stone as proprietors. (Courtesy of Carolyn Wimp.)

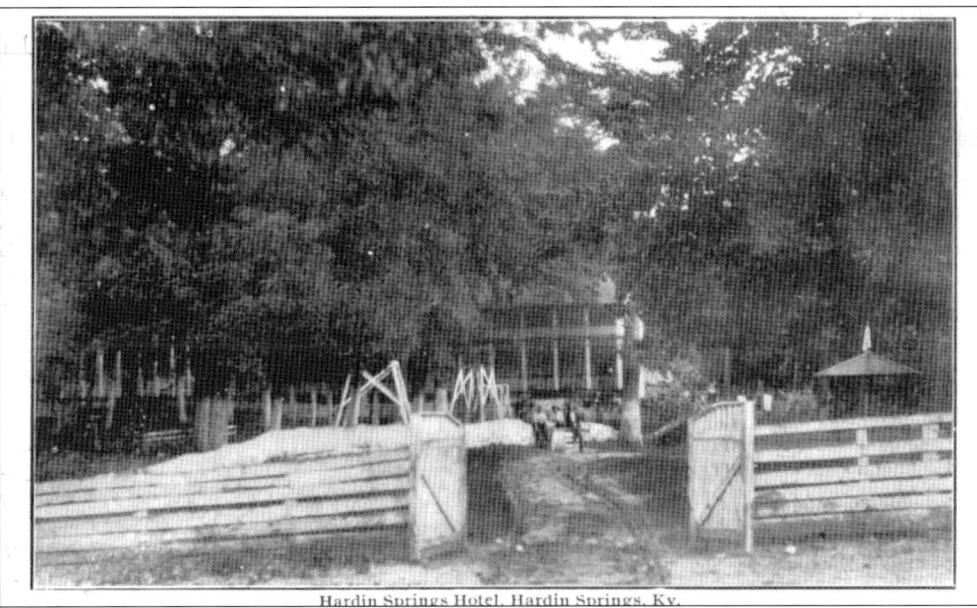

Hardin Springs Hotel, bought by Henry Gotthardt in the early 20th century, had a sulphur spring. It was a vacation spot to drink the spring water and to go horseback riding. Will Goddard owned the hotel before it closed in 1932. This hotel had 34 rooms. Willie Gray tore down the hotel after he bought it. (Courtesy of Carolyn Wimp.)

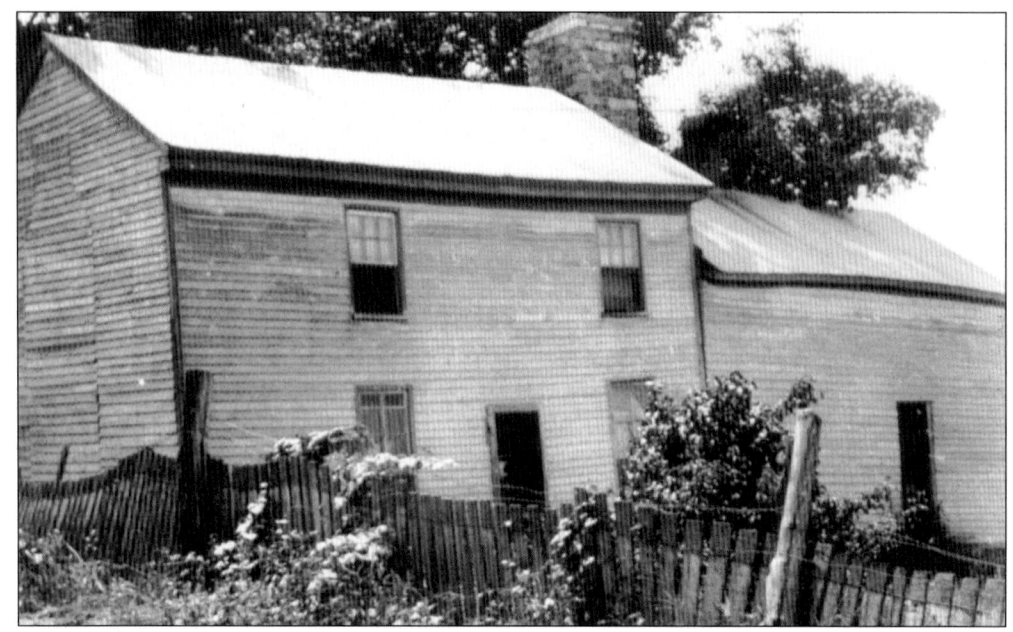

One mile from the Vertrees post office is the home of Joseph (son of Capt. John Vertrees) and Margaret Hodgen Vertrees, built in 1810 between the fork of Vertrees Creek and Rough Creek in Hardin County, Kentucky. This photograph was taken about September 1933. (Courtesy of Pat Sadler.)

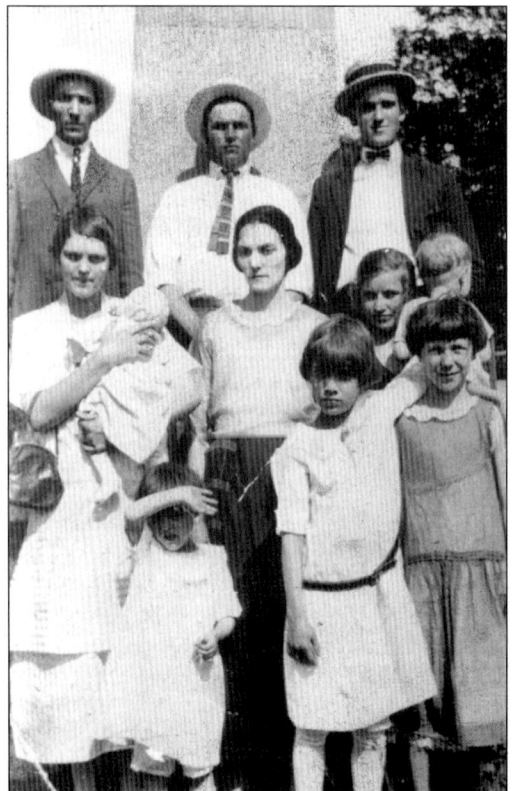

Pictured is the Vertrees family about 1925. From left to right are (first row) Lois Vertrees, Lillian Vertrees, and Lela Mae Vertrees Cain; (second row) Mattie E. Vertrees, Herbert Vertrees Jr., Lula Vertrees Cain, and Magdaline Cain Harper; (third row) Herbert M. Vertrees, William Walter Cain, and Barney Lee Harper. Near the town of Vertrees are the towns of Arch, Grandview, Fairfarm, and Howevalley. (Courtesy of Pat Sadler.)

George Washington Smith built the pictured house at Smith's Mill about 1870. It is located near the site of a former mill on Valley Creek on Bacon Creek Road. This road leads to Star Mills, White Mills, and Buckles Mill. Nearby are Harcourt, Glendale, Homeland Station, Glendale Children's Home, and Nolin. (Courtesy of Brown-Pusey House.)

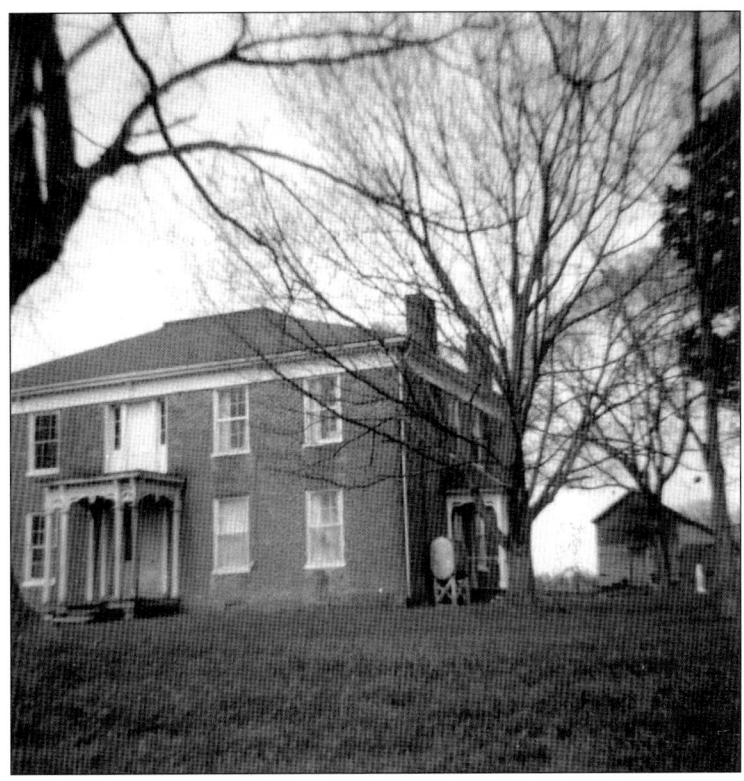

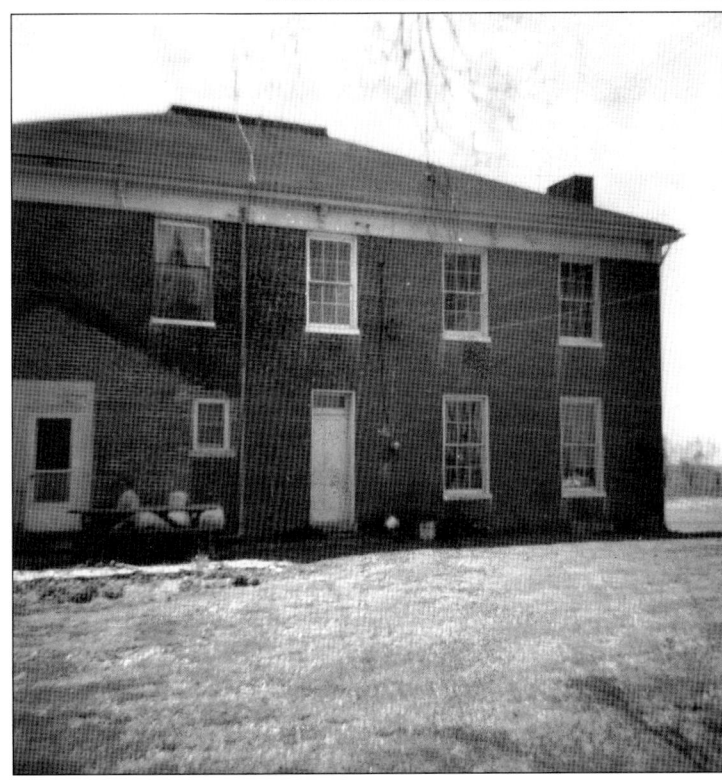

Smith's Mill and the other mills no longer exist. All of the mills used the Nolin River water to operate the gristmills. Valley Creek empties into the Nolin River near Smith's Mill. Part of Valley Creek is in downtown Elizabethtown. W. H. Gardner Implement Company had a lumberyard across the Valley Creek Bridge where items purchased in the late 19th century included buggies, wagons, plows, washing machines, and churns. (Courtesy of Brown-Pusey House.)

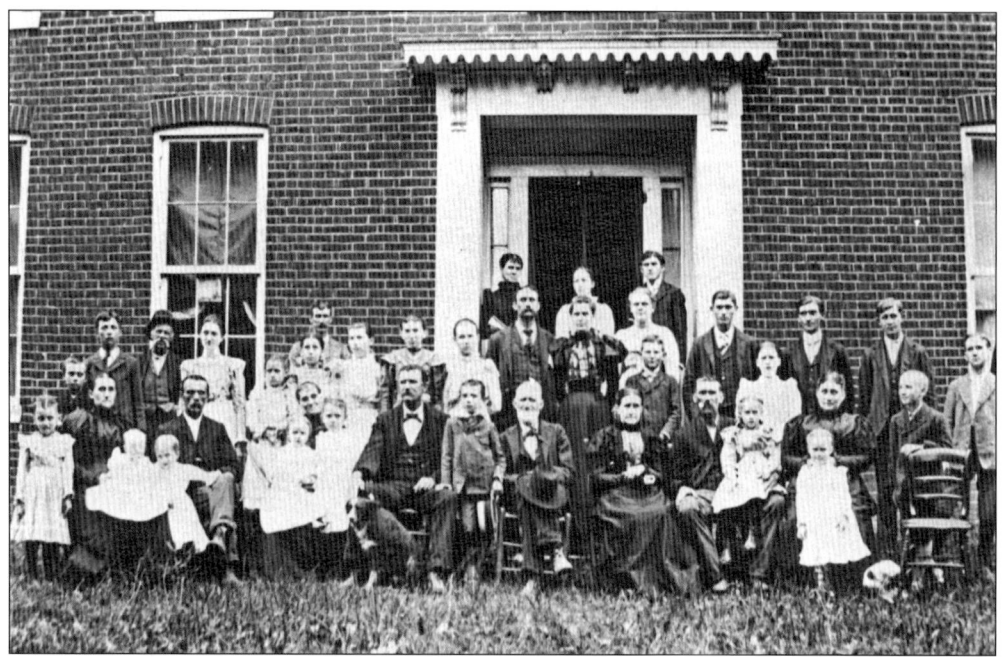

Daniel D. Pickerill's house and family are pictured about 1899. The house is known today as the Bland-Overall House. Seated at left are Elisha G. Scott, his family, and his wife, Elizabeth Ann Pickerill Scott. This building is located on Kentucky 1868, which leads from Glendale to the middle of Kentucky 720, leading to Sonora or Flint Hill. (Courtesy of Brown-Pusey House.)

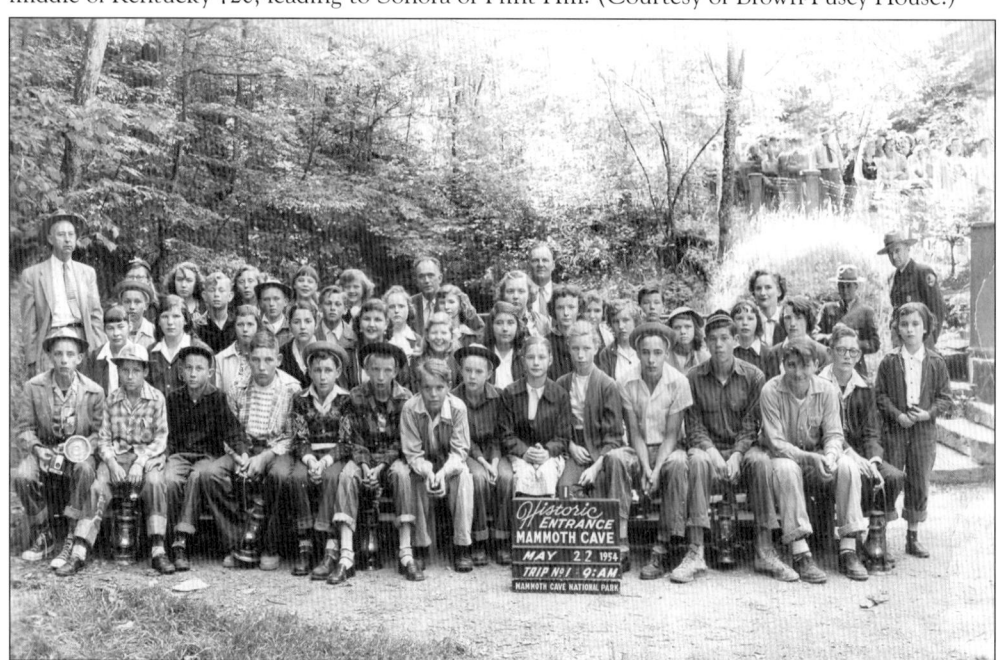

Principal Lindsey of Howevalley Graded and High School and janitor Mr. Flowers took the following children to Mammoth Cave in 1954 for a class field trip: Betty Jo Wilcox, Gene Wimp, Eloise Miller, Vera Gardner, Susan Gardner, James Willyard, Carolyn Wilson, Phyllis Dotson, Virginia Sprinkler, Phillip Addington, Jimmie Dunn, and others. (Courtesy of Carolyn Wimp.)

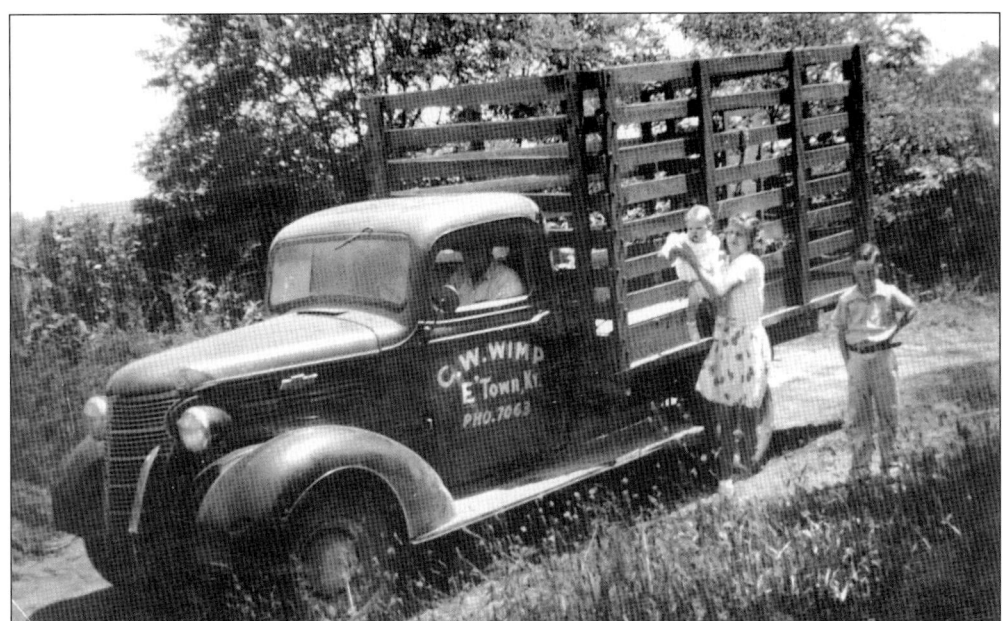

From left to right, Wayne, Carolyn, Iva, and Jimmie Wimp are preparing to deliver products with the truck advertised as "C. W. Wimp, Phone 7063." The telephone operator system was brought into existence in Hardin County in the late 19th century. Following this system were four-digit phone numbers, then five-digit phone numbers, and then seven-digit phone numbers. Telephone directories from 1889 to 2006 of Hardin County can be viewed at the Brown-Pusey House. (Courtesy of Carolyn Wimp.)

Iva, Carolyn, and Kenneth Wimp are pictured from left to right with their house in the 1940s. White Dove flour was manufactured and sold by the Cecilian Milling Company, once owned by M. A. Cooper. It was one of Kentucky's largest businesses in the early 20th century. An advertisement of this business could be seen painted on the side of a building in Elizabethtown as well as a store outlet. (Courtesy of Carolyn Wimp.)

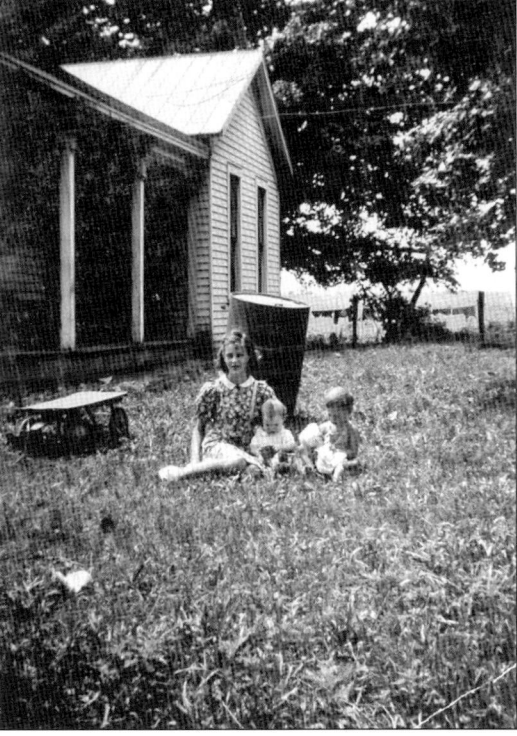

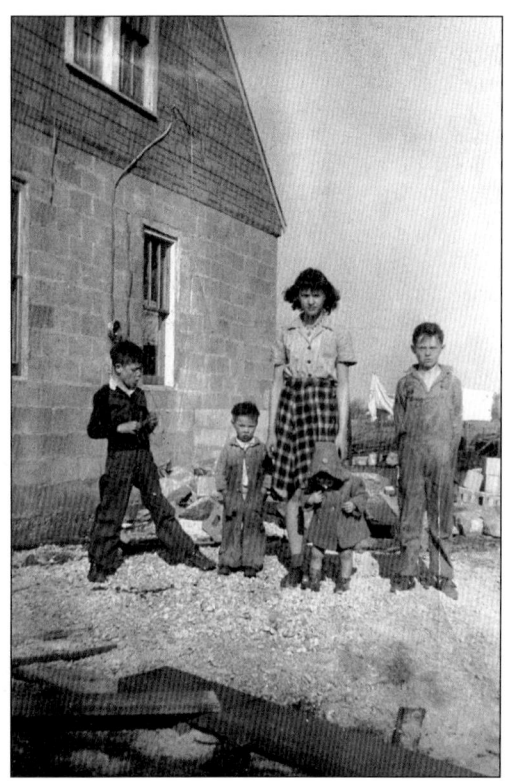

From left to right, Gene, Kenneth, Iva, Carolyn, and Jimmie Wimp are from Cecilia, and their farm is adjacent to the land that once belonged to the Cecilian College. Charles Cecil married Rebecca, the daughter of Denton Geoghegan. Henry Cecil, Charles's brother, was the president of this world-renowned college in 1860. The town of Cecilia was established about 1871 as Cecilian, a railroad town. Cecilian College brought travellers to the area when the railroad was built, and the Cecil brothers continued to operate Cecilian College. (Courtesy of Carolyn Wimp.)

Mayme Lee Wimp and her husband, Wayne Wimp, lived in Cecilia and worked in Cecilia and Elizabethtown. Cecilia had two creeks that flowed through it: West Rhudes Creek and Dry Branch Creek. Some of the early families of Cecilia were Morrison, Slinker, English, Cecil, Mossbarger, Aud, Nusz, Marriott, Heller, Kurtz, Bobo, and Creager. John Heller, born in Germany, operated Heller's Hotel in Cecilia in the late 1880s. (Courtesy of Carolyn Wimp.)

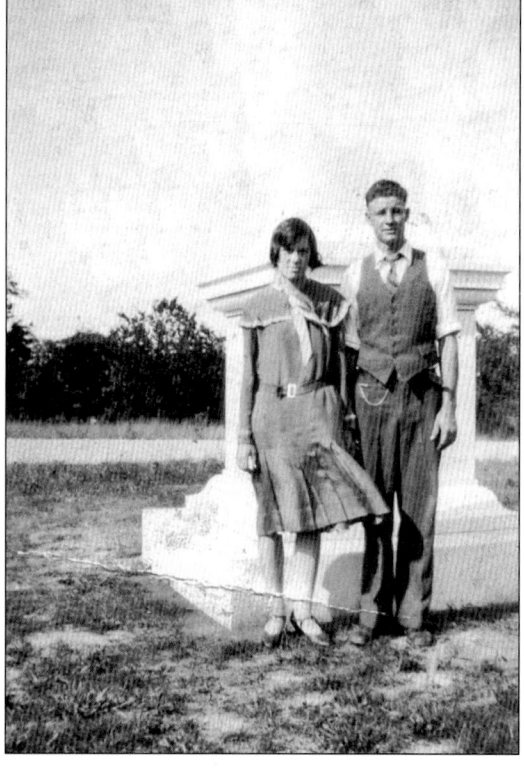

Around 1848, Greenberry Gaither built part of the Hazelnut Hill house, pictured, at Gaither Station. Little information is known about this station on the L&N near Valley Creek and in the middle of the two towns of Cecilia and Glendale. Dr. A. Shore, a vice president of the railroad after the Civil War, built part of this building. (Courtesy of Brown-Pusey House.)

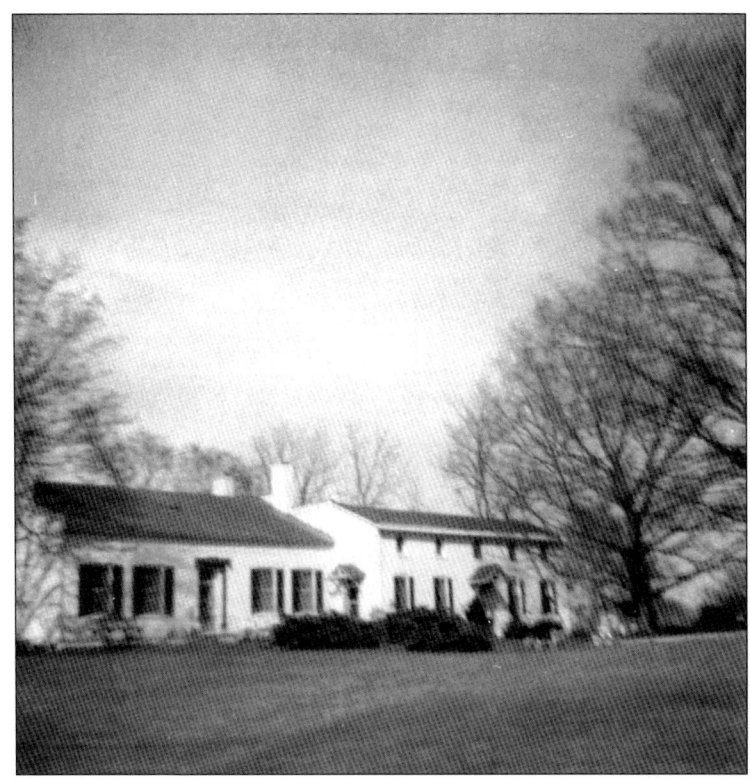

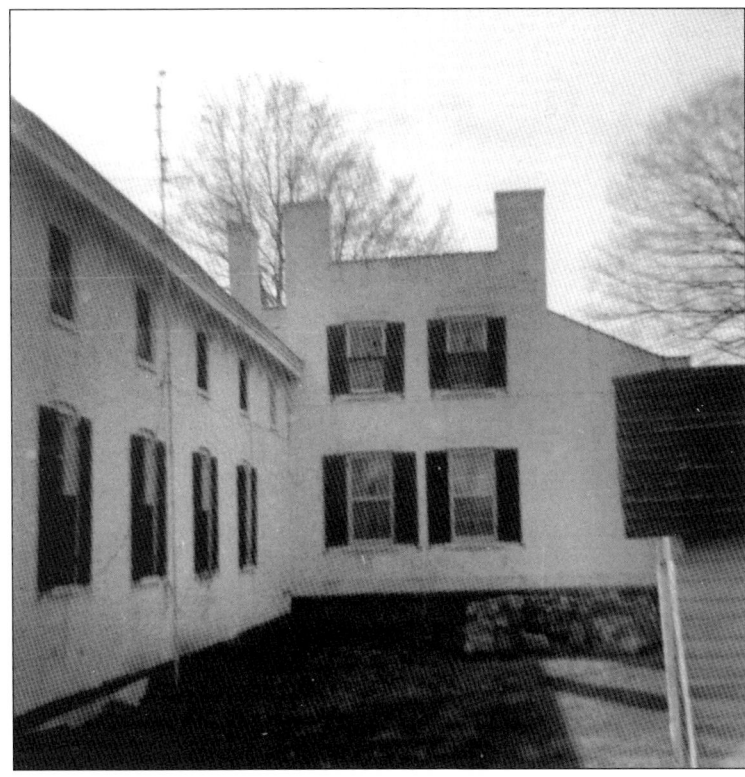

Pictured is the rear view of Hazelnut Hill. (Courtesy of Brown-Pusey House.)

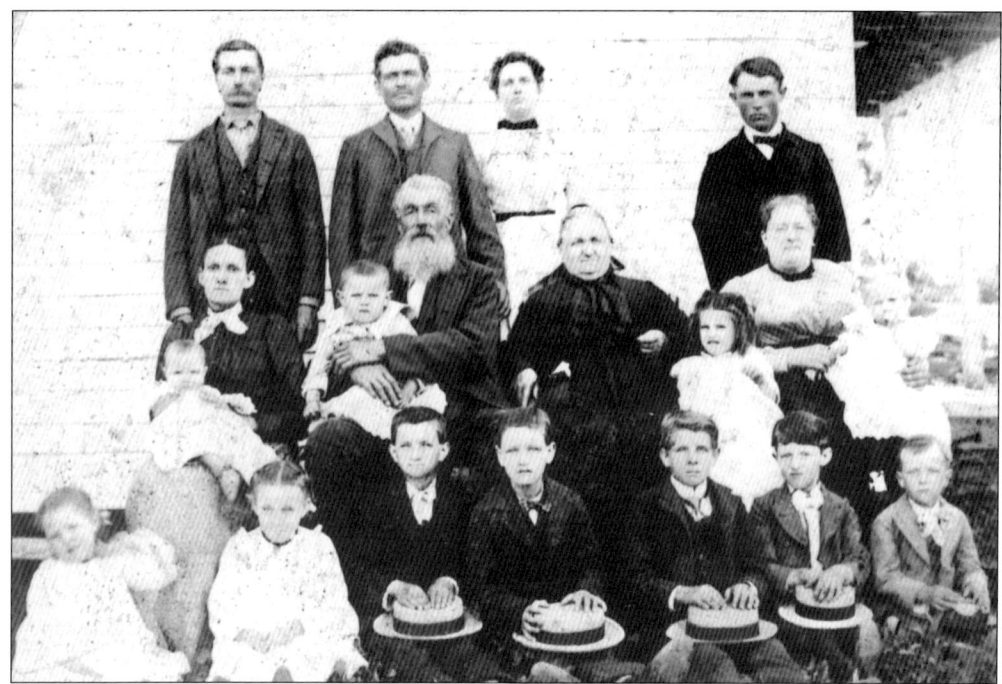

This photograph was taken after February 1899. Identified from left to right are (first row) Cliff Hoskinson's two girls and three boys, Vernie Spradlin, and Eddie Spradlin; (second row) wife of Cliff Hoskinson holding baby, James Mark Hoskinson holding James Spradlin, who was born February 16, 1899, Mary Payne Hoskinson, Pearl Spradlin, and Valeria Hoskinson Spradlin holding Goldie Spradlin Hutcherson; (third row) Clifford Hoskinson, Jody (Fox) Gray, Kate Hoskinson Gray, and Thomas Gray Spradlin. (Courtesy of Brown-Pusey House.)

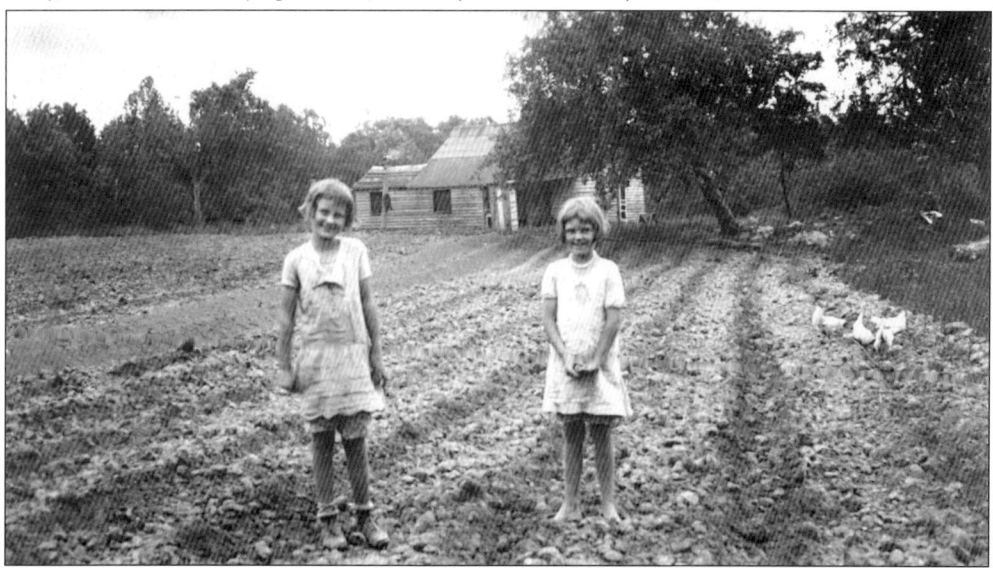

Winsome children were living in surroundings of dilapidation in the early 20th century. The towns west of U.S. 31 West—East View, Link, Limp, Solway, Big Clifty, and Summit—are on the waters of Meeting Creek. In the 1920s, many landowners had five-year mineral leases through W. H. Giltner of Jefferson County, Kentucky. (Courtesy of Brown-Pusey House.)

Five

WARS

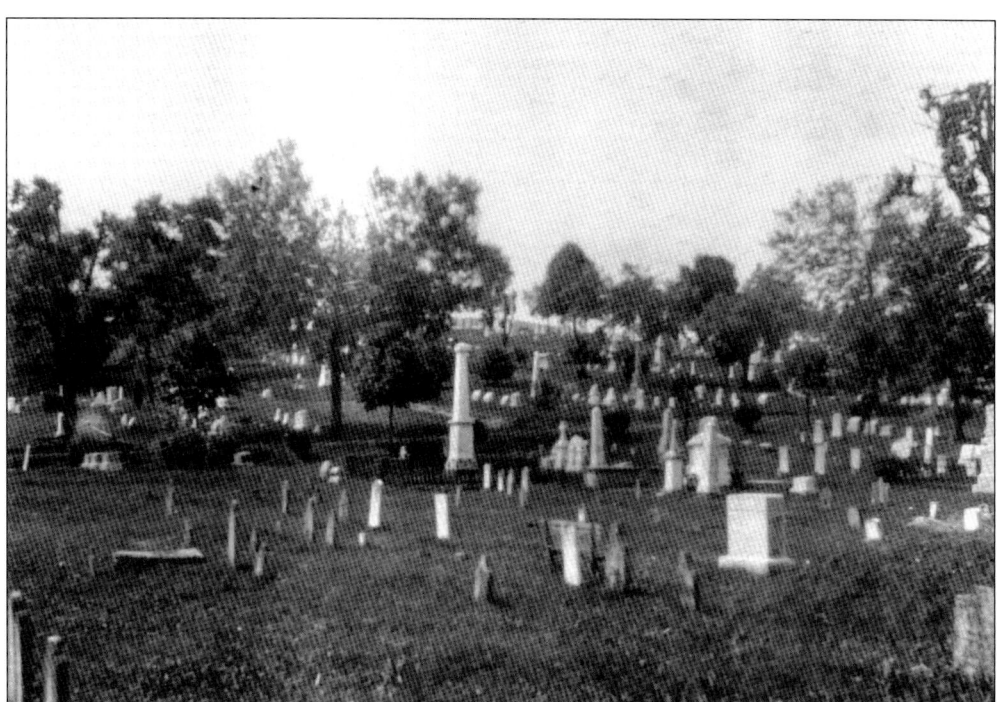

This photograph of the Elizabethtown City Cemetery was taken after 1872 and prior to 1930s. This is part of the site of Andrew Hynes's Revolutionary fort as well as the fort of John Hunt Morgan's troops during his Civil War raid on Hardin County. Gabriel Tichenor, from Sonora, was one of Morgan's soldiers who was captured and imprisoned by Union forces until the end of the Civil War. (Courtesy of Brown-Pusey House.)

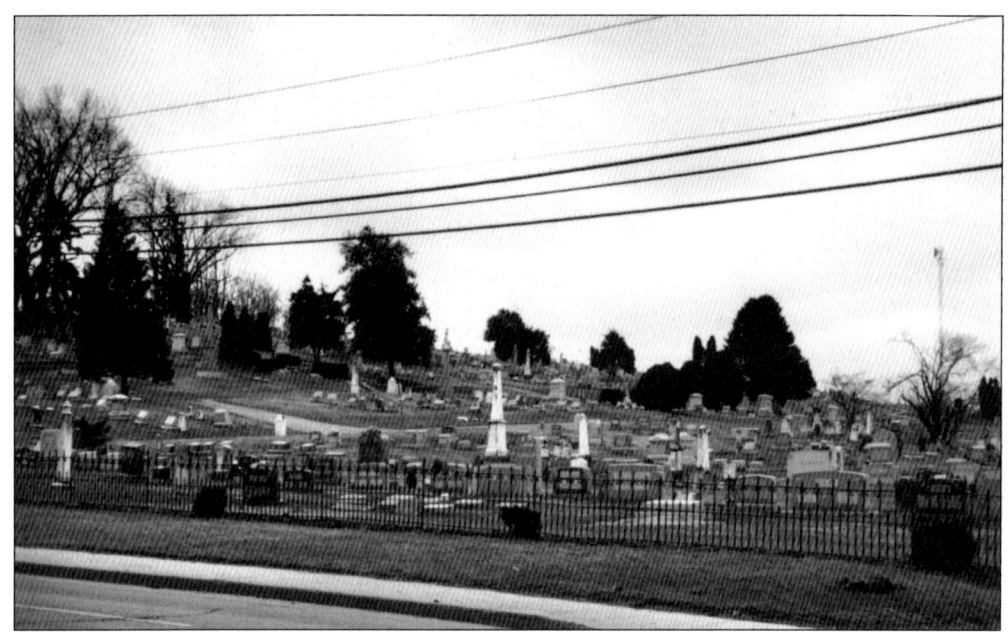

This Elizabethtown City Cemetery photograph, taken in 1996, is similar to the photograph on the previous page. The city purchased much of this land after the Civil War as a cemetery. The grave site of Philip Arnold, the man who was a partner in the great diamond mine hoax of the West in the mid-19th century, is located in this photograph. (Courtesy of Brown-Pusey House.)

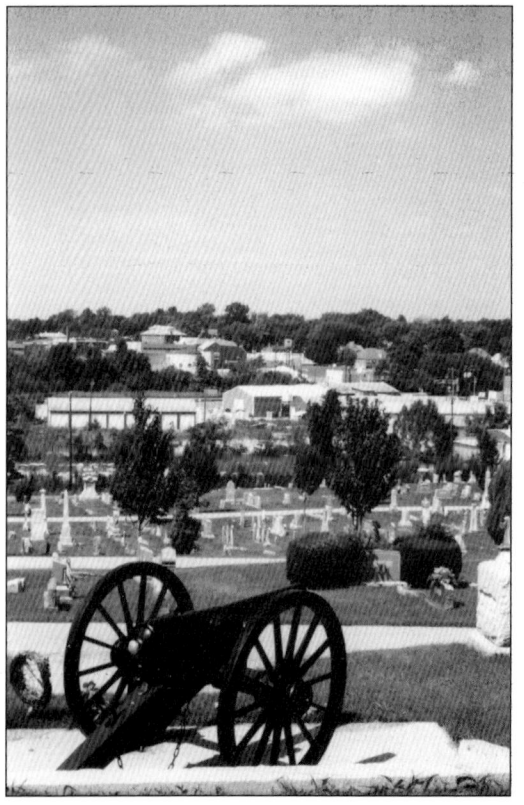

This replica of a Civil War canon that may have been used by the raiders of Confederate general John Hunt Morgan was placed in the Elizabethtown City Cemetery overlooking Elizabethtown. Morgan had traveled throughout the South, including Louisiana, wreaking havoc against the North. Morgan had also eaten at the Hill's Hotel during his raids of the county. Morgan gathered men to terrorize federal troops in Hardin County by destroying two L&N trestles on December 28, 1862, rendering lines impassible for two months. (Courtesy of Millie Robinson.)

John D. Gore recruited Company G of the 9th Regiment Kentucky Cavalry at Elizabethtown on August 15, 1862. They arrived at Eminence in Henry County, Kentucky, where the regiment was organized the next day and mustered into the United States' service at 10 o'clock the night of August 22, 1862. (Courtesy of Brown-Pusey House.)

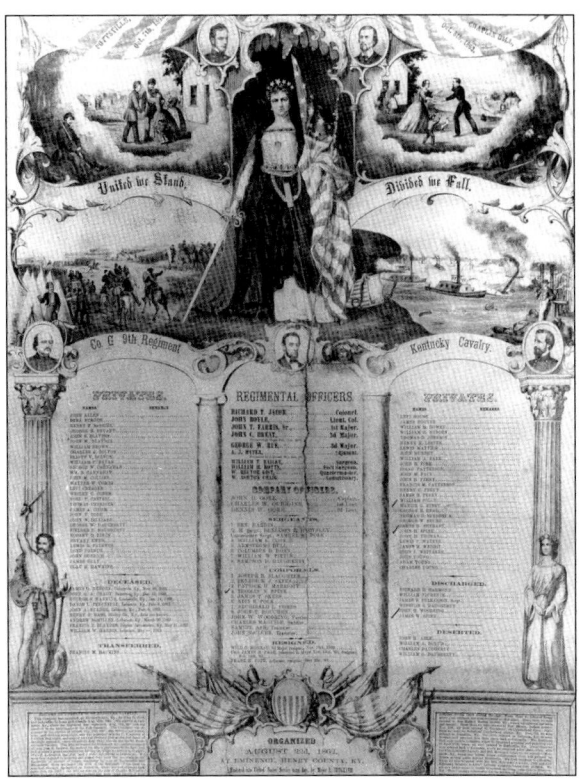

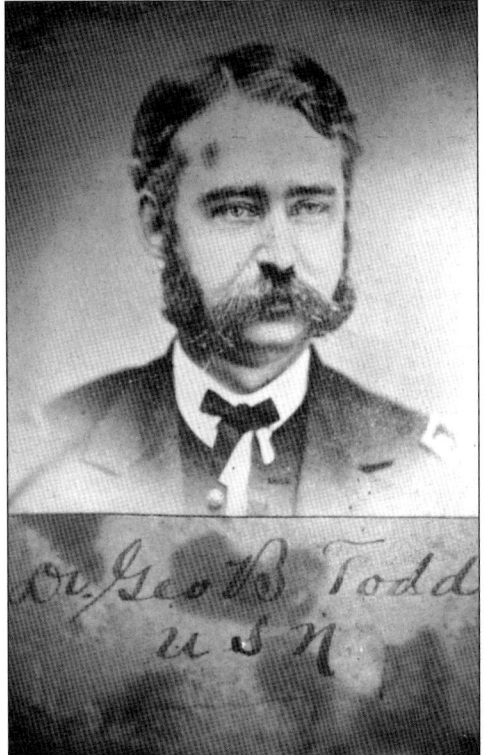

Dr. George B. Todd, pictured, was of the U.S. Navy during the Civil War. In the collection of the Brown-Pusey House are the items from the disbanded local chapter of the United Daughters of the Confederacy. Sallie Cunningham Pusey and Bell Brown Pusey were directly related to Confederate soldiers and veterans of the UDC. (Courtesy of Brown-Pusey House.)

Dr. Robert Burns Pusey graduated from a university in Philadelphia in 1860. This certificate states "that R. B. Pusey of Hardin County, State of Kentucky, claiming exemption on account of disability, has been carefully examined, and is found to be unfit for military duty by reason of contraction of chest, and, in consequence thereof, he is exempt from service under the present draft." It was dated at Shelbyville on December 17, 1863. (Courtesy of Brown-Pusey House.)

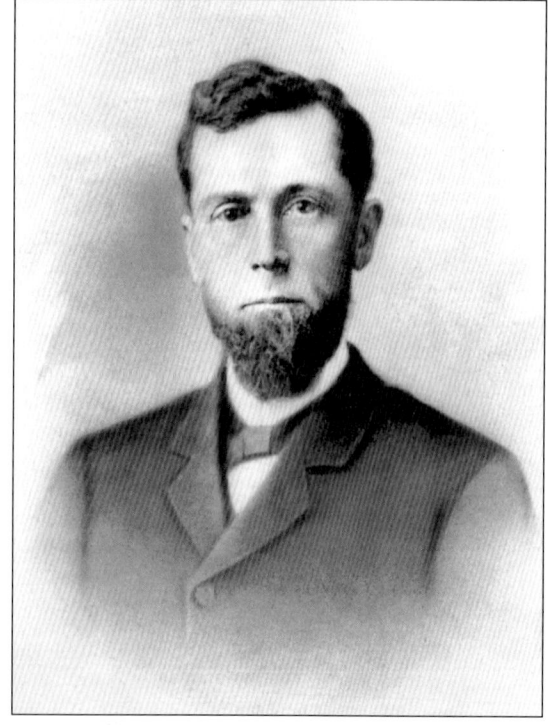

This is a retouched photograph of Robert Burns Pusey that was used in the oil painting by Katherine Helm in 1890. Photography has always been manipulated with additions and deletions of items. The retouching on this photograph shortened Robert's long beard. (Courtesy of Brown-Pusey House.)

Alfred Brown Pusey was in the U.S. Navy during World War I. Alfred was born in 1869 and went by the name of Brown Pusey. His father, Robert Burns Pusey, died in 1889. Alfred's memorabilia, such as his boots from the 1870s, his doctoral diploma in a metal case, and opium certificates from the Prohibition era, are all on display at the Brown-Pusey House. (Courtesy of Brown-Pusey House.)

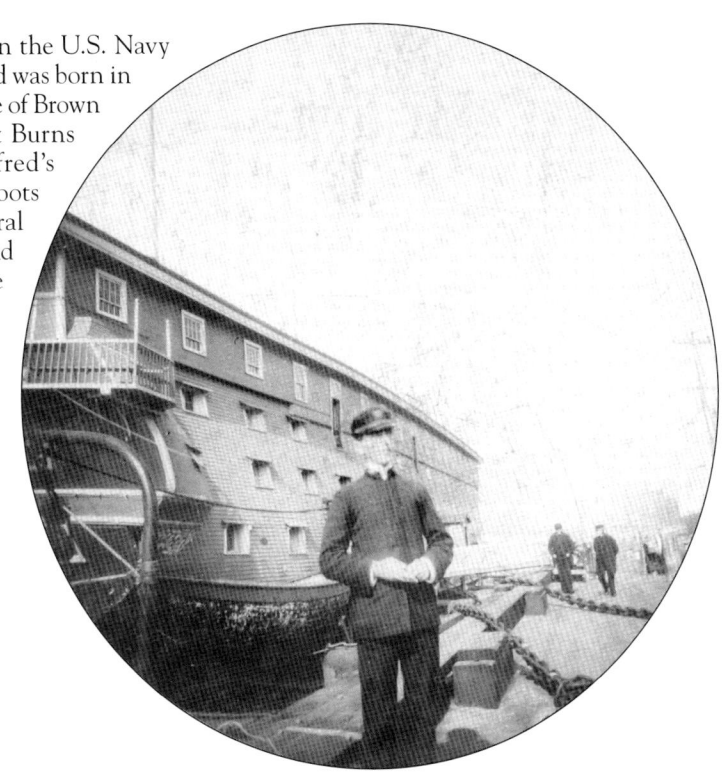

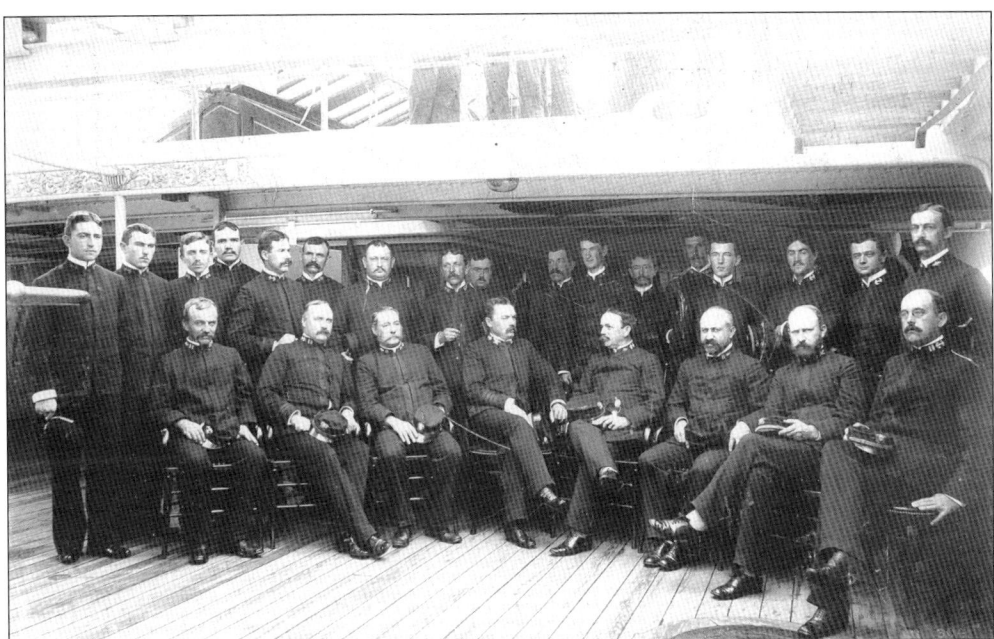

Pictured is a U.S. Navy crew during World War I with Alfred Brown Pusey (standing fourth from the right) and his fellow sailors. Included here are Payne, Sawyer, Waldo Evans, Andrew Gaffney, Lt. W. C. Neville, Lieutenant Dillingham, Lieutenant Colwell, Lieutenant Mayer, Kavanagh, Graham, and others who are unidentified. The naval sword of Dr. Alfred Brown Pusey is on display at the Brown-Pusey House. (Courtesy of Brown-Pusey House.)

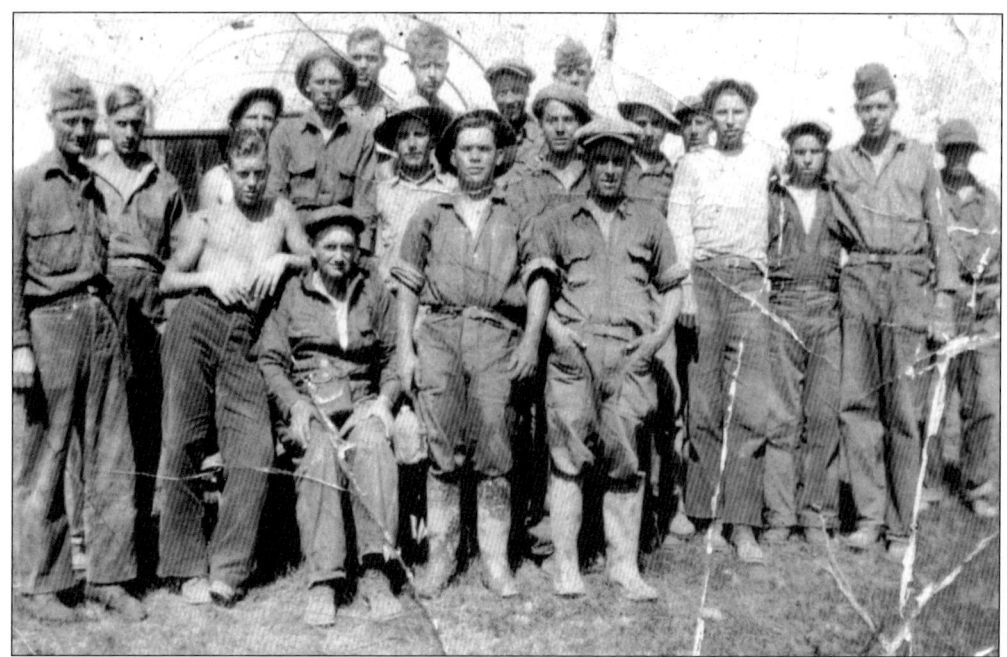

The author's great-grandfather, William Alfred Miller, pictured among his regiment of the 105th Infantry of the U.S. Army and the Medical Department of the Kentucky National Guard, was in World War I. Ben Miller, William's brother, was not drafted into the military. William died in 1945 from tuberculosis. The Hardin County Tuberculosis Committee sold the house at the top of Glendale Hill to William's widow for one dollar in 1950. (Courtesy of Helen Glasgow.)

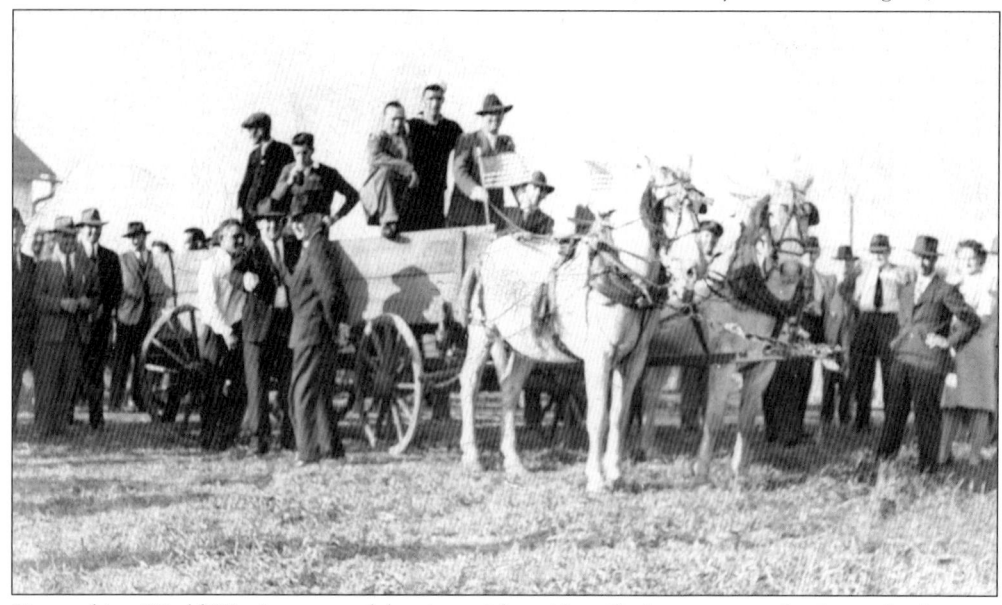

Pictured is a World War I wagon celebration with unidentified men except for the author's great-grandfather, William Alfred Miller. William was born to John Miller and Molly Ann Tharp in Sonora. This town is on U.S. 31 West and straddles the county line of Hardin and Larue Counties. The records of people from Sonora as well as Upton can be found in three counties: Hardin, Larue, and Hart. (Courtesy of Helen Glasgow.)

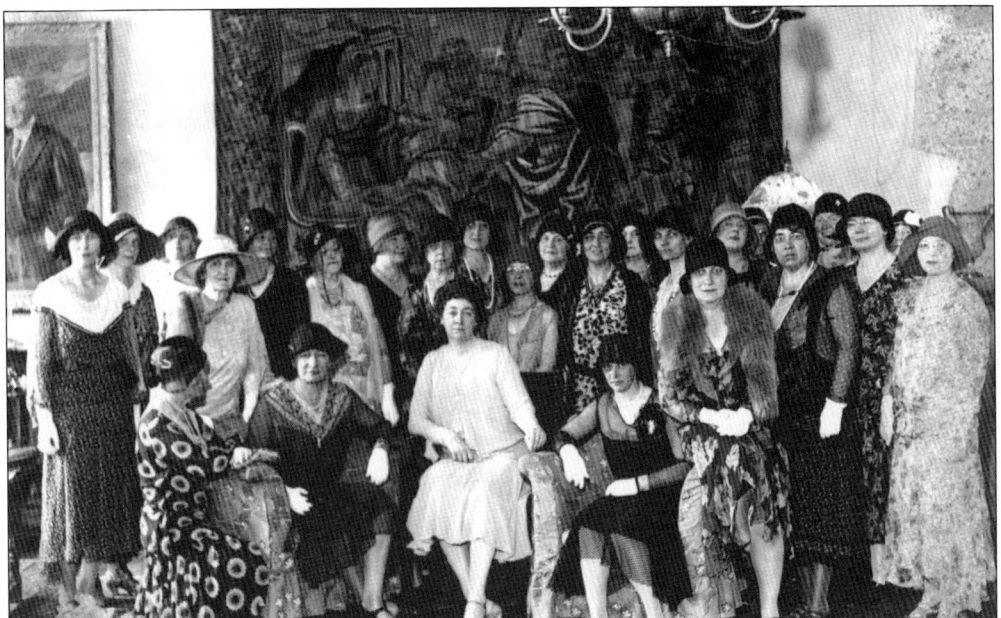

Sallie Cunningham Pusey traveled extensively. In July 1931, she visited the home of John M. Moorhead, who was the U.S. ambassador to Sweden, in Stockholm, and the office of the National Federation of Social Democratic Women in Sweden. Sweden remained neutral in World Wars I and II. Memorabilia from each of Sallie and Dr. William A. Pusey's travels, such as trips to Cuba, Alaska, Mexico, and Europe, are in the archives of the Brown-Pusey House. (Courtesy of Brown-Pusey House.)

Bettie Runner is pictured at Fort Thomas, Kentucky, during World War II. She is the great-granddaughter of Lydia Ann Cunningham and Dr. Ambrose Geoghegan. World War II affected the entire nation in some form, making it difficult even to continue on with life as normal. H. O. Craycroft, chairman of the Board of Trustees of Vine Grove, installed a new sewer system in the town during World War II. (Courtesy of Brown-Pusey House.)

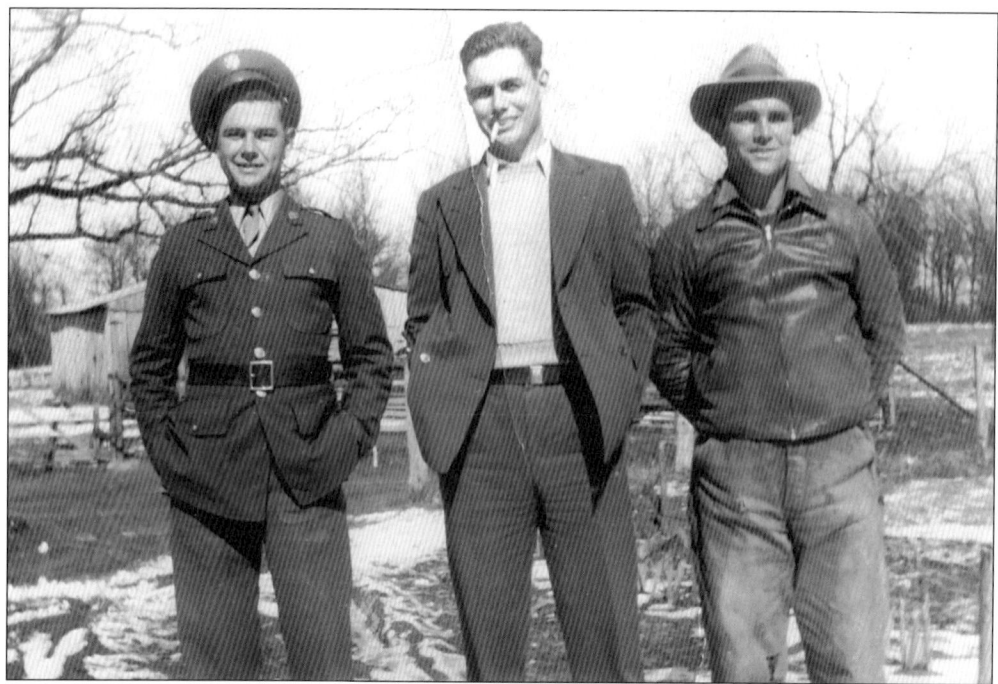

Pictured from left to right are Howard (born 1921), Louis "Bullseye" (born 1915), and Marshall Walters in February 1946. All three served in the U.S. Navy during World War II. Forty-eight states sent thousands of boxcars of wheat by railroad to France. After the war, the county seat received a gift of a handmade wool scarf from the French Gratitude Train, which the people of France used to send gifts as a token of appreciation. The scarf is on display at the Brown-Pusey House. (Courtesy of Michelle Walters.)

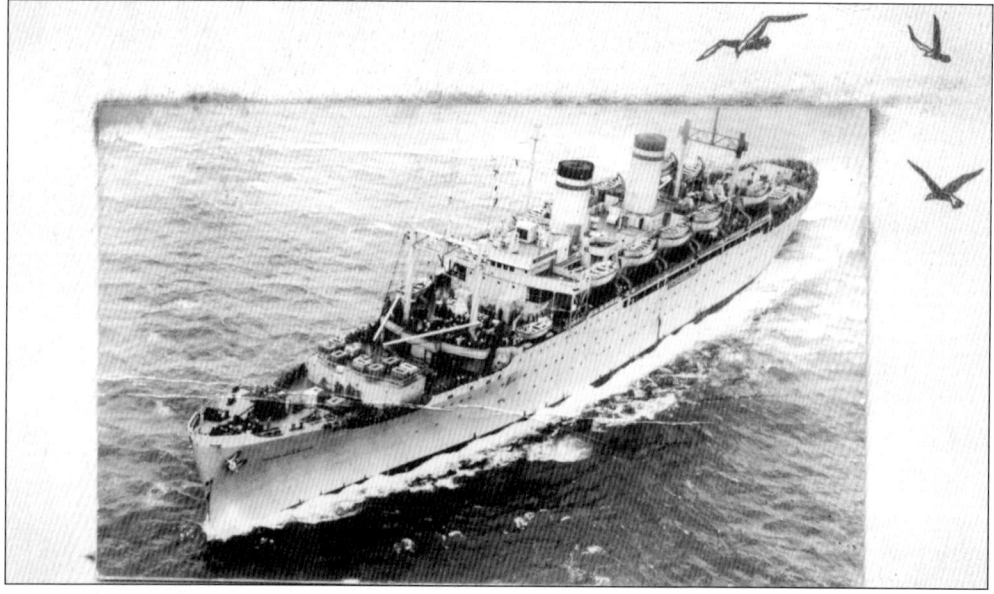

Raymond Lee Miller, the author's great-uncle, was in the Marines during the Korean War. Pictured is the USNS *Gen. N. M. Walker* that carried Raymond from Hollywood and San Francisco in California to Japan. (Courtesy of Helen Glasgow.)

Six
EAST OF U.S. 31 WEST

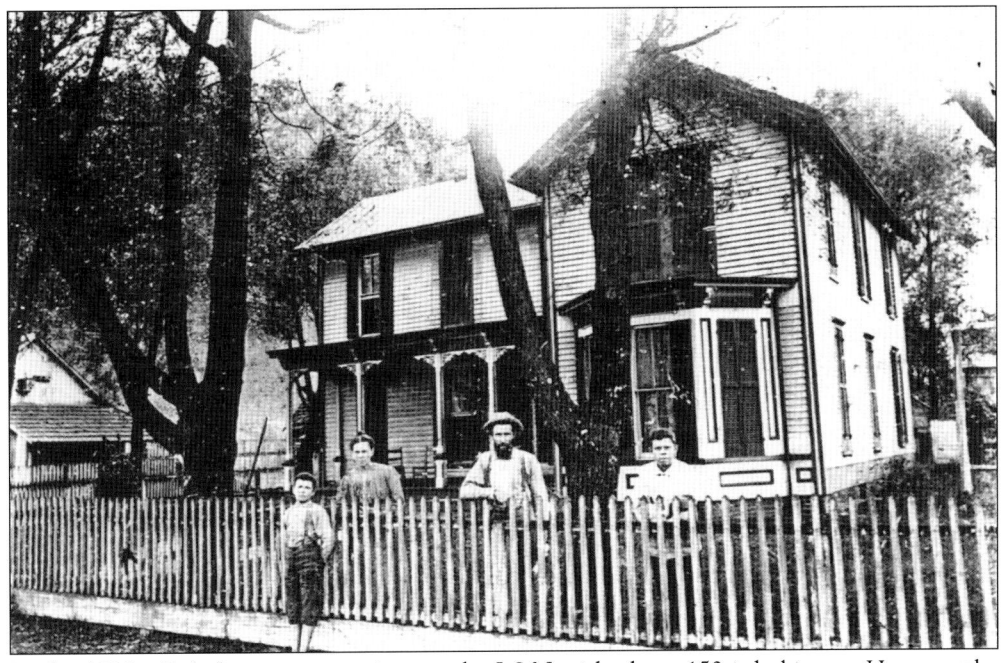

In the 1880s, Colesburg was a station on the L&N with about 150 inhabitants. Hogs, cattle, lumber, tanbark, and large quantities of hay were shipped. Pictured from left to right, an unknown boy, Susan A. Miller Pardee, Cassins A. Pardee, and Albert Pardee are standing in front of their house in Colesburg next to St. Clare Catholic Church; presiding was Rev. J. L. Abell. Cassins operated a sawmill and flour mill in Colesburg. Susan A. Miller Pardee was the sister of Margaret Catherine Miller. (Courtesy of Brown-Pusey House.)

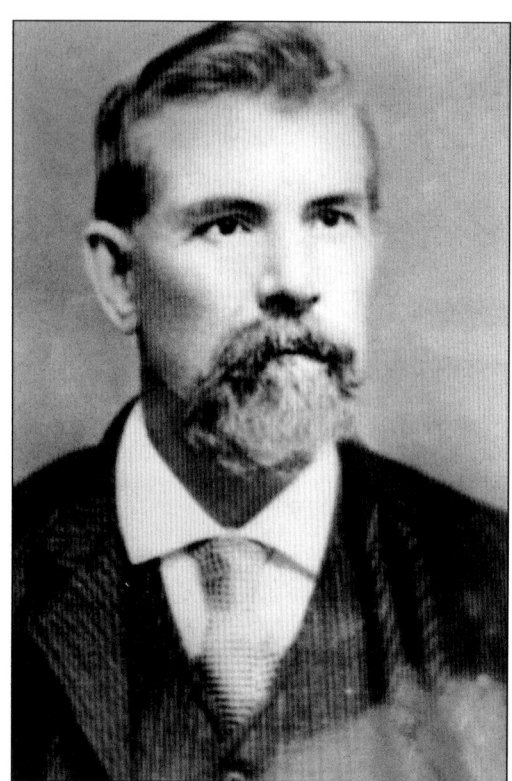

James Alfred Stovall, born 1840 and died in 1913, was a moonshiner and merchant in the Colesburg area. Jesse James supposedly gave a horse to Stovall during a stay in Colesburg. (Courtesy of Brown-Pusey House.)

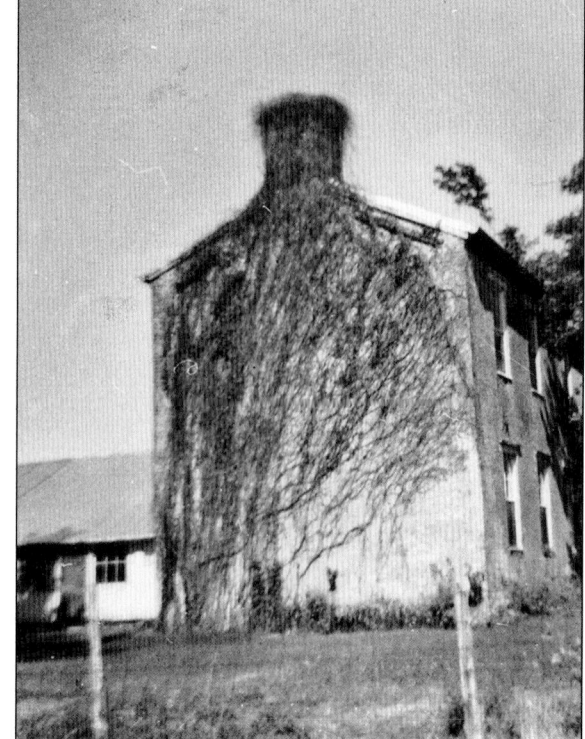

Irwin House is located on Battle Training Road. In 1881, Boothe's Station, 10 miles north of the county seat, had only a farmhouse, post office, and a station on the L&N. P. Booth was the postmaster and hay dealer. (Courtesy of Brown-Pusey House.)

Sally Miller and John Lyons Miller had several children, including Margaret Catherine Miller, who was born about 1861. Her daughter, Ruby May Miller, was born in 1892, married Francis Asbury Caldwell, and lived in Tennessee. (Courtesy of Brown-Pusey House.)

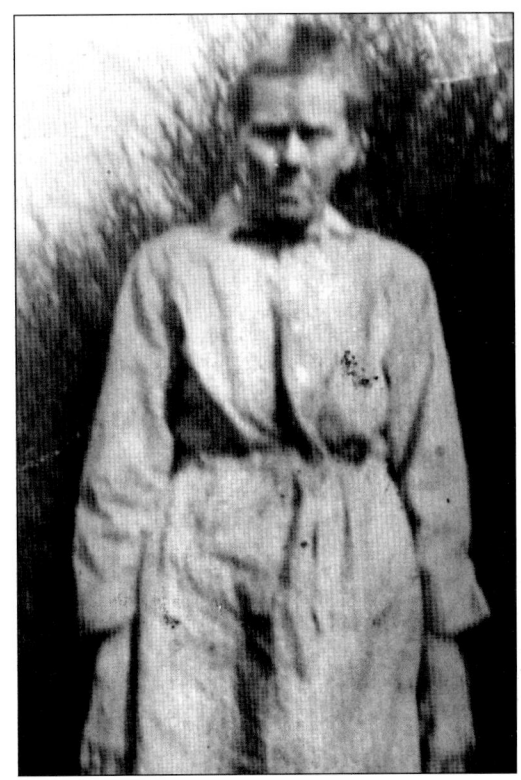

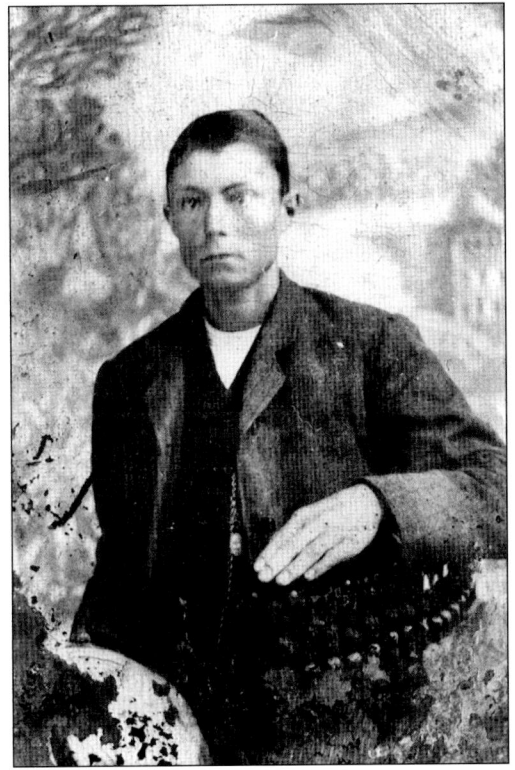

Arthur Miller, by oral tradition, was a Native American. The records in Hardin County do not contain any genealogy information about Native Americans. (Courtesy of Brown-Pusey House.)

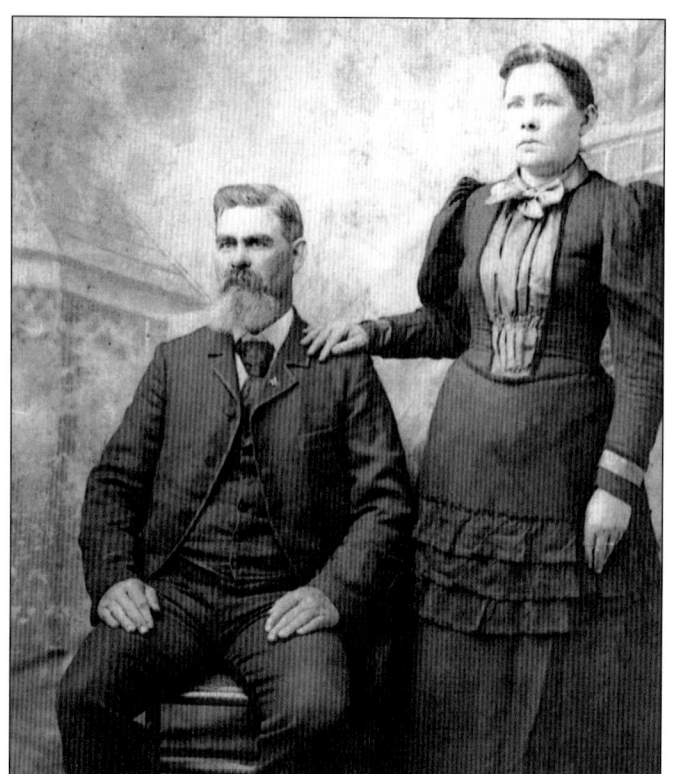

William Spradlin, pictured, was born in Bedford County, Virginia. Hannah Gray, pictured, married William on April 23, 1868. (Courtesy of Brown-Pusey House.)

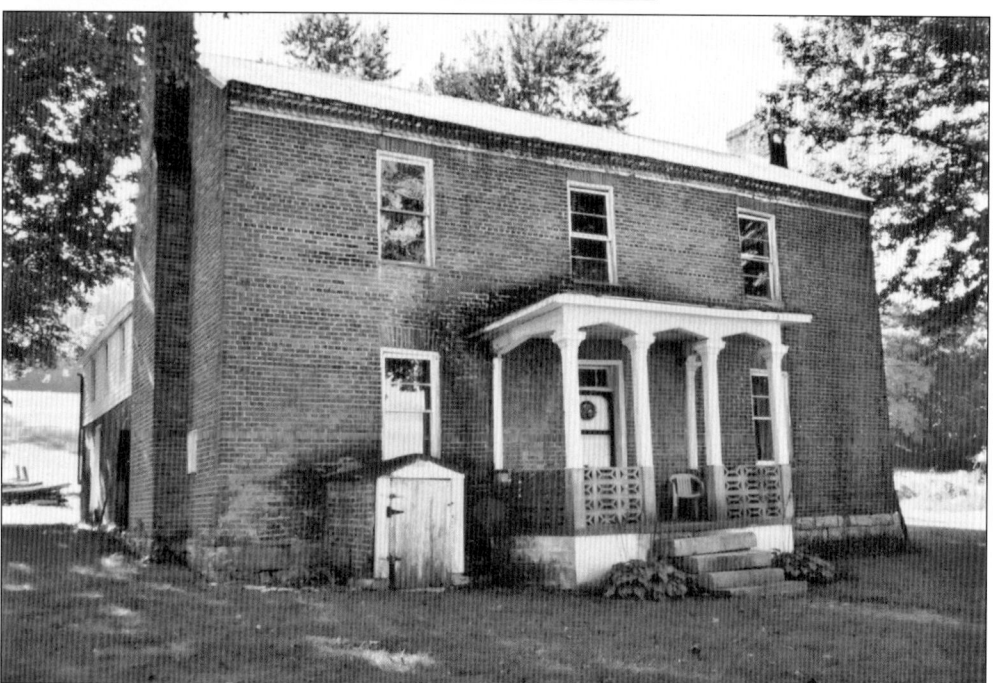

The Rolling Fork River flooded from winter rains several times. Travelers such as Andrew Jackson and John Hunt Morgan, per oral history, may have rested at the Hamilton House, pictured. Hance Hamilton, who had built the house, died in 1838. (Courtesy of Millie Robinson.)

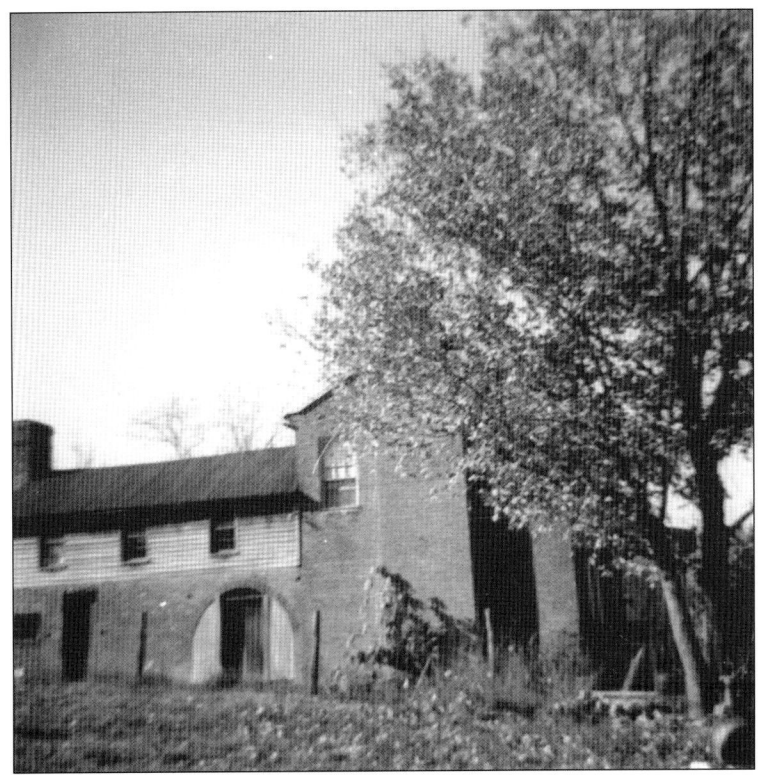

Pictured is the side view of Hamilton House in Youngers Creek. (Courtesy of Brown-Pusey House.)

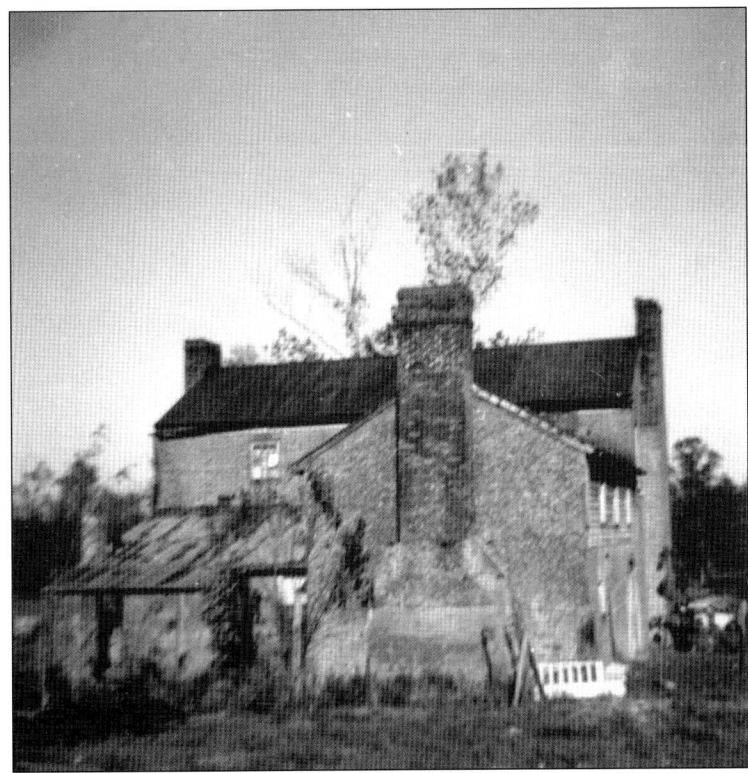

Pictured is the back view of Hamilton House. (Courtesy of Brown-Pusey House.)

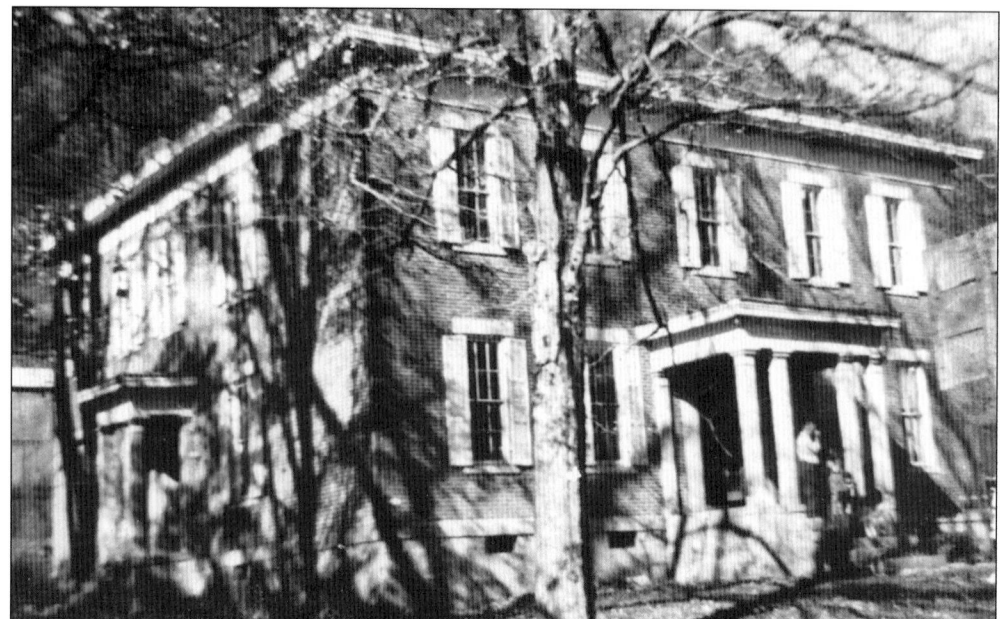

John Hart House pictured in 1969, is in Youngers Creek near Hall Hill. Hall Hill is a narrow road with steep drop-offs on one side and the side of a knob on the other side. Youngers Creek has many knobs in its landscape. Youngers Creek Road intersects with U.S. 31 East at New Haven, the Kentucky Railroad Museum town. Tourists can ride a passenger train at this station. (Courtesy of Brown-Pusey House.)

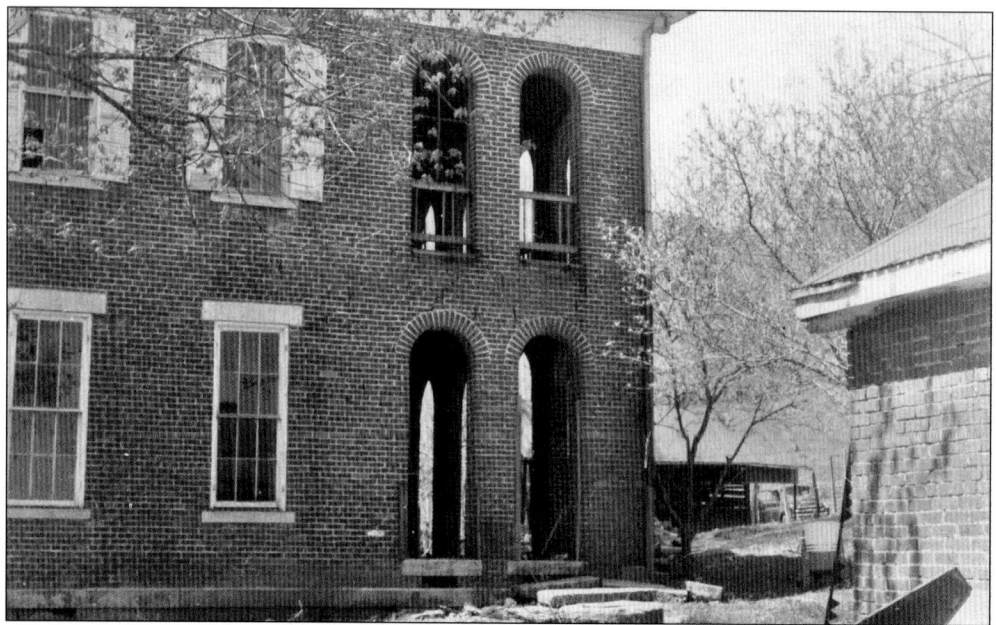

John Hart House at Youngers Creek is pictured. From the intersection with Youngers Creek Road, U.S. 31 East leads to the Lincoln Boyhood Farm and then into downtown Hodgenville. These roads were an important part of the daily life of Thomas Lincoln and other residents of the three counties—Hardin, Nelson, and Larue—in the early 19th century. (Courtesy of Brown-Pusey House.)

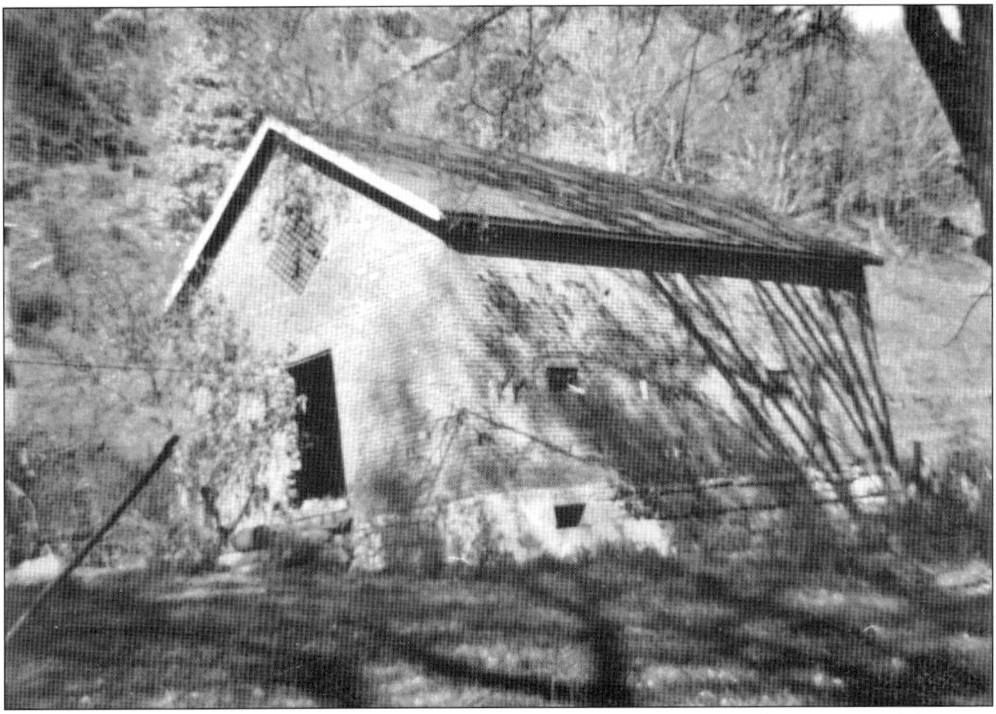

The storehouse of the Hart Place is pictured in Youngers Creek. (Courtesy of Brown-Pusey House.)

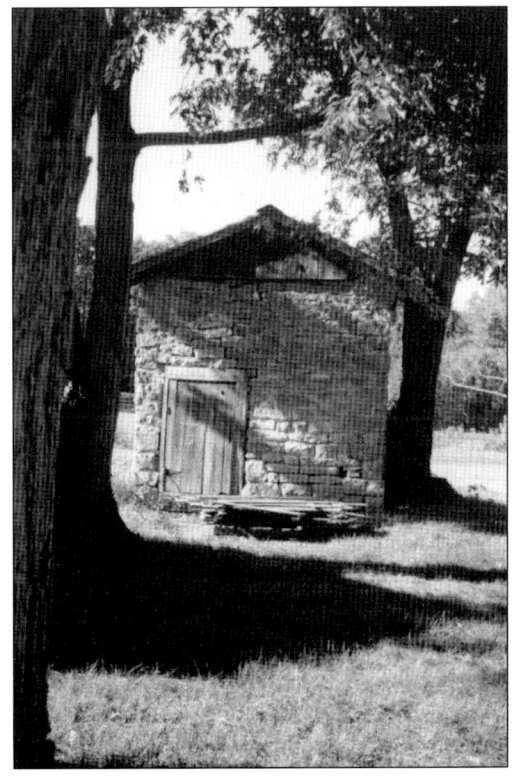

Pictured is an ice house at Hamilton House in the Youngers Creek community. The Elizabethtown Ice Company began operation in the late 19th century and continues today as Bluegrass Ice. Ice was gathered during the winter months from the creeks and streams in the nearby areas and stored in an ice house. The ice was covered in salt or sawdust and used until the next freeze. In the late 19th century, ice shredders cut ice into slivers for drinks. (Courtesy of Brown-Pusey House.)

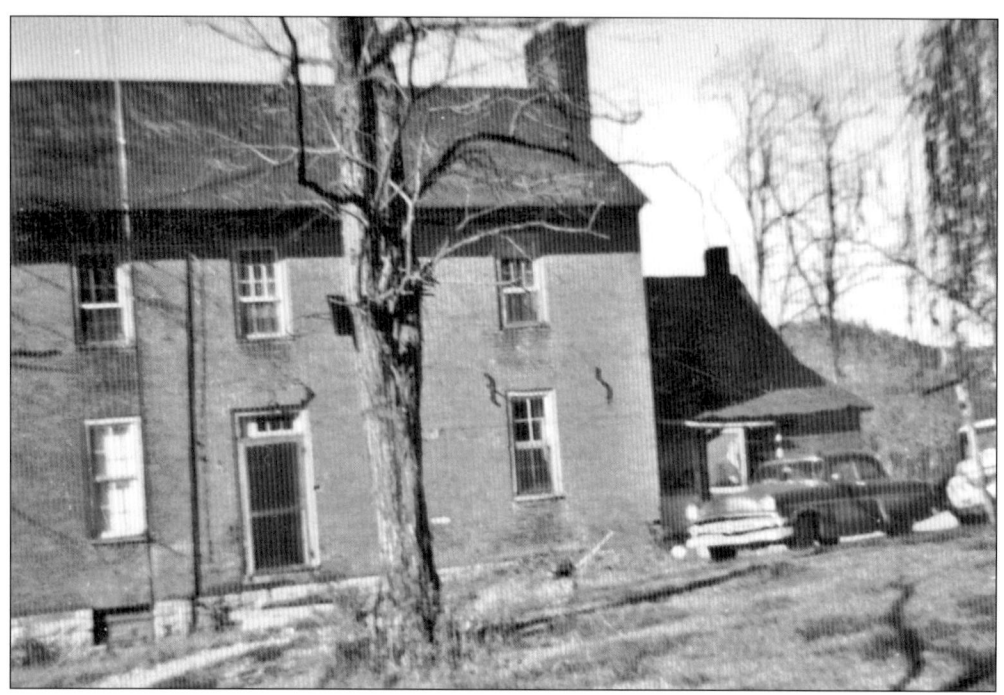

Anthony Vernon built a house in 1795 in the Youngers Creek area. The two-story structure has a stone foundation. A cemetery behind the house has fieldstones as grave markers. (Courtesy of Brown-Pusey House.)

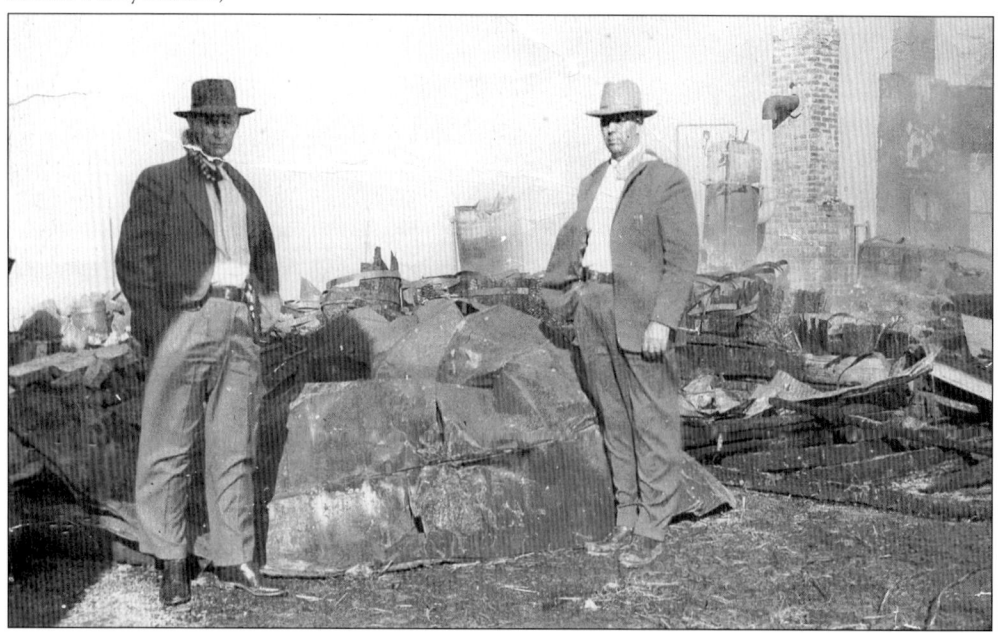

Deputy Sheriff Harvey Tabb, on the left, and High Sheriff Jake Nall are pictured here somewhere in Hardin County about 1949. They are in front of the remnants of a moonshine still and house, in which the still caught the house and the still on fire. Alcohol was allowed in Hardin County, except during the Prohibition era. Between 1939 and 1942, the county went dry, and illegal distilleries became a popular trade. (Courtesy of Hardin County clerk Kenny Tabb.)

Seven
Hill's Hotel

This License Number 4081 was dated from May 1, 1863, to September 1, 1863. "Mrs. Rebecca Davis [Stone] Hill of the Town of Elizabethtown in the county of Hardin and State of Kentucky [is] to carry on the business or occupation of Seventh Class Hotel at No. _ Street . . . having paid the tax of Ten dollars." The Hill's Hotel began in the 1840s and continued as the Hill's Hotel until about 1895, when her stepson, James H. Hill, sold the building to his wife. (Courtesy of Brown-Pusey House.)

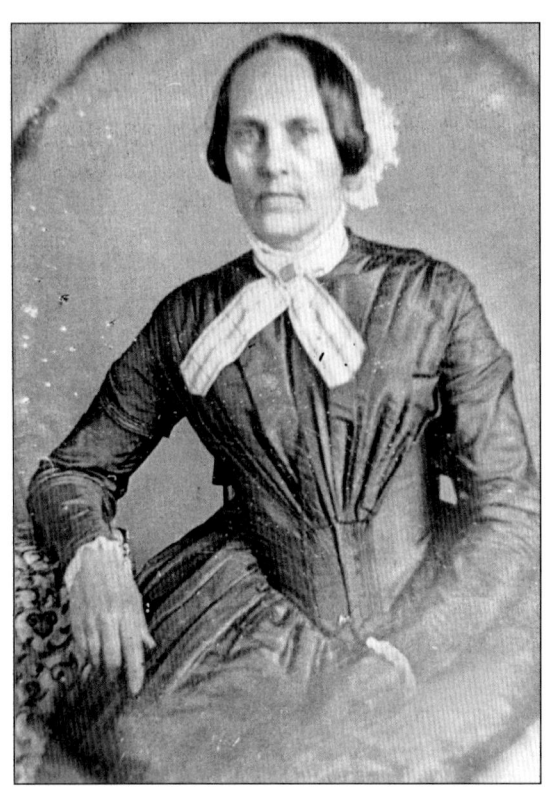

Rebecca Davis Stone, pictured, had married the widower John Y. Hill on August 14, 1827, near Bloomfield, Nelson County. John Y. Hill (born August 14, 1799) married his first wife, Eliza Heyser (born December 6, 1803), on January 1, 1822, in Sheperds Town, Jefferson County, Virginia, where they both were born. The first child of John Y. and Eliza was Mary Ellen Hill, who died on October 23, 1823, near Zanesville, Ohio, and was buried in the public graveyard. Their second child, James H. Hill, was born on January 7, 1825, in Elizabethtown. Eliza died on September 16, 1825, in Elizabethtown and was buried at the Elizabethtown City Cemetery. (Courtesy of Brown-Pusey House.)

In 1868, the county taxes at the rate of 30 percent on each hundred dollars on Rebecca Hill's property were on four town lots and one horse, and a tax of one dollar was levied on one dog. During the Civil War, she was taxed on three and four Elizabethtown lots; three slaves over the age of 16; one horse; five cattle; a tavern license; gold, silver, and other metals; watches; clocks; and a piano. After the Civil War, "Aunt Beck" Hill freed her slaves, and they stayed with her until death. (Courtesy of Brown-Pusey House.)

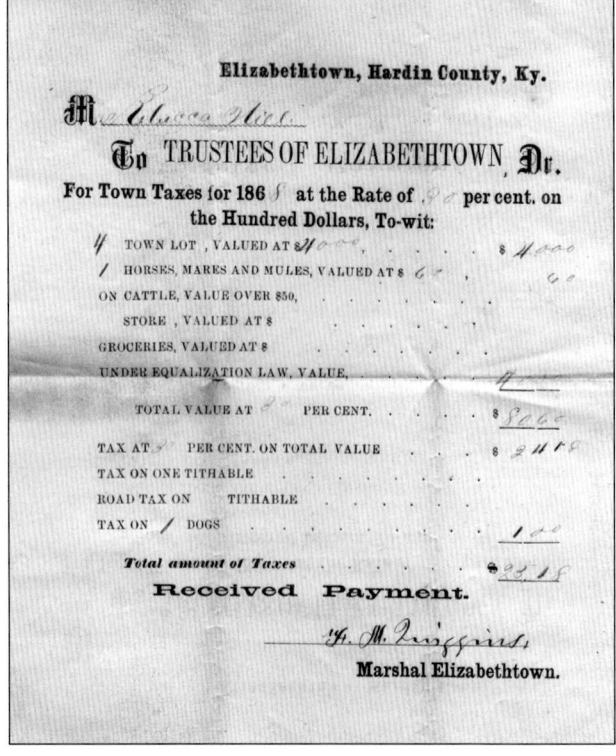

This claim, *Rebecca Davis Hill v. United States* in 1865, stated that on February 15, 1863, Hill had given 27 meals to the detachment of Company D, 30th Kentucky Mounted Infantry, at 50¢ per meal agreed upon by a lieutenant. Also by the order of a Lt. Luturan, the 48th Kentucky Cavalry agreed upon seven meals to the soldiers at 50¢ per meal. Aunt Beck was awarded her due from the federal government. The officers and the soldiers had eaten at the Hill's Hotel in 1863. (Courtesy of Brown-Pusey House.)

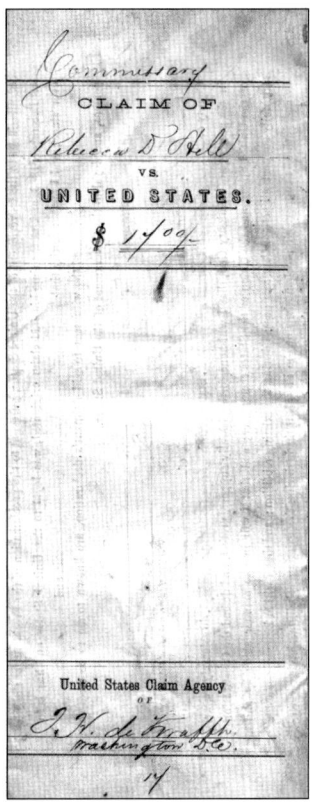

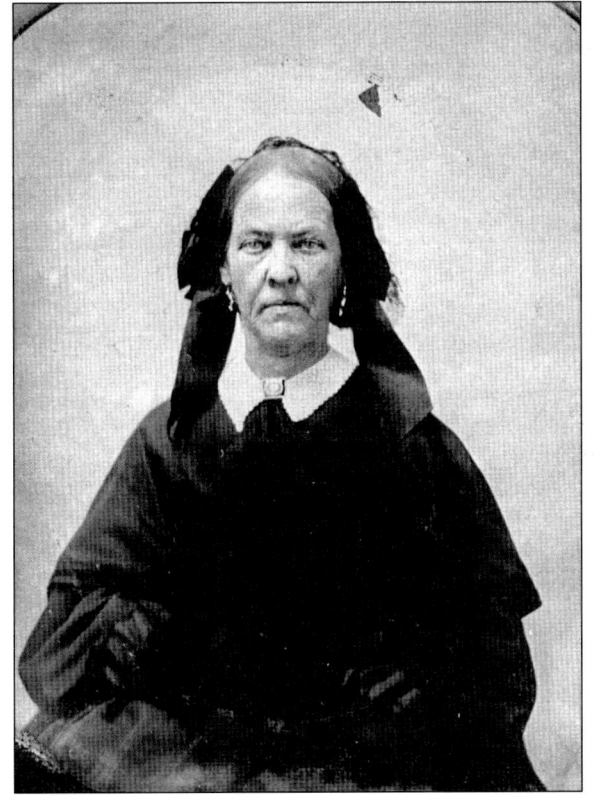

Rebecca Davis Stone was born on November 17, 1803, near Bloomfield, Nelson County. She married the widower John Y. Hill. They operated Hill's Hotel from the 1840s until her death. John Y. Hill died either on August 1 or 2, 1859, from pneumonia. The first of August was the 12th day that Prof. J. Isaacs, an oculist and aurist of Philadelphia, formerly of Leyden, Holland, was to practice in Elizabethtown at the Hill's Hotel. He used Brazilian pebbles for eyeglass lenses and could be consulted on all diseases of the eye and ear. (Courtesy of Brown-Pusey House.)

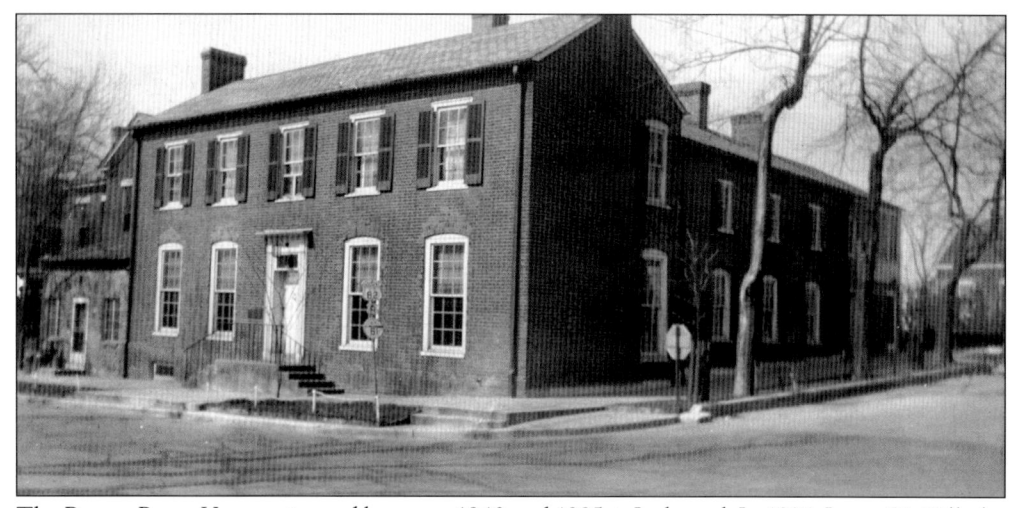

The Brown-Pusey House, pictured between 1940 and 1985, is L-shaped. In 1894, James H. Hill, the stepson of Rebecca D. Hill, sold this property to his wife, Emma S. Hill, who in turn sold it to A. D. McCanns in 1895. McCanns operated it as a boarding house from 1895 to 1913. Then McCanns sold the property to A. J. Bush, who in turn sold it to J. M. Smith. The Smith Hotel Annex, which was the property sold from James H. Hill to McCanns, was purchased and renovated by doctors William Allen Pusey and Alfred Brown Pusey in 1922. (Courtesy of Brown-Pusey House.)

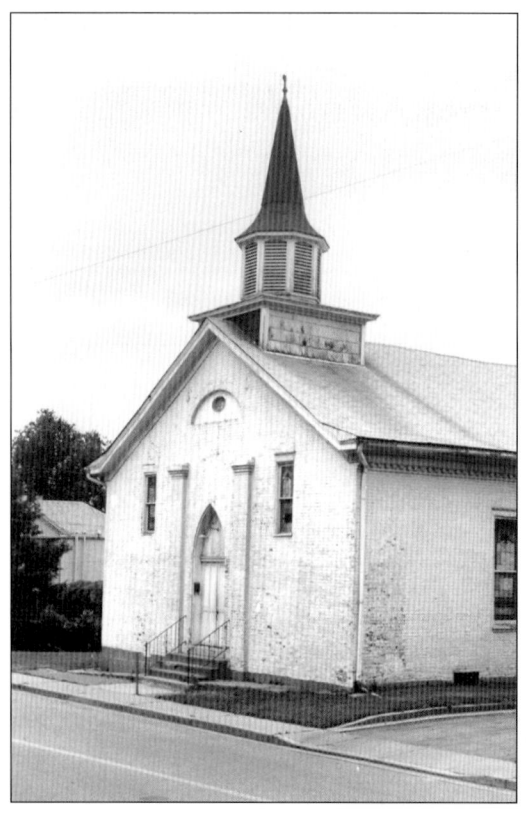

John Y. Hill built Severns Valley Baptist Church in 1834. The building has had many functions, such as a school, hospital, and meetinghouse. Adjacent to this property on the corner of North Mulberry Street and West Poplar Street was the Hardin Academy. The academy had to locate 6,000 acres of land pursuant to legislature acts in 1798 and 1825. John Y. Hill acquired 4,000 acres of land in Livingston County and in Tennessee for the Hardin County Seminary. In 1827, John Y. Hill built the seminary in exchange for the acreage above. (Courtesy of Brown-Pusey House.)

The building of the Skaggs Brothers Barber Shop is diagonally across from the Brown-Pusey House. This building has been remodeled several times but has some definition of antiquity left according to the Elizabethtown Sanborn Fire Insurance Map of 1871. Presently it is the archive room of the Hardin County Clerk's Office. (Courtesy of Brown-Pusey House.)

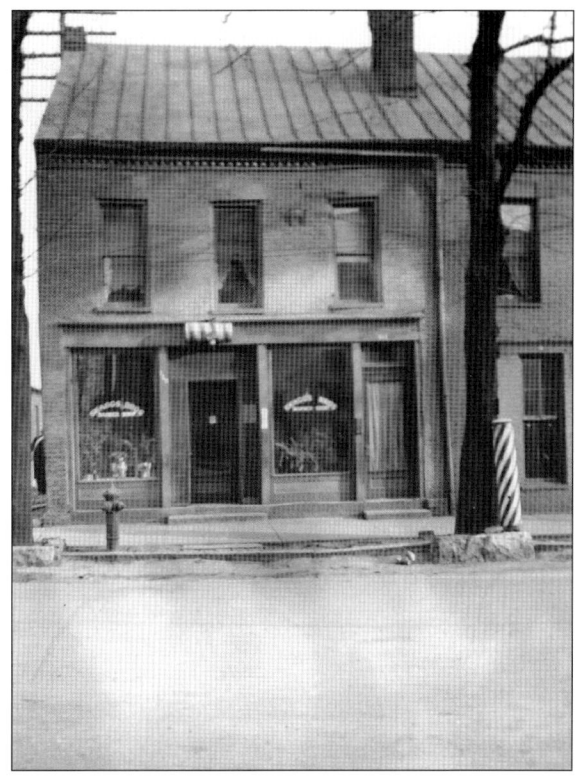

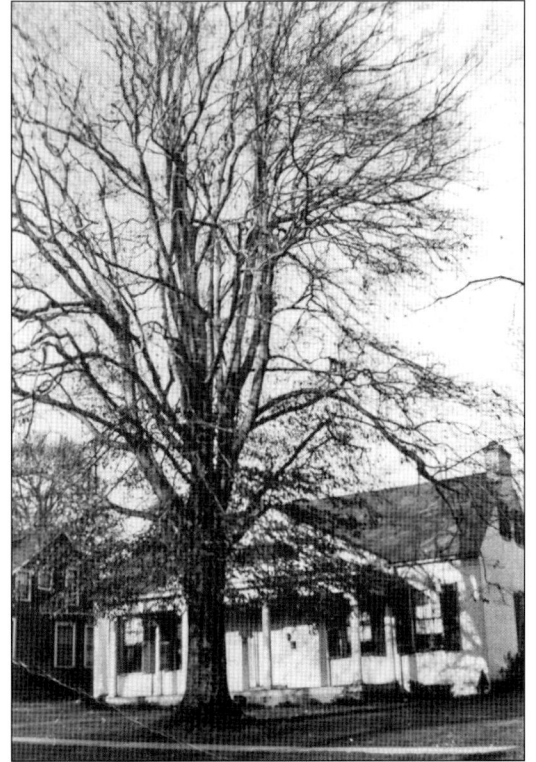

The Buck Tree in front of Margaret Wintersmith's house was 100 years old in the spring of 1942. Alfred Mackenzie Brown wrote an article about the preservation of trees in the late 19th century. One will find many old trees in Hardin County due to the teachings from Brown, the CCC, and other organizations throughout the years. (Courtesy of Brown-Pusey House.)

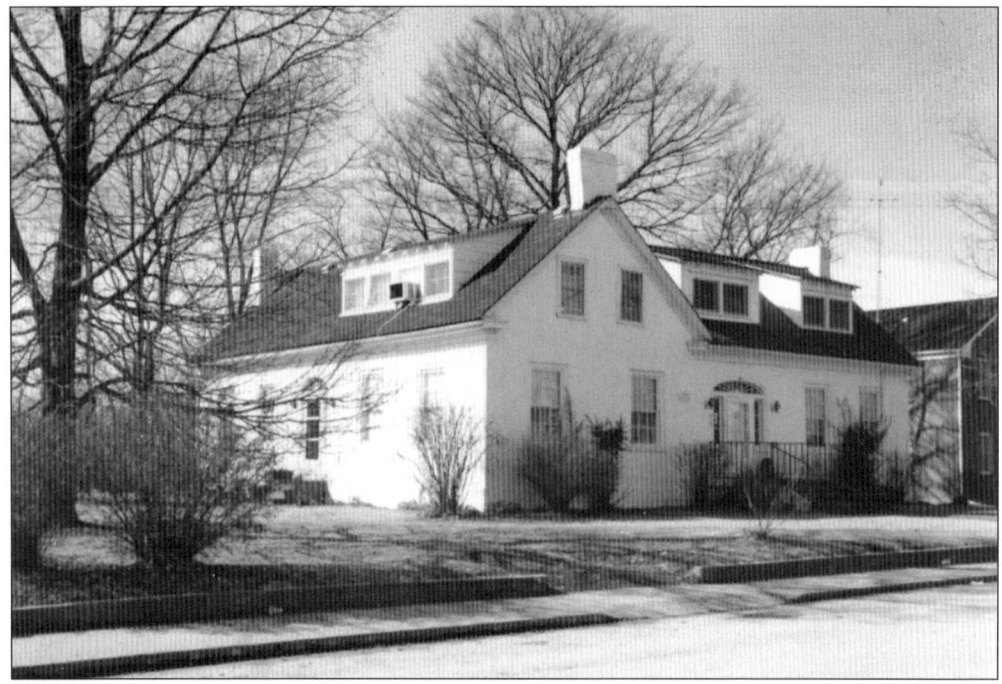

This is the site of the first brick house built by Ben Hardin Helm, and it burned in 1882. Harriet Barney, the wife of Commo. Joshua Barney, lived on this site before the fire and had filed a claim in the Hardin County Circuit Court in 1821, concerning who owned what land. Joshua Barney had acquired 2,000 acres of land near the "Knoll Linn" Station and Middle Creek from the heirs of Andrew Hynes, Philip Phillips, John May, John Banister, Kennon Jones, Thomas Shore, and Christopher McConnico. (Courtesy of Brown-Pusey House.)

FUNERAL NOTICE.

The funeral of
MRS. R. D. HILL
will take place from her house to-morrow (Thursday) December 14th at 2 o'clock p. m. Interment in the town cemetery.

Elizabethtown, Ky., December 13, 1882.

The funeral of the widow Rebecca Davis (Stone) Hill took place at her house, Hill's Hotel, the day after her death of December 13, 1882. She was interred in the Elizabethtown City Cemetery. John Y. Hill arrived in Hardin County in 1825, and in 1827, he bought one half of a town lot and had two slaves. By 1829, he had acquired 116 acres of land in Hardin County and retained the half town lot for himself, and obtained 4,600 acres of land in Livingston County, Kentucky, on the Cumberland River for the Hardin Academy. (Courtesy of Brown-Pusey House.)

Dr. William Allen Pusey is pictured about 1900 in Chicago, Illinois. He had practiced for one year in Elizabethtown from 1889 to 1890 after the death of his father in order to settle the estate. After the death of his grandfather A. M. Brown in 1903, he was in charge of all estates that concerned the widows and children of Hill, Hastings, Brown, and Pusey. (Courtesy of Brown-Pusey House.)

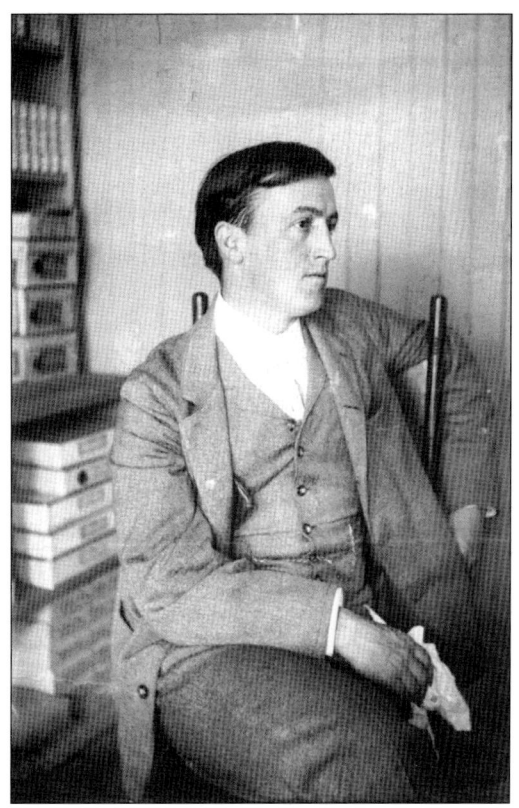

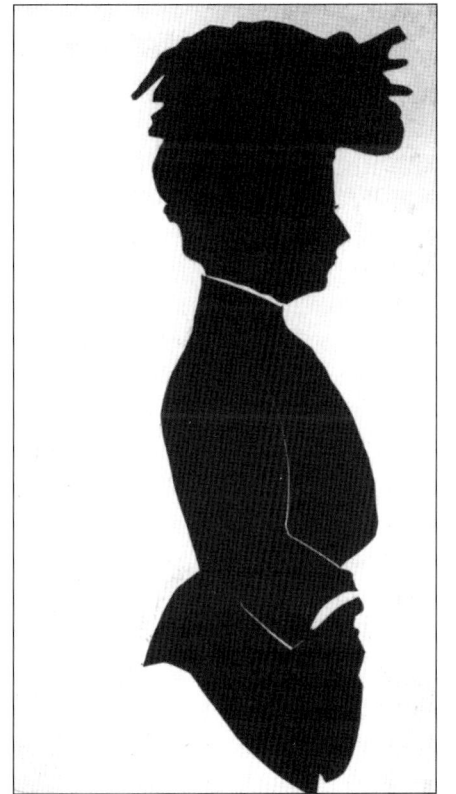

The silhouette of Sallie Pusey in October 1905 was one of many items on display at the Brown-Pusey House, formerly called the Hill's Hotel. After Rebecca Hill died in 1882, the Brashear family rented the hotel and operated it as a hotel until 1889. One winter the snow so deep that it drifted to the lower sill of the front windows, which were about five feet from the sidewalk. To get from the dining room to the kitchen it was necessary to go out onto an open porch. The cook, Millie Munford, was paid $1.25 per week. (Courtesy of Brown-Pusey House.)

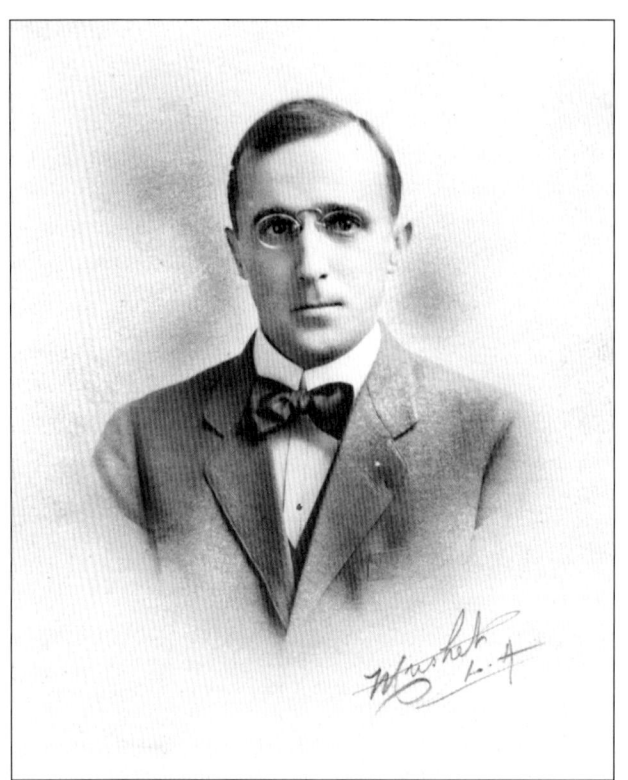

Hill Hastings, the son of Edith Brown Hastings, contributed to the restoration of the Hill's Hotel. When the Brashears left the hotel, the Middleton family operated the building as a hotel. John, Lizzie, Ann, Julia, and Tom Harris helped to run the house. John Harris, the brother to Mrs. Middleton, met the train as a Red Cap, a stagecoach or buggy chaperone who led guests to the Hill's Hotel. Lizzie was the cook. Tom fed the hog and performed other chores. Ann and Julia took care of the rooms and waited on the tables. John Stewart, who lived near Tunnel Hill, visited the hotel every day except Sunday as long as the Middletons operated the hotel. (Courtesy of Brown-Pusey House.)

Edith Brown Hastings, who died at an early age, is pictured with a boy child. Bell Brown Pusey raised her three children in the late 19th century. Bell Brown Pusey died in 1922, and her sons and stepsons restored the Brown-Pusey House in her honor. Bell visited the hotel when the Middletons operated it until 1890. Jack Vanmeter, Clint Haycraft, and Mattie Fenton were regular guests, and Jim Bowman and his wife were regular boarders. (Courtesy of Brown-Pusey House.)

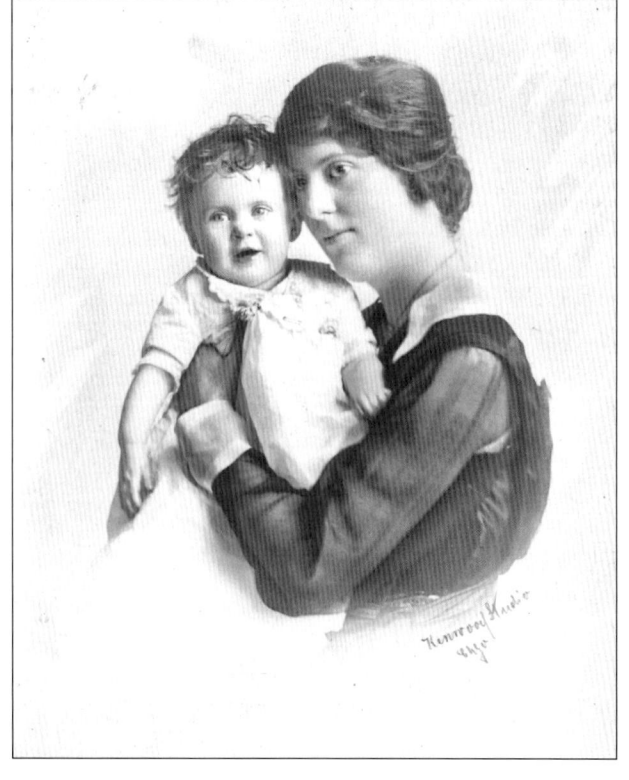

Mary Garvin Brown Hastings, who died in 1910, was the first wife of Hill Hastings. Her father was George Garvin Brown, and she was the biological mother of Robert P. Hastings. George organized a wholesale liquor business with his half-brother, John Thompson Street Brown Jr. Today it is the Brown-Forman Company. George died in 1917, and during Prohibition, most of the barrel goods were for medicinal spirits. (Courtesy of Brown-Pusey House.)

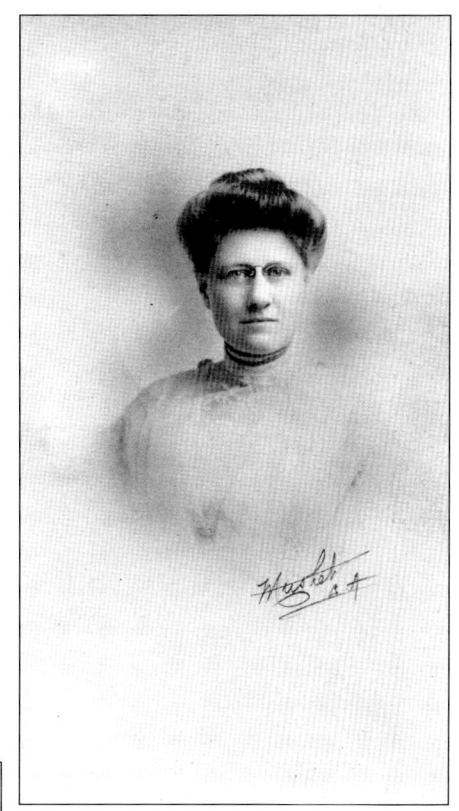

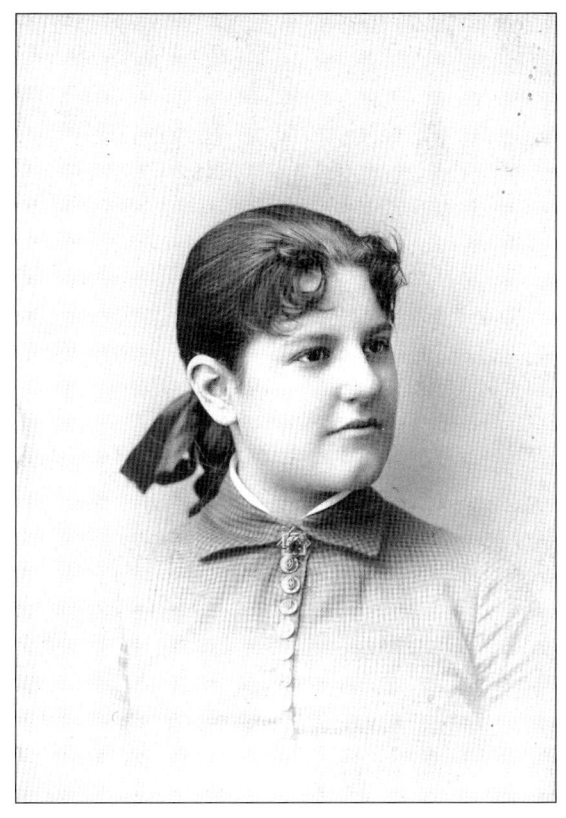

Julie Roberson, pictured, was the daughter of George Garvin Brown, who married Emily Swanengen in Louisville in December 1886. (Courtesy of Brown-Pusey House.)

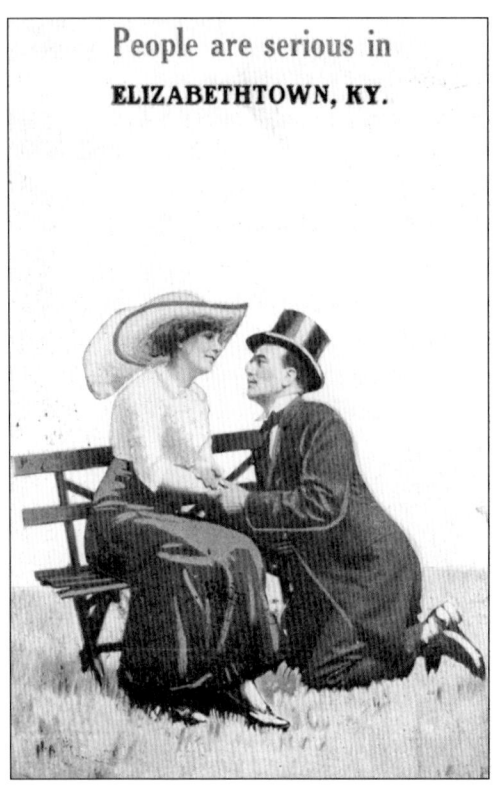

The formal Cunningham garden of the Brown-Pusey House is a romantic place to marry your sweetheart or to renew your vows. The garden is maintained by the Sallie C. Pusey Trust, the Garden Club of Elizabethtown, the Hardin County Detention Center, and the Brown-Pusey House. The holly trees—one male and one female—near the Poplar Street sidewalk in the garden are a popular spot for winter weddings. The rose-covered brick pergola near the old Morris House and the rear patio draped by the Magnolia trees are other wedding altars for the bride and groom. (Courtesy of Meranda Caswell.)

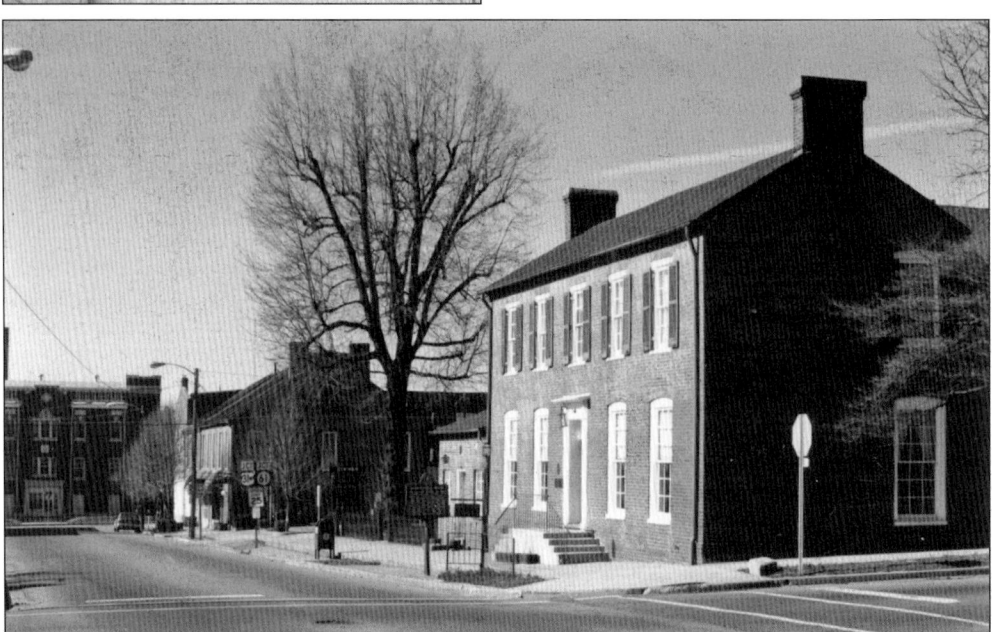

This view is of the Brown-Pusey House, located on the corner of North Main Street and Poplar Street, looking toward the Hardin Courthouse in the 1980s. The author watched the filming of a scene of a boy on a bicycle from Cameron Crowe's movie *Elizabethtown* in July 2004 here. The 1896 wrought-iron fence in front of the Morris House, the building adjacent to the Brown-Pusey House, is seen in the movie. (Courtesy of Brown-Pusey House.)

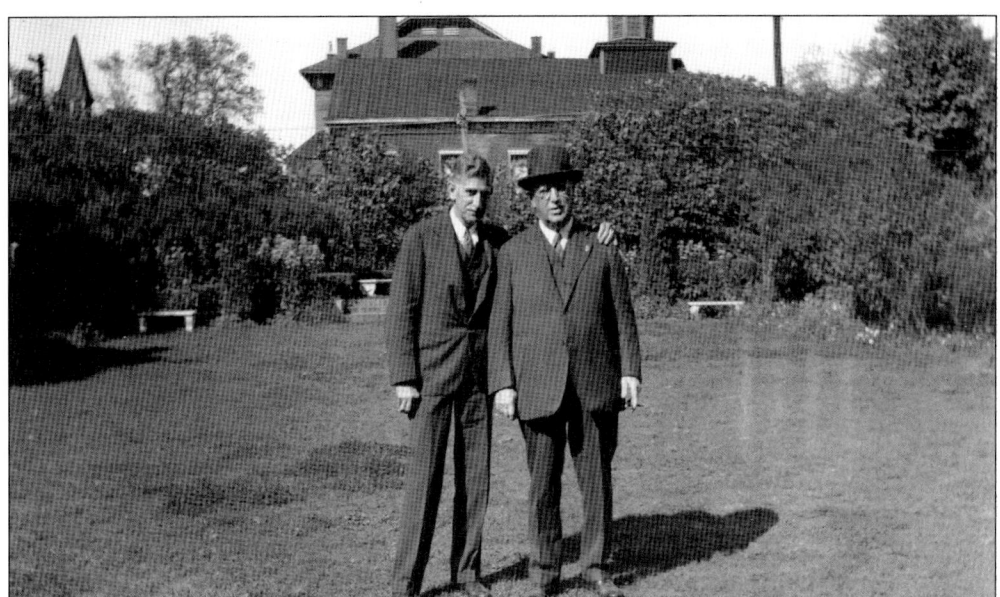

Alfred Brown Hastings (left) and Dr. William Allen Pusey are standing in the Cunningham garden behind the Brown-Pusey House on October 21, 1934. The buildings in the rear are the first brick Severns Valley Baptist Church and the second Masonic Temple. Severns Valley Baptist Church had a church on U.S. 31 West in the late 19th century. William Christen, a shoemaker, lived on the corner where the Baptist church once stood on U.S. 31 West. He was later confined to an asylum. (Courtesy of the Brown-Pusey House.)

From left to right, Susan and Bob Hastings, Sallie Pusey, and Mrs. George Garvin Brown (Gertrude) stand in the Cunningham garden in the summer of 1941. The door to the left has been bricked in. The stone path in front of the door is now a handicap ramp. The ivy has been removed from the building. The official state tree was the Kentucky coffee tree until 1994, and it then was changed to the tulip poplar tree, which is actually a magnolia tree. The tree adjacent to the ramp is a tulip magnolia. (Courtesy of Brown-Pusey House.)

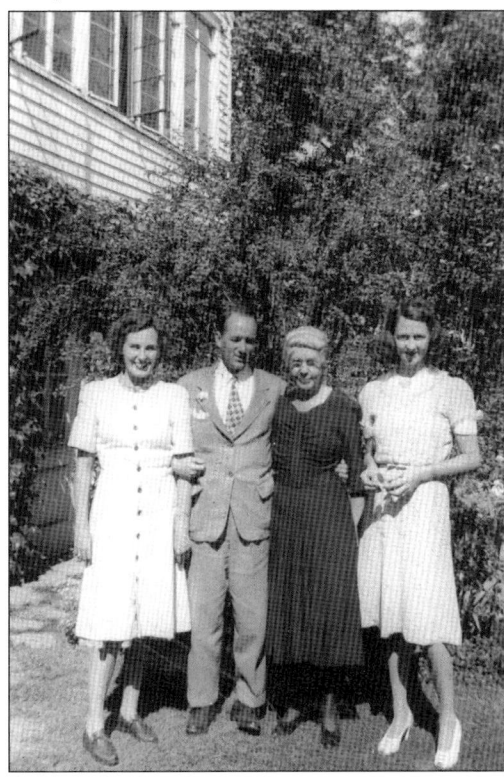

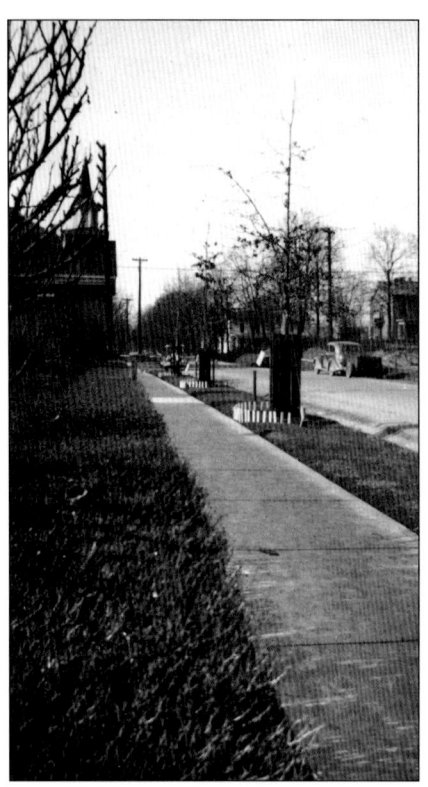

On West Poplar Street near the sidewalk are trees that were planted in the 1930s by Sallie Pusey. Sallie Pusey had played Tom Thumb in the late 19th century. Blind Tom from the Tom Thumb wedding in the 1870s came to Hardin County and gave a performance at Bryans Hall. He occupied the one-story room of the Hill's Hotel that opened onto the street. He had a piano in the room, and at dusk he practiced. Severns Valley Baptist Church is on the left side of the street, shown in January 1939. (Courtesy of Brown-Pusey House.)

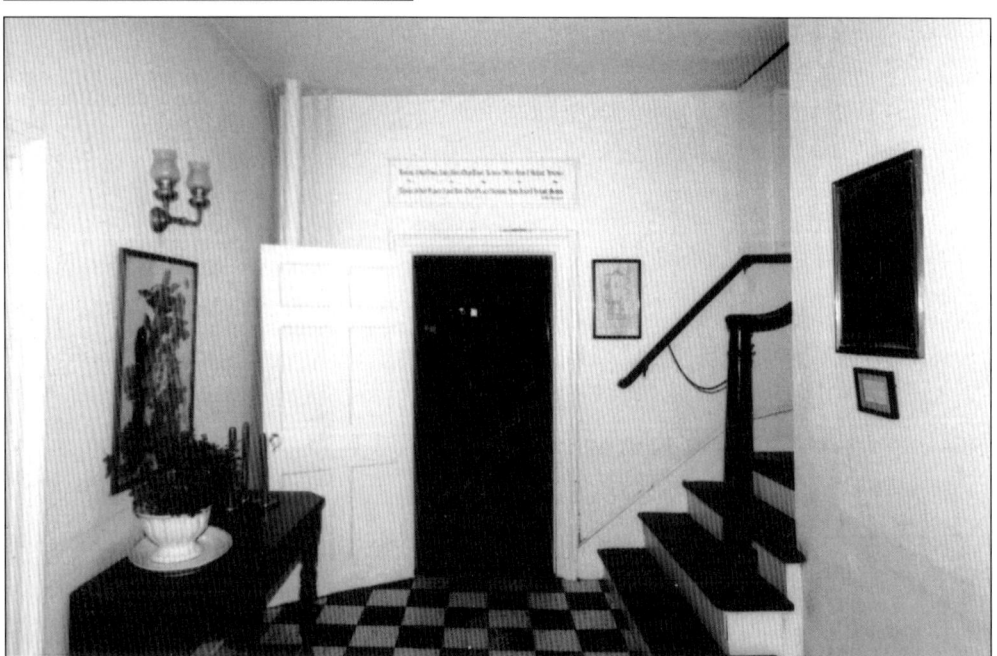

When one enters the front door of the Brown-Pusey House, this is the view that is seen. However, the linoleum has been removed to expose the floor planks from 1825. The Audubon print of the pileated woodpeckers has been moved to the stairwell. John James Audubon and Rozier had a merchandising store in Elizabethtown in the early 19th century. (Courtesy of Brown-Pusey House.)

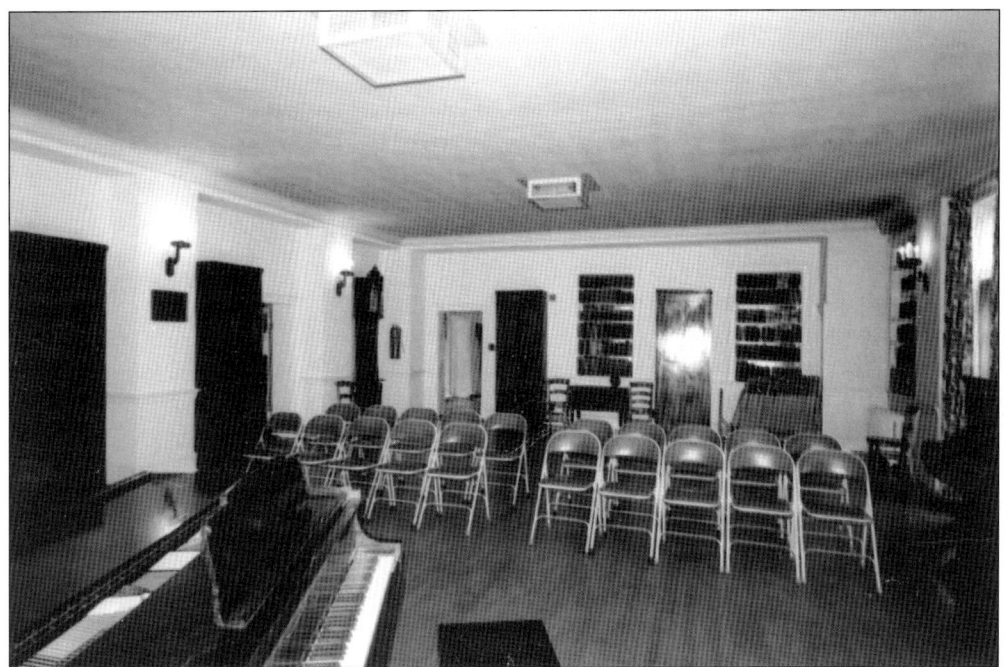

This is the ballroom of the Brown-Pusey House in the 1980s with the cabinets from the library days, a grandfather clock near the entrance of the ballroom, and an upright piano near the French doors on the right. Everything except the grandfather clock and the baby grand piano has been removed from this room. (Courtesy of Brown-Pusey House.)

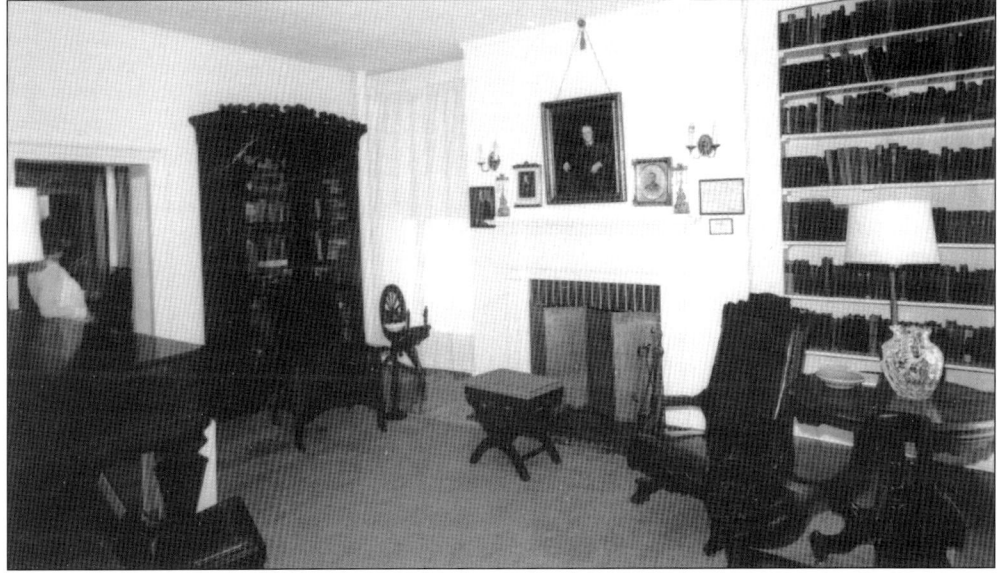

The parlor of the Brown-Pusey House is shown here with a square piano, an étagère, and a flax wheel. The woodwork in the room was hand done by John Y. Hill in 1825. Electricity was added to the building about 1900 by Alex D. McCann, renovated in 1922 by the Pusey family, and updated several times until 1995. The square piano, which went out of style by 1900, is from the Peters, Webb, and Company in Louisville from between 1859 and about 1890. (Courtesy of Brown-Pusey House.)

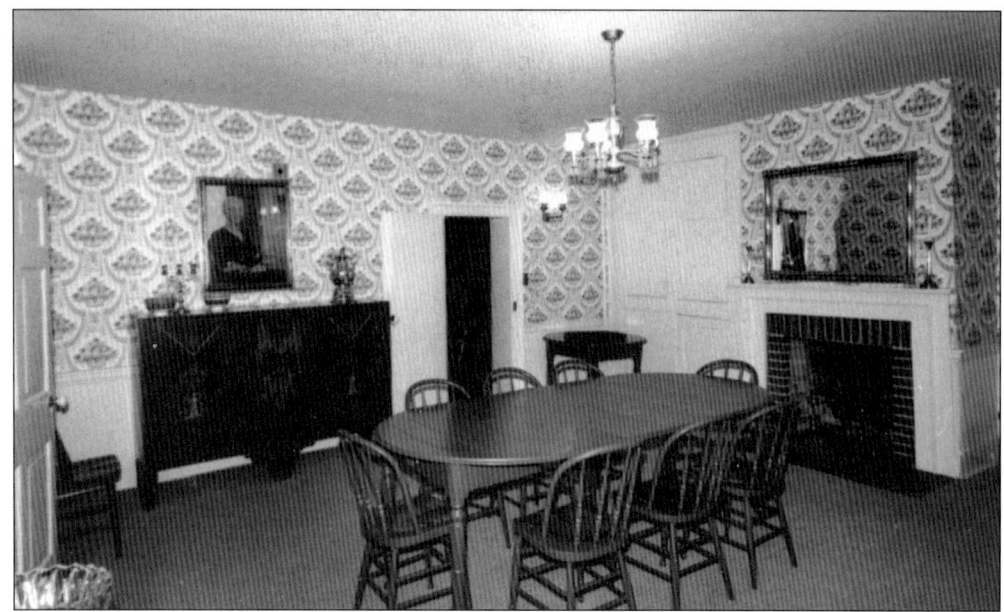

This photograph shows what was at one time Rebecca Davis (Stone) Hill's bedroom. It was the dining room of the Hill's Hotel and later the Brown-Pusey House, and the sideboard was made about 1850. Many people resided at the hotel for days to years at a time. Dr. Bryan R. Young, a Hardin County doctor, coroner, and manufacturer of medicine, lived for many years and died in 1882 in this building. The Masonic lodge in Hodgenville is named after B. R. Young because he was a Mason and was the grand master of the order in the state in 1845. (Courtesy of Brown-Pusey House.)

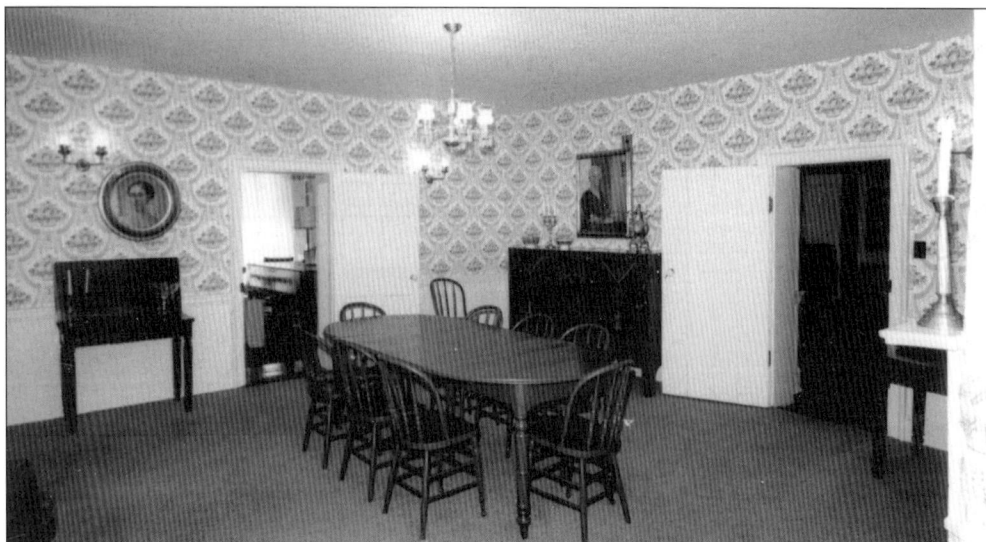

On the other wall of the dining room is an oil painting of Malvina Warfield Cunningham painted by Katherine Helm in the 1880s. Katherine was the daughter of Gen. Ben Hardin Helm, who died at Chickamauga in 1863, and the granddaughter of Kentucky governor John Larue Helm. The door opening to the right leads to the parlor room. The door opening to the left leads to the ballroom. The ballroom was added on in 1922 after the previous room was demolished. There used to be a two-story room with doors to the boarding rooms. (Courtesy of Brown-Pusey House.)

Dr. Robert Burns Pusey's saddlebags, on display at the Brown-Pusey House, were the standard medical kit of a country doctor in the 1870s and 1880s. Bell Brown, wife of Robert Burns Pusey, was the second vice president of the local chapter of the United Daughters of the Confederacy in 1901. Her daughter-in-law, Sallie Pusey, joined the same year. (Courtesy of Brown-Pusey House.)

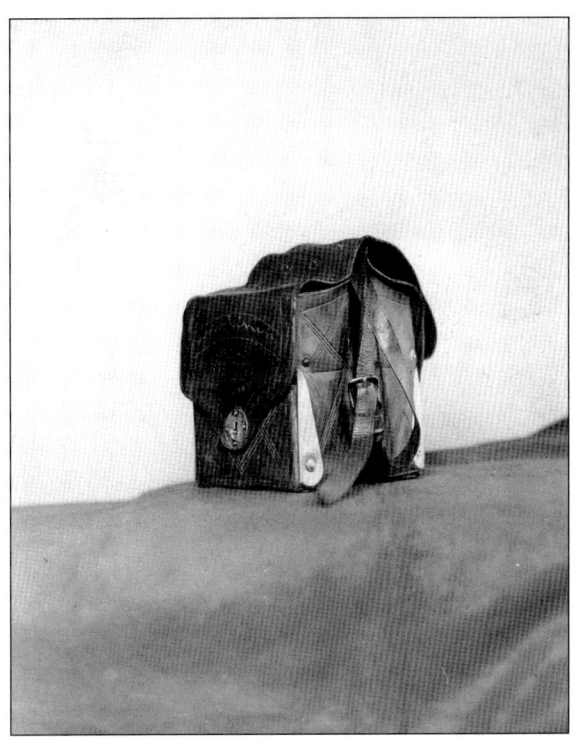

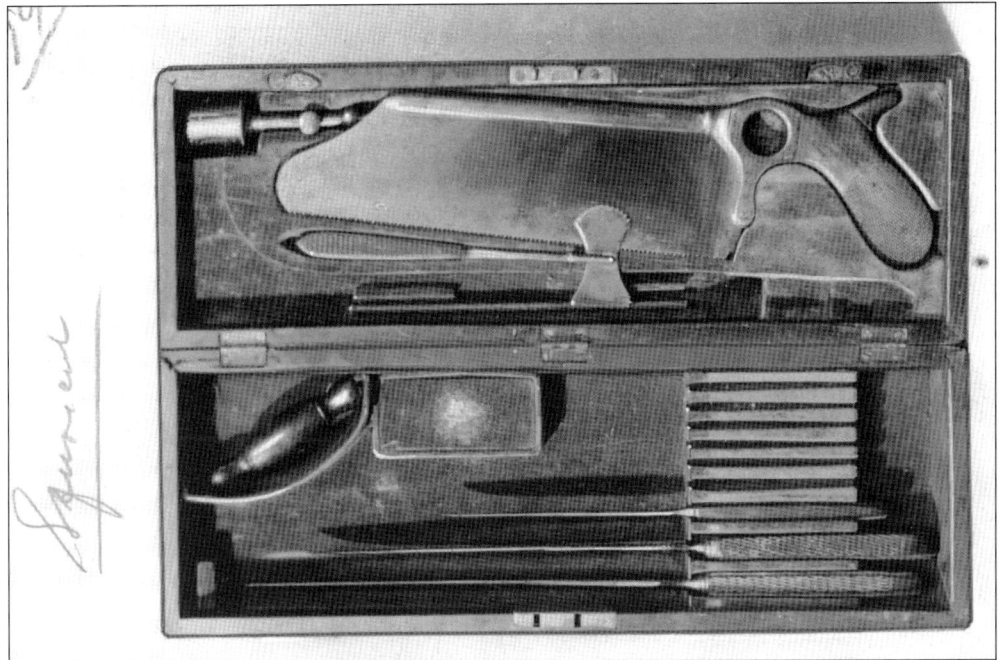

This photograph of Dr. Robert Burns Pusey's surgical operating tool kit, which included a bone saw, is on display at the Brown-Pusey House. The lancets, mortar, spittoon, whiskey medicine, scale, syringes, and other medical items, such as his nameplate, his ledgers, and accounts, are displayed. Dr. Pusey was well known and liked by the people of Hardin County. (Courtesy of Brown-Pusey House.)

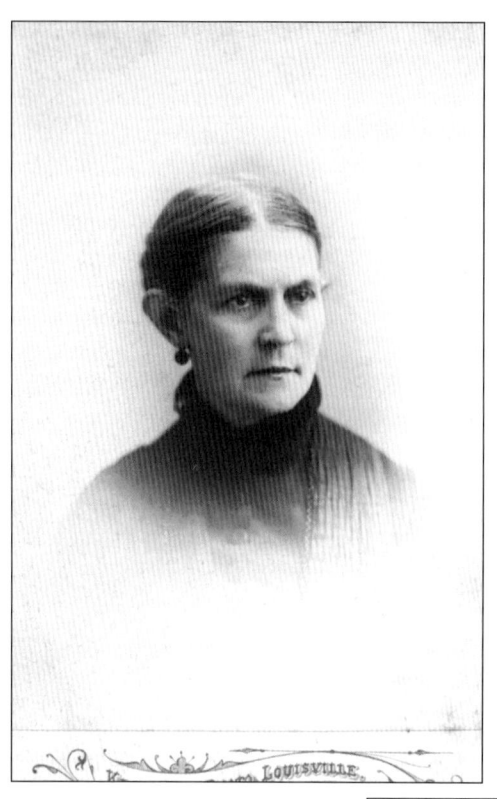

In 1832, Anthony Hundley Cunningham had married Caroline Wintersmith, the daughter of Elizabeth Hodges and Horatio G. Wintersmith. Their daughter, Elizabeth "Lizzie" Cunningham, married William Curd of Louisville. Elizabeth and William Curd were rebels during the Civil War and were banished to the South due to their rebellious activities. Her brother, Washington Whittaker Cunningham, died in 1866 after serving in the Confederate army. (Courtesy of Brown-Pusey House.)

This photograph is possibly Joseph McMurtry, the father of Stephen McMurtry, in 1859. Howesvalley, situated on Rough Creek, contained a Methodist Episcopal church with Rev. J. B. Barnett presiding; a Masonic lodge, Fitch Lodge No. 309; one water flour mill, run by Glover and Morrison, who were also the proprietors of a carding machine; one water sawmill, owned by G. Neff; one general store, Spiers and Straus; two physicians, Stephen McMurtry and James Goodman; two magistrates, John Tabor and J. F. Hill; and one distiller, T. C. French. (Courtesy of Brown-Pusey House.)

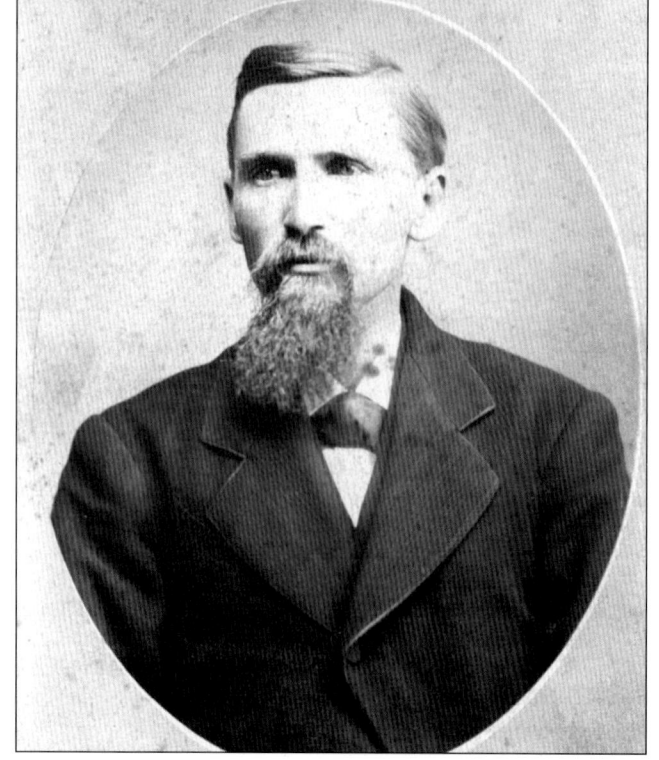

John Wilton Cunningham was born in Leitchfield, Grayson County, on June 12, 1824, and married Samantha Ingram on September 17, 1846. This photograph was made in California when he was 90 years old in 1914. He was the minister of the Methodist church in Elizabethtown and the brother of Anthony Hundley Cunningham. His parents were Susan Major Hundley and William Cunningham, who arrived in Kentucky in 1795 and settled on Rough Creek near Green's Water Mill. (Courtesy of Brown-Pusey House.)

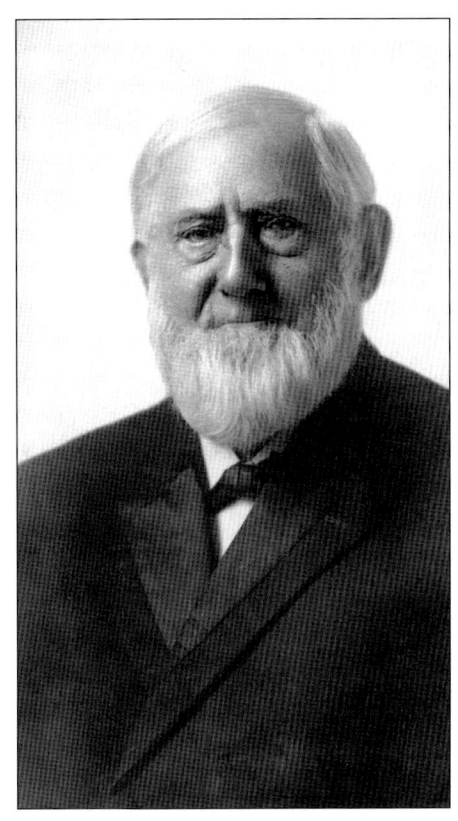

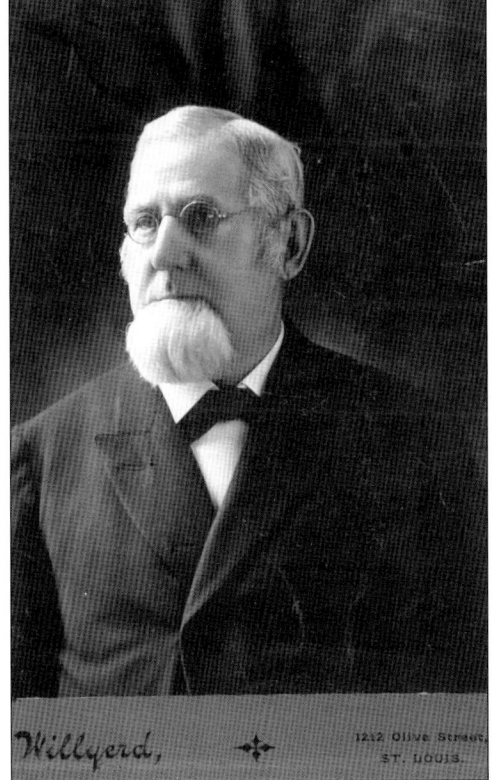

John W. Cunningham's status during the Civil War is not known, but his brother Anthony was imprisoned for Confederate sympathies. Mr. Middleton, who operated the Hill's Hotel in the 1880s, spent four years in the Confederate army as a captain of Company H of the 39th Georgia Regiment, Having gone through the suffering of prisons, marches, hunger, and other trials, he had tramped from Virginia to his Georgia home after Sherman's surrender. In Georgia prior to the Civil War, he was sheriff of Chattooga County and postmaster of the town of Summerville. He went home without a job, removed his family to Louisville and met John Turner of Elizabethtown, who hired Middleton to build a house. (Courtesy of Brown-Pusey House.)

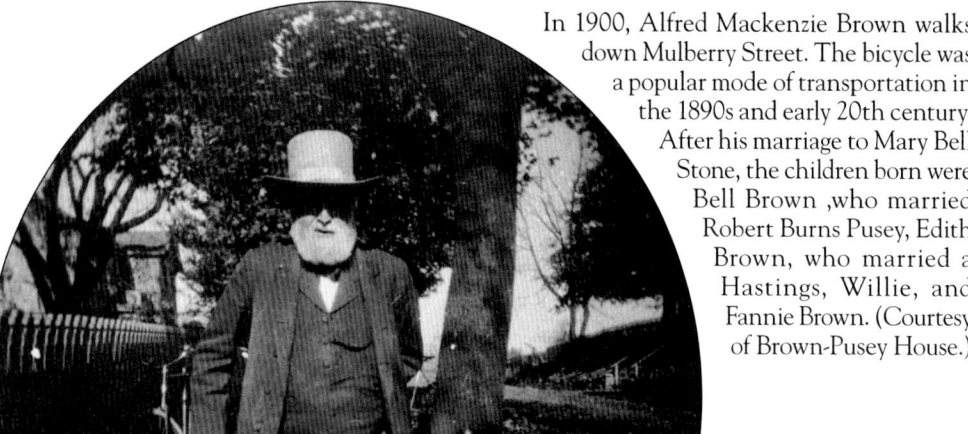

In 1900, Alfred Mackenzie Brown walks down Mulberry Street. The bicycle was a popular mode of transportation in the 1890s and early 20th century. After his marriage to Mary Bell Stone, the children born were Bell Brown, who married Robert Burns Pusey, Edith Brown, who married a Hastings, Willie, and Fannie Brown. (Courtesy of Brown-Pusey House.)

Willie Brown, pictured, died in March 1859 from scarlet fever along with his sister, Fannie. Willie and Fannie were the children of Alfred M. and Mary Bell Stone Brown. Mary Bell was half-sister to Rebecca Davis Stone Hill. John Y. Hill, the husband of Rebecca, died on August 1, 1859, from pneumonia. The Browns lived on Mulberry Street, one block from the Hill's Hotel. (Courtesy of Brown-Pusey House.)

Eight
19TH CENTURY SCENERY AND PEOPLE

Two ladies and two children (unidentified) in the 1880s are dressed for the winter and are next to a tree with ice on it and a picket fence. Photography began in 1839, and the pictures were produced on metal and glass. This photograph was from the first Kodak camera that was released to the public in the 1880s. The photographs produced were round on rectangular paper. Notice these photographs throughout the book. (Courtesy of Brown-Pusey House.)

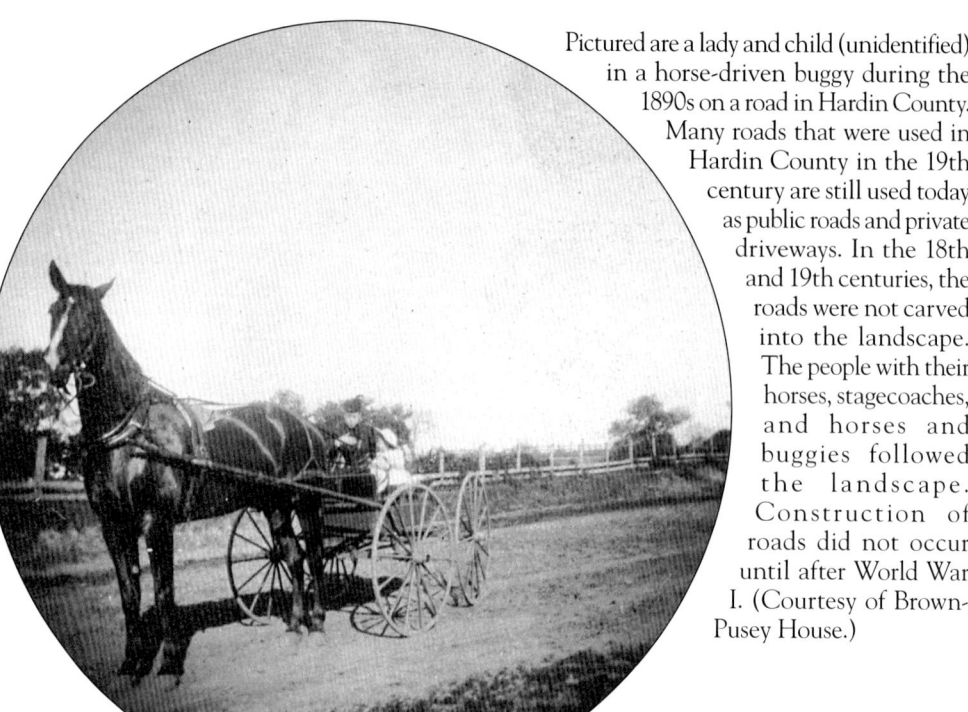

Pictured are a lady and child (unidentified) in a horse-driven buggy during the 1890s on a road in Hardin County. Many roads that were used in Hardin County in the 19th century are still used today as public roads and private driveways. In the 18th and 19th centuries, the roads were not carved into the landscape. The people with their horses, stagecoaches, and horses and buggies followed the landscape. Construction of roads did not occur until after World War I. (Courtesy of Brown-Pusey House.)

Pictured is a snow-covered fork in the road during the 1890s in Hardin County with its destination unidentified. People have enjoyed taking photographs of the scenery since photography began. Dr. William Allen Pusey authored the book *The Wilderness Road to Kentucky*. In this book, he photographed many roads, landscapes and areas of the late 19th century and early 20th centuries that his great-grandfather had written about in his journal and he had walked in the late 18th century. His photographs and slides are in the archives of the Brown-Pusey House. (Courtesy of Brown-Pusey House.)

Sallie Pusey (at left) and two others are riding horses near the Warfield home in the 1890s in Hardin County. Sallie's mother, Malvina Penelope Warfield, was the daughter of Roderick Warfield and Ann Stockett. Malvinia married first an Adams and then Anthony H. Cunningham. The two children born were Sallie Warfield and Malvina Hundley Cunningham. Malvina Cunningham first married Garnett Duncan Ripley and had a daughter, Mary Louise Ripley. Then she married Harry McGoodwin. (Courtesy of Brown-Pusey House.)

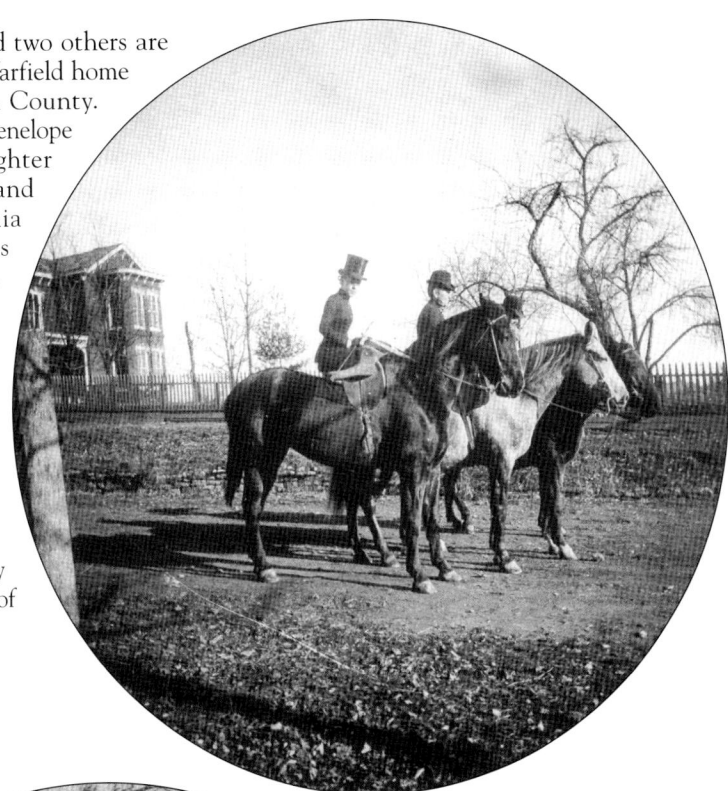

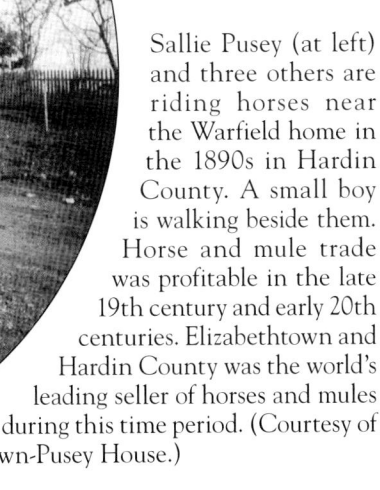

Sallie Pusey (at left) and three others are riding horses near the Warfield home in the 1890s in Hardin County. A small boy is walking beside them. Horse and mule trade was profitable in the late 19th century and early 20th centuries. Elizabethtown and Hardin County was the world's leading seller of horses and mules during this time period. (Courtesy of Brown-Pusey House.)

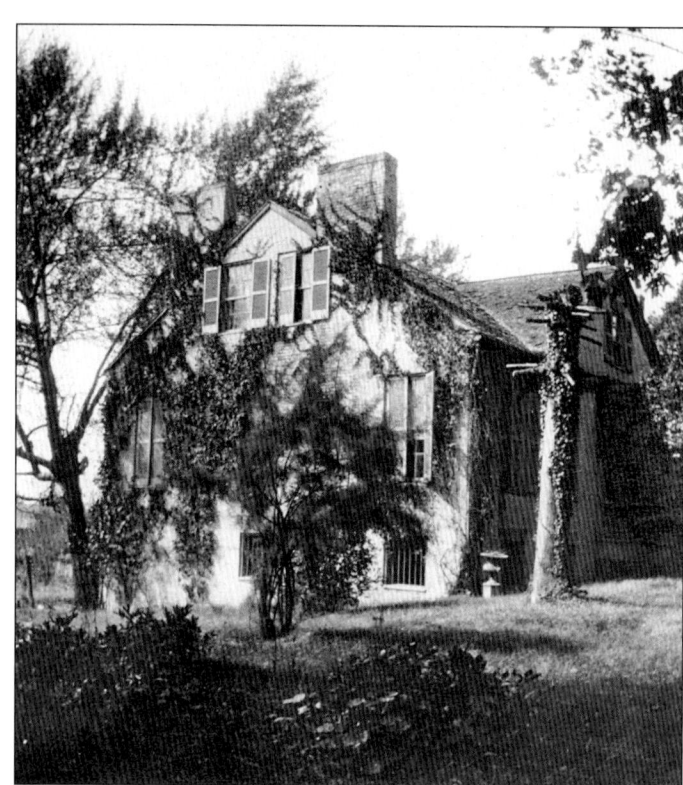

Pictured before 1920 is the McKinney home where Elizabeth Robinson, Mrs. Hardin Helm, and the wife of the late Hobson James lived in Elizabethtown. This house, like the Pusey House before it, was torn down and rebuilt on Mulberry Street in the 1870s. Dr. Robert Burns Pusey and Bell Brown had their first son, William Allen Pusey, in 1865. Their second son, Alfred Brown Pusey, was born in 1869. (Courtesy of Brown-Pusey House.)

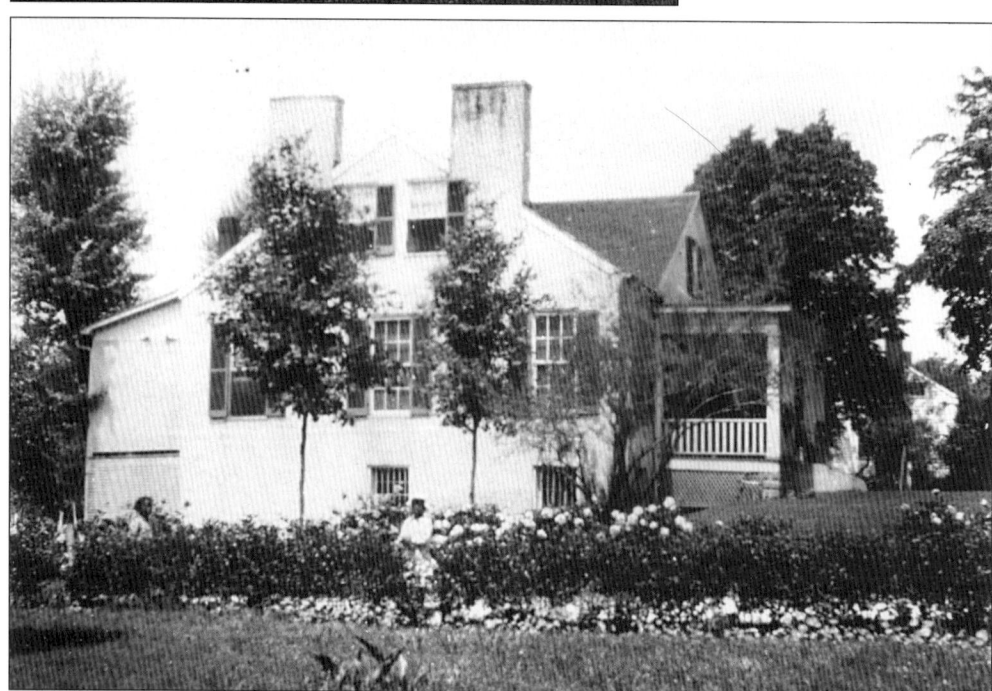

The McKinney home, where a Robinson, a Helm, and a James had lived in Elizabethtown, was, like the Pusey House before it, torn down and rebuilt on Mulberry Street. Notice the addition of the front porch and people working in the garden area after 1920. (Courtesy of Brown-Pusey House.)

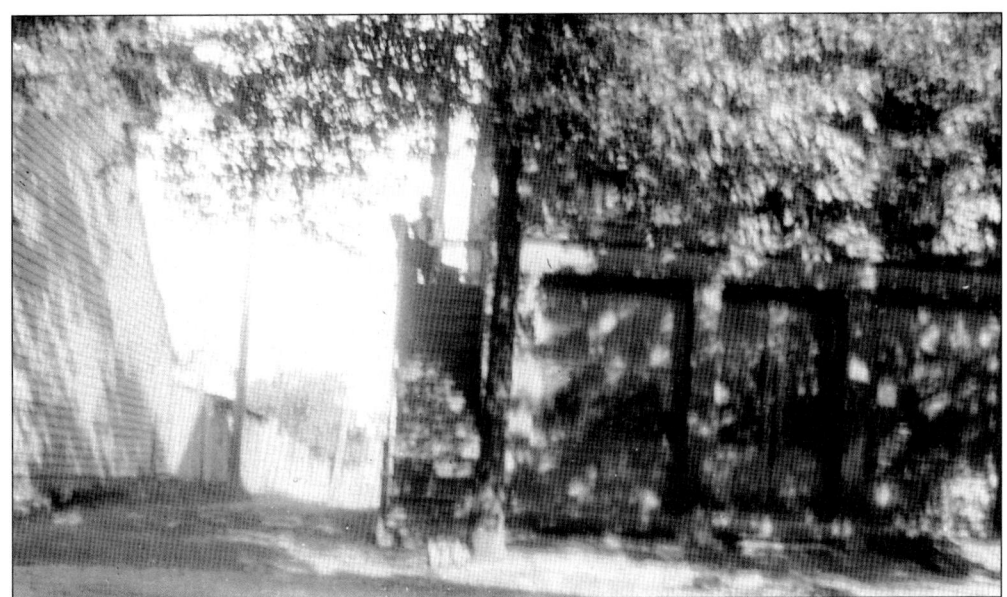

This building is located in Elizabethtown on North Mulberry Street. Roderick Warfield lived on this street. He died in 1862. His wife, Ann, took care of their children Thomas Noble, Joshua, George, Roderick, John Augustus, Mary (who married a Haynes), Malvina P. (who married an Adams), Eleanor (who married a McGill), Rachel (who married a Johnson), and Manelid Warfield. John Augustus Warfield drowned crossing the Ohio River in 1863. His personal effects are at the Brown-Pusey House. (Courtesy of Brown-Pusey House.)

Sallie and Bell Pusey are on the stairs of the side entrance to the Pusey house on Mulberry Street. This house is across street from the current Kelley law office. Bell Brown Pusey was a supporter of community activities, especially ones for children. A YWCA and a YMCA were created in Elizabethtown with subscriptions from local people such as Bell Pusey, Lena Johnson, Louis Goldnamer, Lucy Robertson, Bess English, and many others. The space rented for this community center was above Marshall Jewelers on the Public Square. (Courtesy of Brown-Pusey House.)

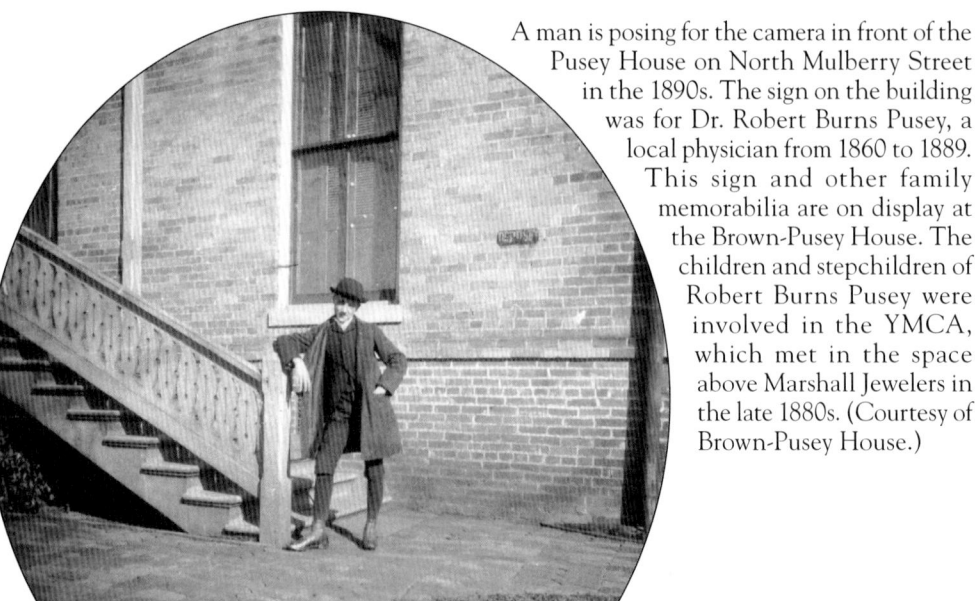

A man is posing for the camera in front of the Pusey House on North Mulberry Street in the 1890s. The sign on the building was for Dr. Robert Burns Pusey, a local physician from 1860 to 1889. This sign and other family memorabilia are on display at the Brown-Pusey House. The children and stepchildren of Robert Burns Pusey were involved in the YMCA, which met in the space above Marshall Jewelers in the late 1880s. (Courtesy of Brown-Pusey House.)

This photograph is reversed. The printing process could invert the image even in the 1890s. The man carrying a trunk from the Pusey house is actually walking out onto North Mulberry Street. Sallie Warfield Cunningham visited this family house often from the 1880s to 1950. Malvina Penelope Warfield married an Adams and then Anthony Hundley Cunningham. Their daughter, Sallie, married Dr. William Allen Pusey in Missouri. (Courtesy of Brown-Pusey House.)

Sallie Pusey is riding her horse, Boon, on Mulberry Street. Sallie's aunts attended Bethlehem Academy in the 1840s and 1850s. Photographs and other personal effects of the students (most are not known) from Bethlehem Academy are in the archives of the Brown-Pusey House. The students known are George McMurtry, Lizzie McCawley, Della McSean, T. S. Burnam, Susan Thomas, C. F. McCarty, T. G. Scott, and Samuel B. Young. (Courtesy of Brown-Pusey House.)

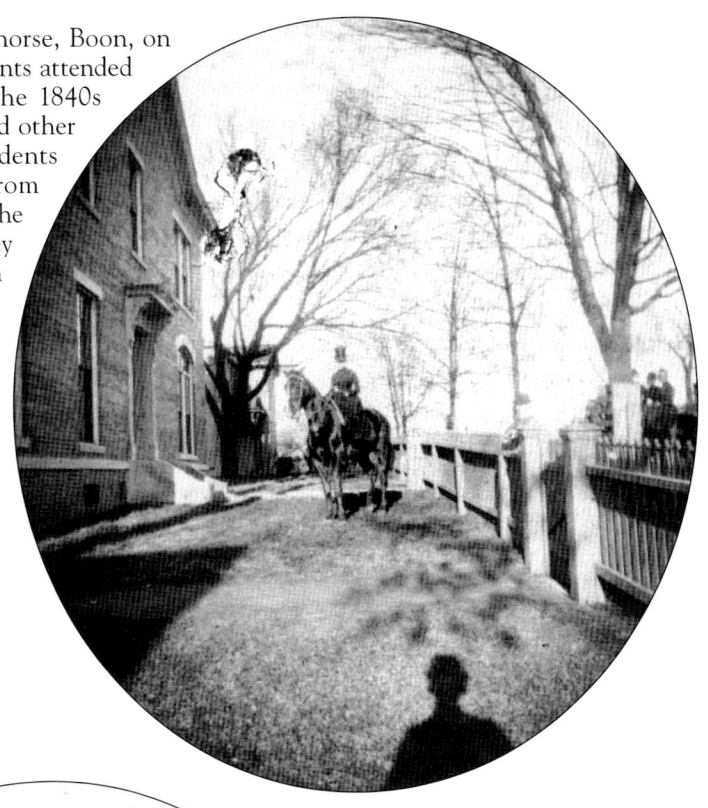

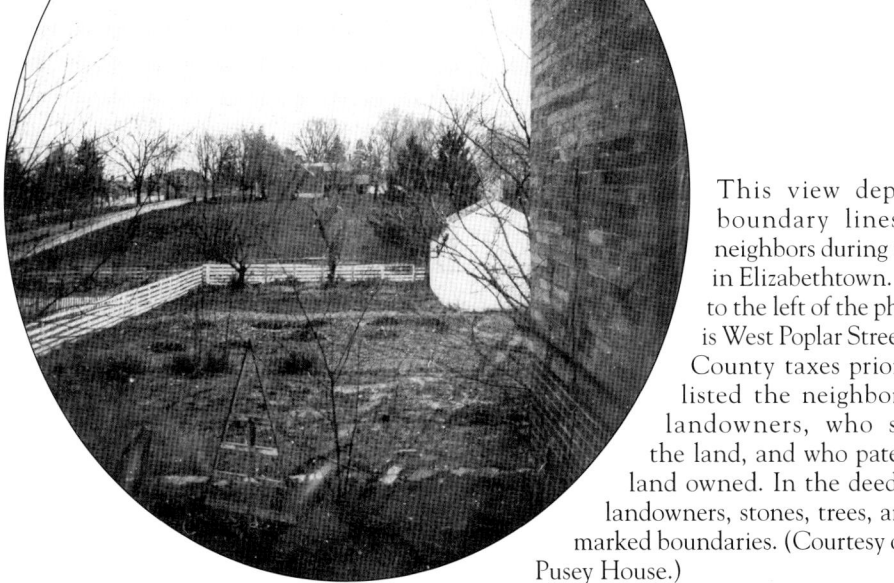

This view depicts the boundary lines of the neighbors during the 1890s in Elizabethtown. The road to the left of the photograph is West Poplar Street. Hardin County taxes prior to 1875 listed the neighbors of the landowners, who surveyed the land, and who patented the land owned. In the deed records, landowners, stones, trees, and creeks marked boundaries. (Courtesy of Brown-Pusey House.)

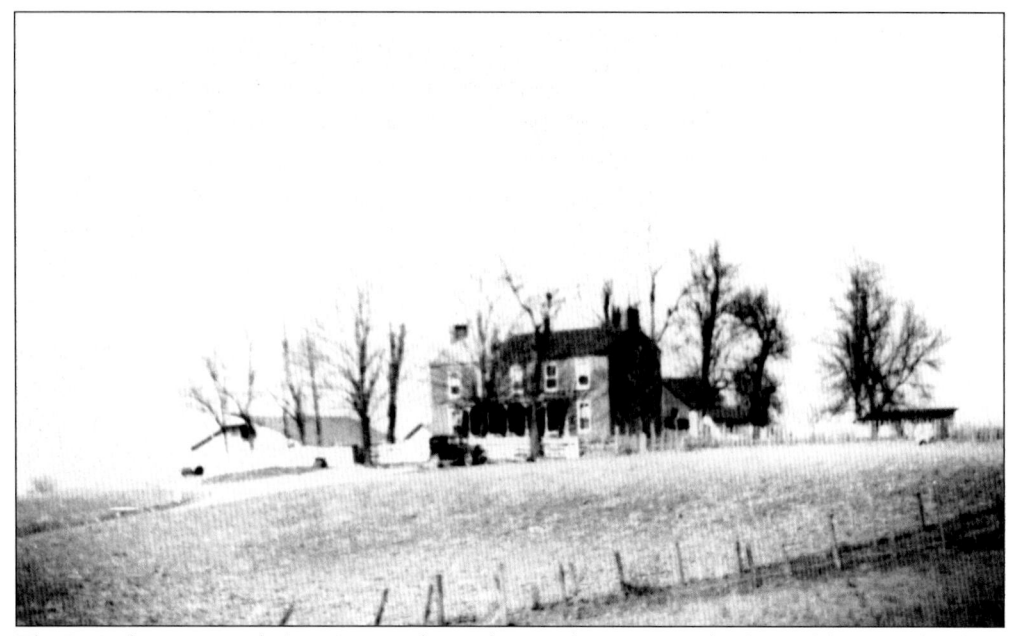

The Pusey farm, pictured after 1920, was located in Hardin County. This farm of the Pusey brothers was one of many properties purchased in the 1920s. The Pusey brothers owned one-fourth of Elizabethtown from the 1920s to 1950s and rented the properties to businesses. The Pusey brothers owned most of the Public Square. Most of the Public Square had been rebuilt after the Great Fire of 1869 and the fires of the late 1870s and 1880s. (Courtesy of Brown-Pusey House.)

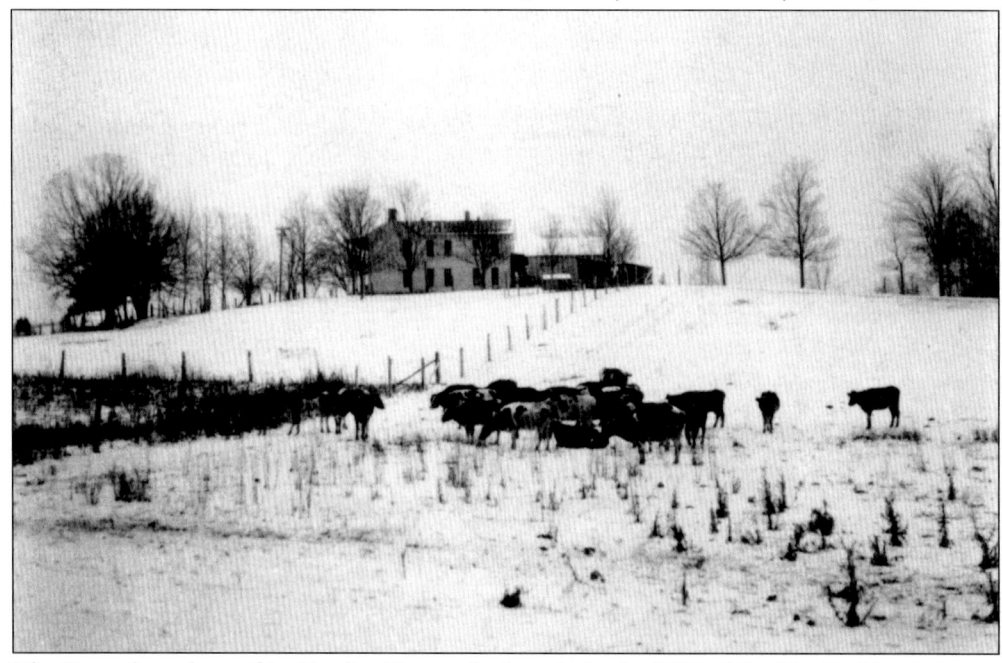

The Pusey farm, located in Hardin County, had cattle in the 1920s. The Hardin County taxes from 1830 to 1845 specified how many head of cattle the landowner had and the value of the cattle. John Y. Hill, the great-uncle of the Pusey brothers, had ventured in the cattle and hog enterprise in the 1850s. (Courtesy of Brown-Pusey House.)

Two young boys who are making faces for the camera are unidentified. This view is the rear of the Pusey and Brown homes in Elizabethtown, located on North Mulberry Street, in the 1890s. Entertainment in Hardin County has varied from the 19th century to the present. Outrageous exhibits, like eight-foot mummies, were brought to the county by the way of fairs, circuses, carnivals, and traveling salesmen. The city charged each traveling band a fee per day to have an event. (Courtesy of Brown-Pusey House.)

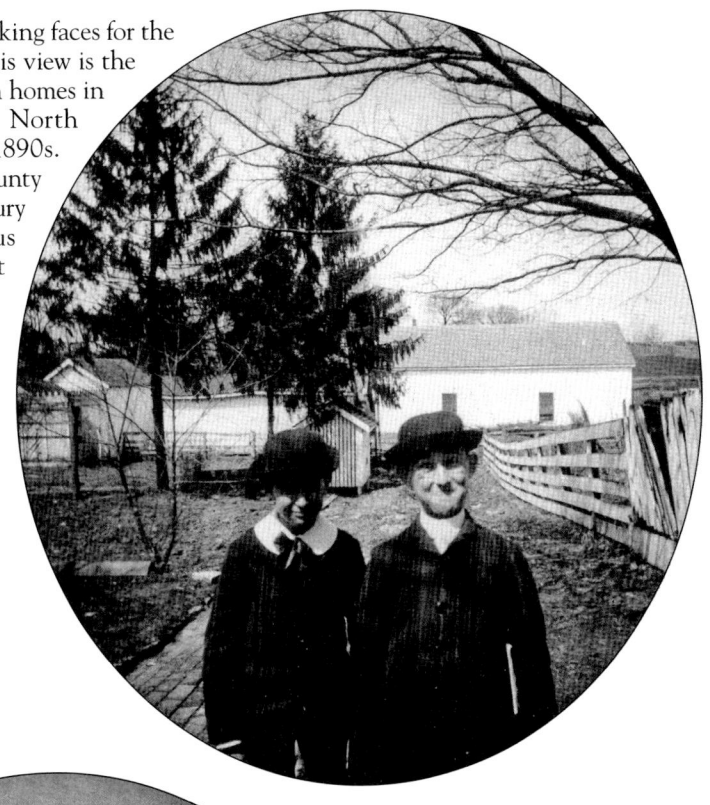

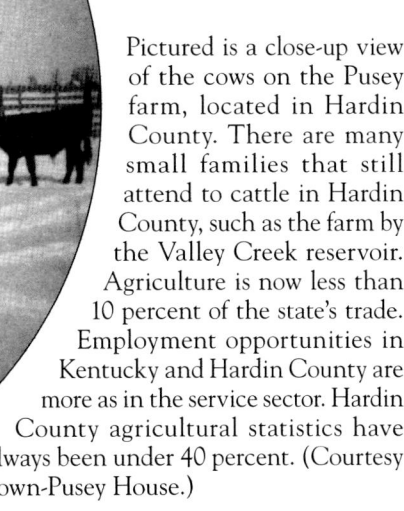

Pictured is a close-up view of the cows on the Pusey farm, located in Hardin County. There are many small families that still attend to cattle in Hardin County, such as the farm by the Valley Creek reservoir. Agriculture is now less than 10 percent of the state's trade. Employment opportunities in Kentucky and Hardin County are more as in the service sector. Hardin County agricultural statistics have always been under 40 percent. (Courtesy of Brown-Pusey House.)

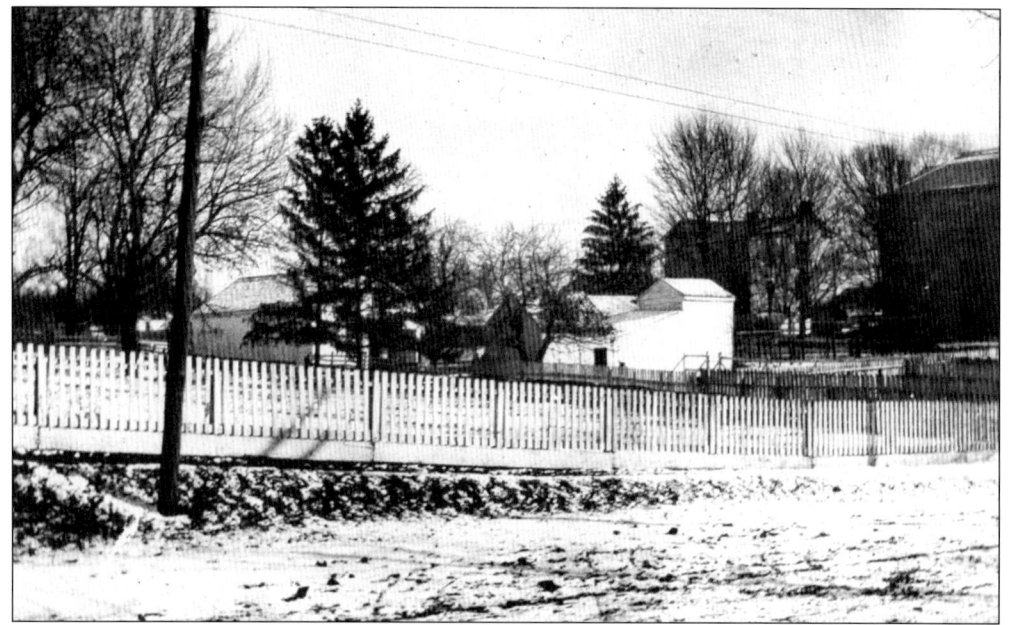

This view about 1920 is taken from West Poplar Street looking toward the Brown residence and the Pusey residence on North Mulberry Street. East Poplar Street was extended in 1835, beginning on Main Street 50 feet above the clerk's office and running 40 feet wide and at right angles back to Haycraft's Quince Alley. The roads of Hardin County have been changed, modified, and rerouted since the beginning of Kentucky exploration. (Courtesy of Brown-Pusey House.)

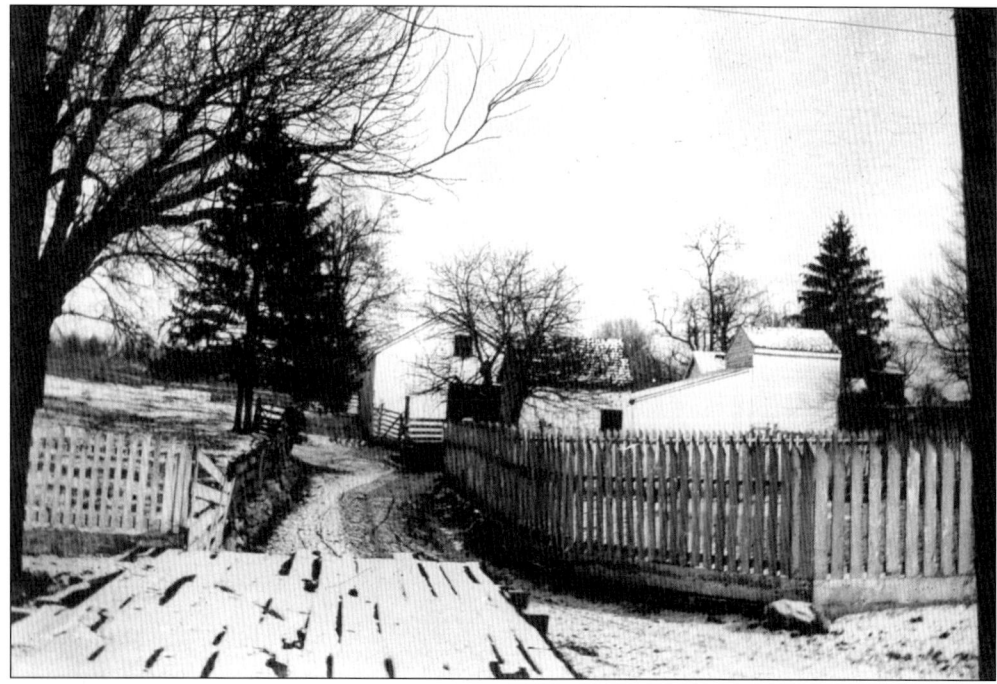

This view is the alley close to the intersection of North Mulberry and West Poplar Streets. Today the law office's parking lots would be located on the right side of this fence. (Courtesy of Brown-Pusey House.)

Pictured are stables behind the Robert Burns Pusey residence and the Alfred Mackenzie Brown residence in the 1890s. This photograph was taken with a Kodak camera. (Courtesy of Brown-Pusey House.)

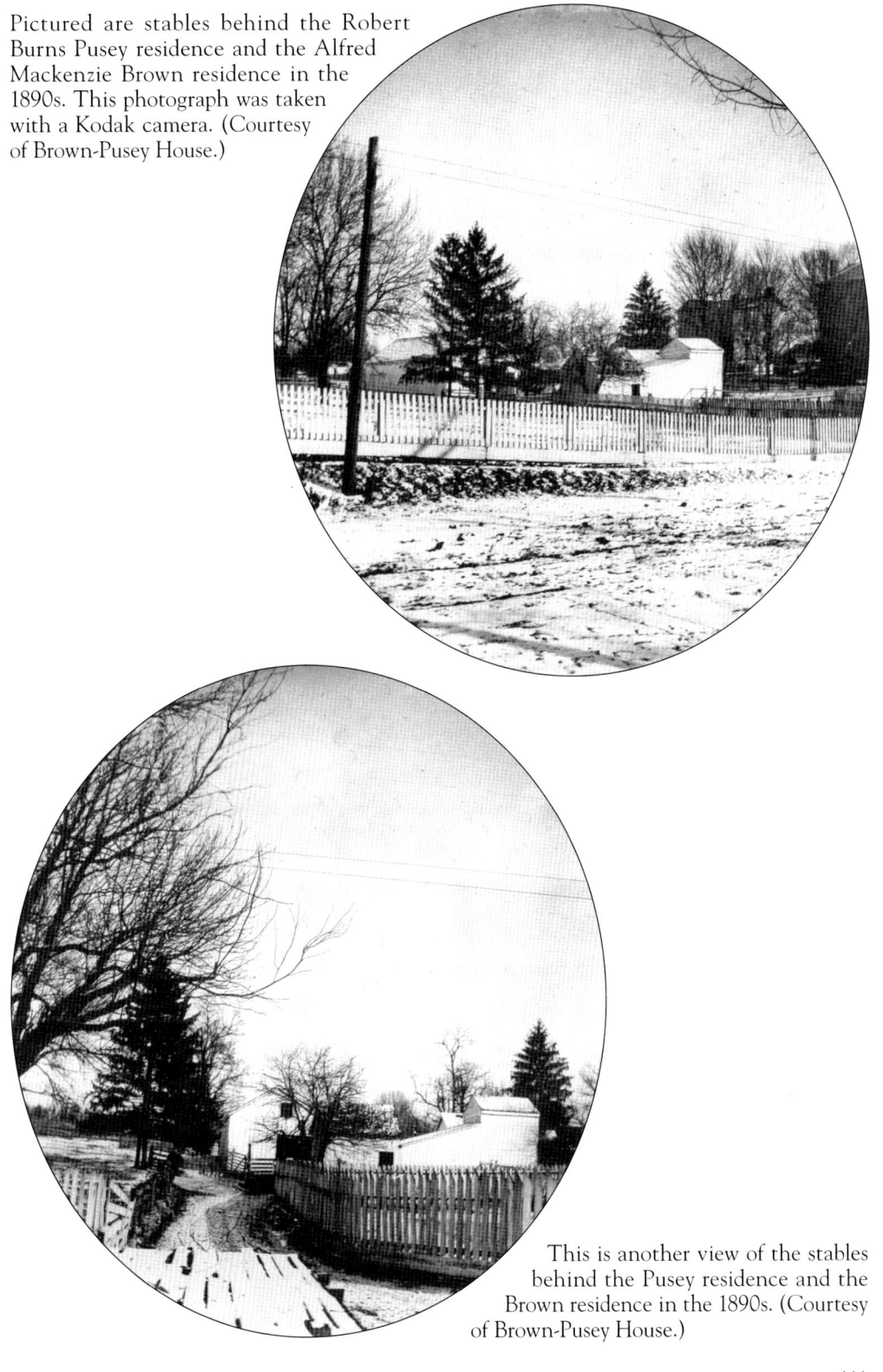

This is another view of the stables behind the Pusey residence and the Brown residence in the 1890s. (Courtesy of Brown-Pusey House.)

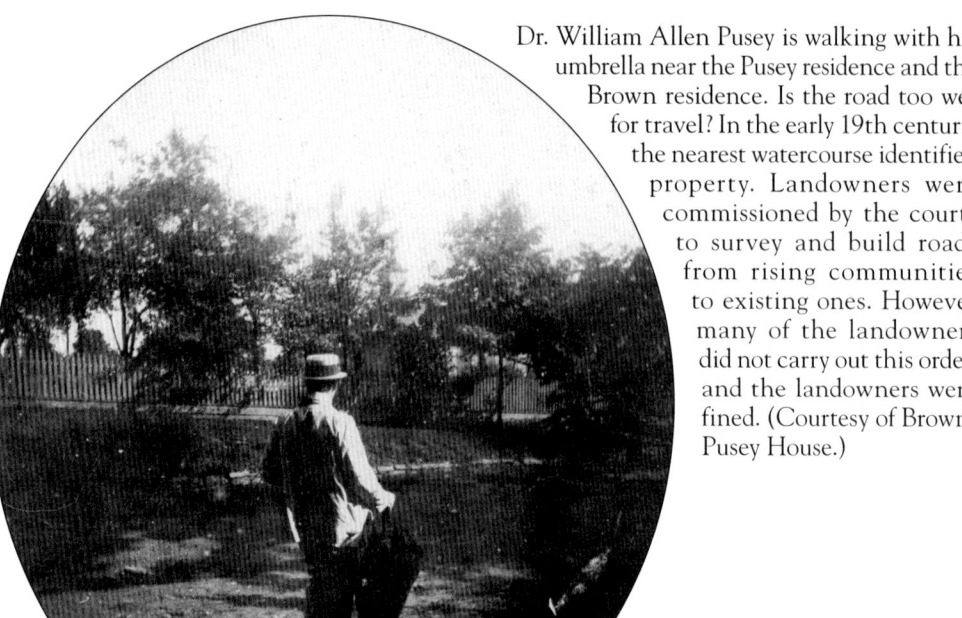

Dr. William Allen Pusey is walking with his umbrella near the Pusey residence and the Brown residence. Is the road too wet for travel? In the early 19th century, the nearest watercourse identified property. Landowners were commissioned by the courts to survey and build roads from rising communities to existing ones. However many of the landowners did not carry out this order, and the landowners were fined. (Courtesy of Brown-Pusey House.)

Pictured is Helen Newlin Hastings with her child, Newlin Hastings. Bell Brown Pusey and Robert Burns Pusey raised the Hastings children. One of the Hastings children married Helen Newlin. The Pusey family has no descendants. The Hastings family has descendants. (Courtesy of Brown-Pusey House.)

Ellen Wathen is pictured at the age of 25 during the 1880s. The Wathen family name can be found in Hardin County records as Wortham or Wathen. Names in the early records were written phonetically. Thomas Geoghegan had married the only daughter of John B. Wathen, and he died soon after his arrival to Elizabethtown about 1804. (Courtesy of Brown-Pusey House.)

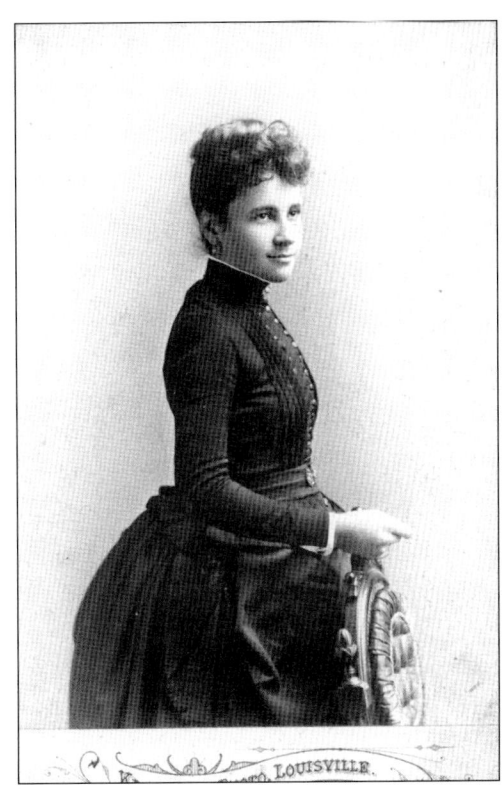

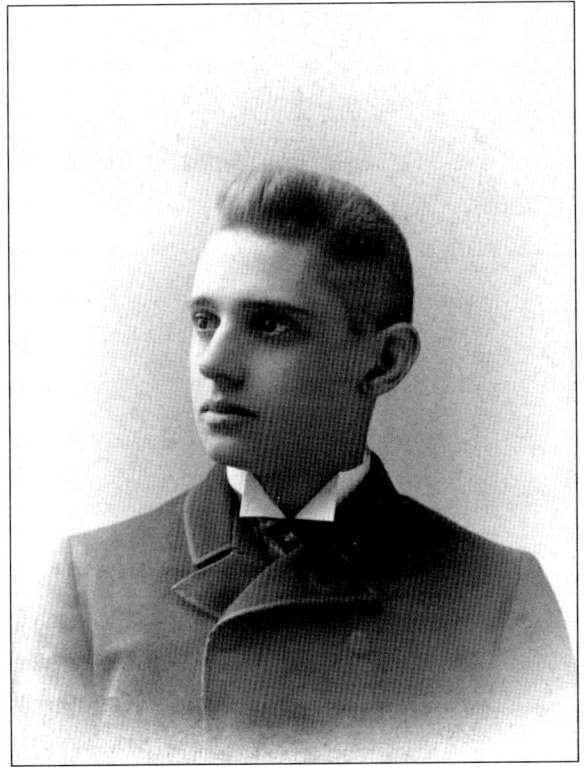

Photographed in 1887 is Edward Hundley Cunningham, the son of Rev. John Cunningham. John was one of five sisters and three brothers. Edward's uncle, Anthony, studied in Elizabethtown in 1818. He partnered with Whittaker and Helm in 1832 and operated a store on Dixie Avenue in Elizabethtown from 1837 to 1869. (Courtesy of Brown-Pusey House.)

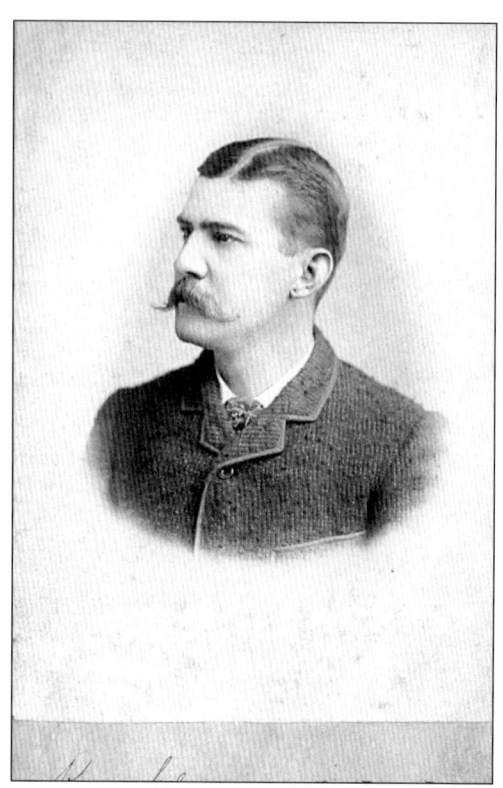

William Cunningham was another son of Rev. John and Samantha Cunningham. The Cunningham family was related to the Geoghegans. Reverend John's sister, Lydia Ann, married Dr. Ambrose Geoghegan in 1842. Ambrose's grandparents, Peggy Zelman and Ambrose Geoghegan, arrived in Elizabethtown about 1804. (Courtesy of Brown-Pusey House.)

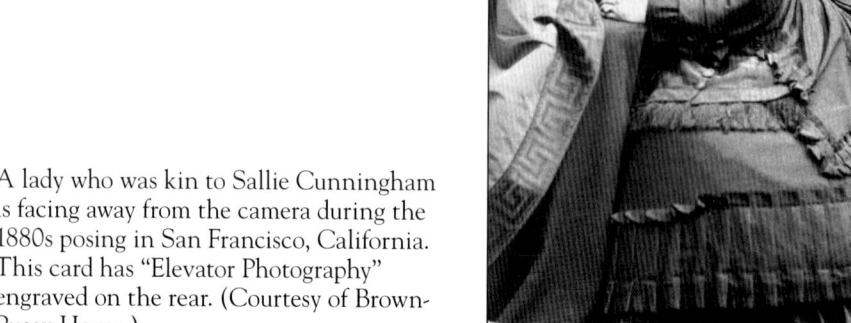

A lady who was kin to Sallie Cunningham is facing away from the camera during the 1880s posing in San Francisco, California. This card has "Elevator Photography" engraved on the rear. (Courtesy of Brown-Pusey House.)

Jenne Warfield lived in Cloverport in 1886. She was the daughter of Thomas Hobb Warfield and Martha Hambleton. (Courtesy of Brown-Pusey House.)

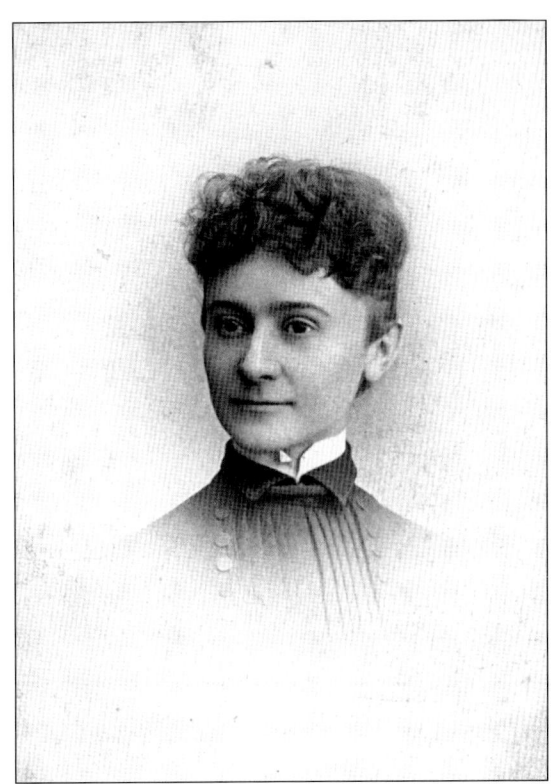

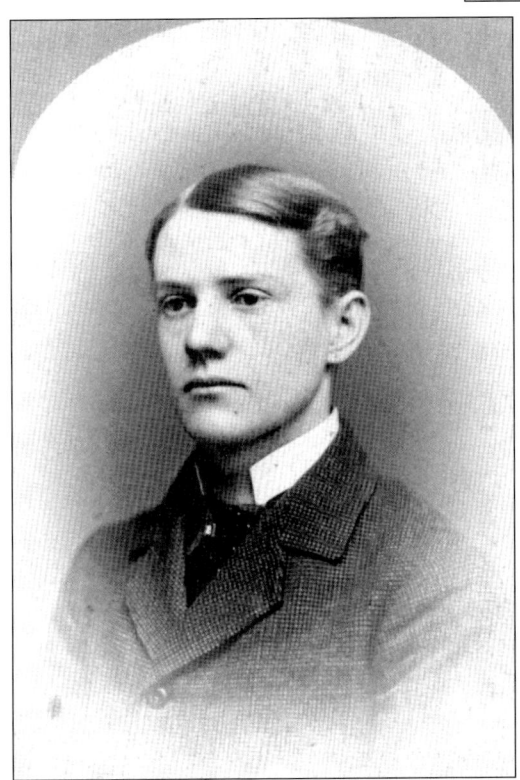

Charles Adams Cunningham, pictured, was the son of Rev. J. and Samantha Cunningham. This photograph was taken by Mrs. J. H. Fitzgibbon, photographer, at 927 Olive Street, St. Louis, Missouri. (Courtesy of Brown-Pusey House.)

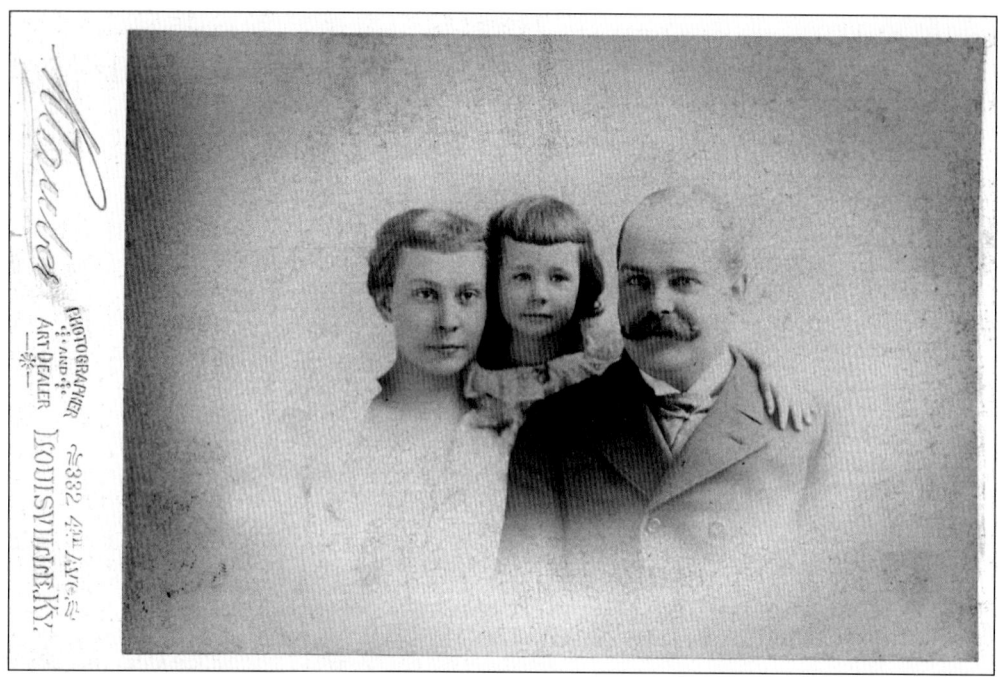

Mr. and Mrs. Harry McGoodwin and their child, Louise, are pictured in this photograph that was taken at E. Klauber, photographer and art dealer, who was located at 332 Fourth Avenue, Louisville, Kentucky. (Courtesy of Brown-Pusey House.)

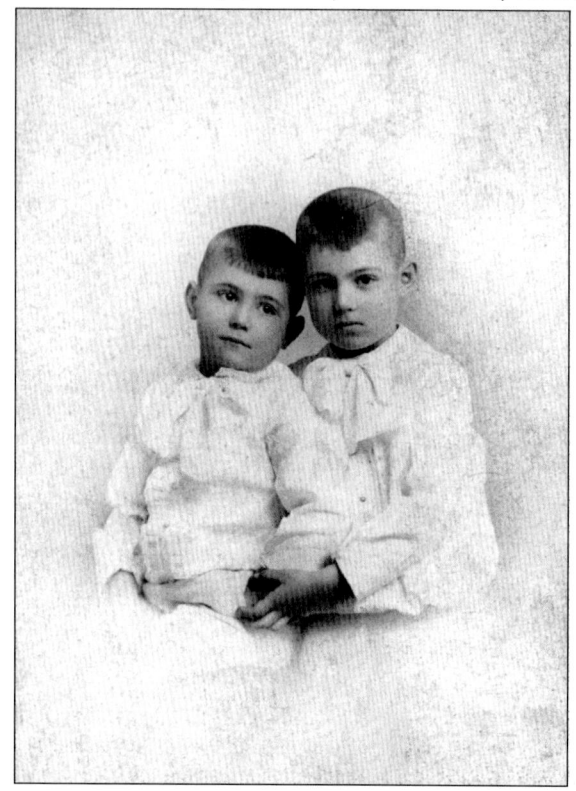

John Taylor (five) and his brother Joe, seven, the sons of Ella Cunningham Taylor (daughter of Rev. J. and Samantha Cunningham), sent this photograph to their cousin, Lizzie Curd. This photograph was taken at Da Lee's Art Gallery on Tennessee Street in Lawrence, Kansas. (Courtesy of Brown-Pusey House.)

This photograph was mailed to Aunt Hundley McGoodwin. It has been retouched to indicate ruffles on the dress as well as to add accessories. Photographs were retouched in the 1880s. (Courtesy of Brown-Pusey House.)

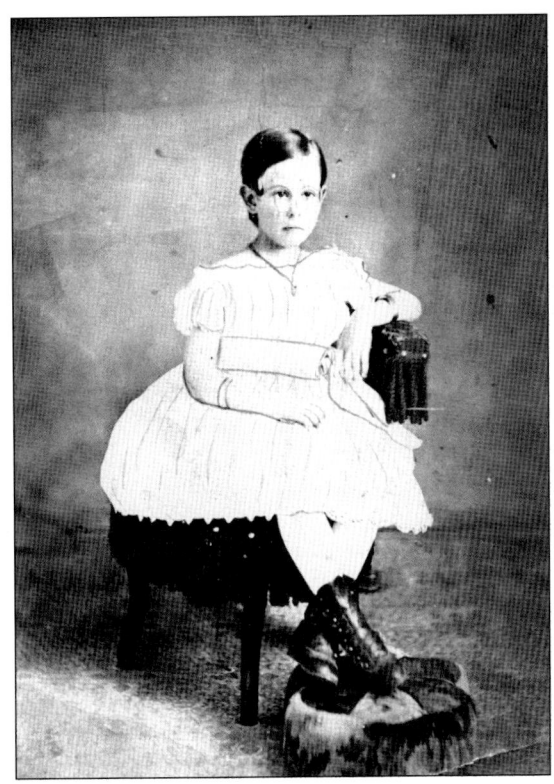

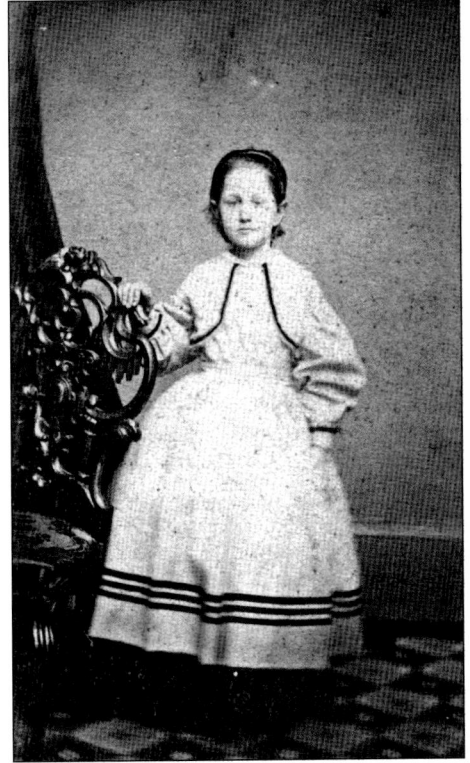

This photograph of an unidentified student, age seven, at Bethlehem Academy was found in a Cunningham album. The image was taken in the 1850s by Jennings, a photographer at 66 Fourth Street in Louisville, Kentucky, located over G. W. Robertson. (Courtesy of Brown-Pusey House.)

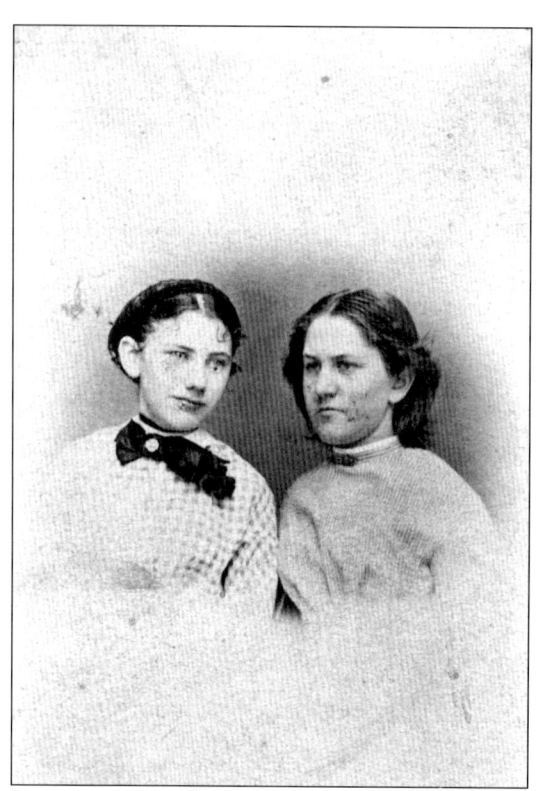

This photograph and other photographs of unidentified students at Bethlehem Academy in the 1850s were found in a Cunningham album. Frank Wybrant, located on 144 Market Street, between Fourth and Fifth Streets in Louisville, Kentucky, was the photographer. (Courtesy of Brown-Pusey House.)

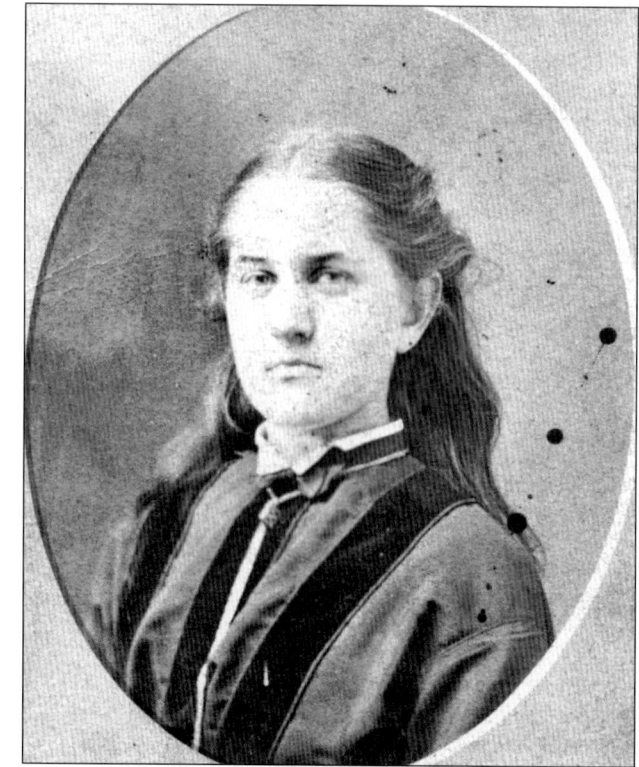

This photograph of an unidentified student was found in a Cunningham album in the 1850s; it was photographed by Frank Wybrant. On the back are the initials H. C. C. (Courtesy of Brown-Pusey House.)

In the late 19th and early 20th centuries, wood fences like this one were placed near the rim of a knob in order to keep the farm animals from roaming. (Courtesy of Brown-Pusey House.)

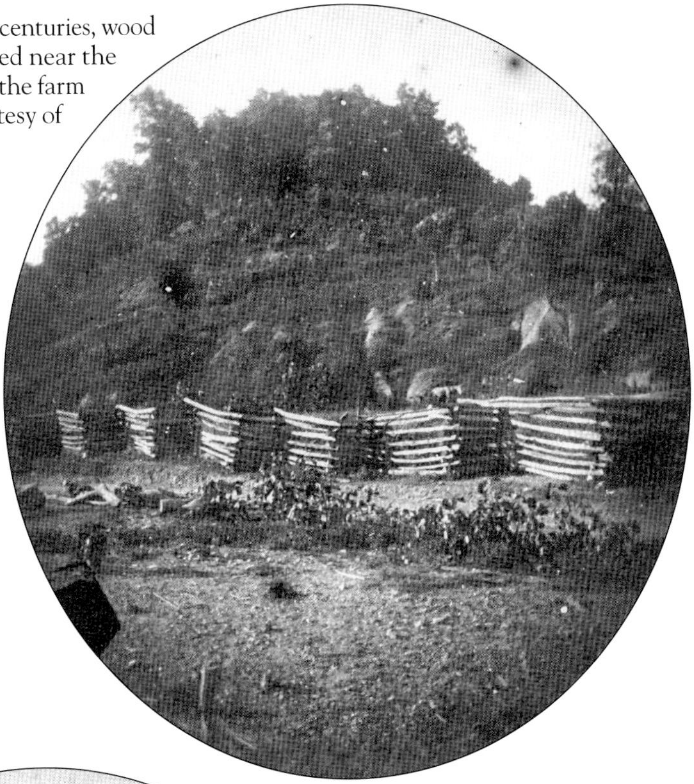

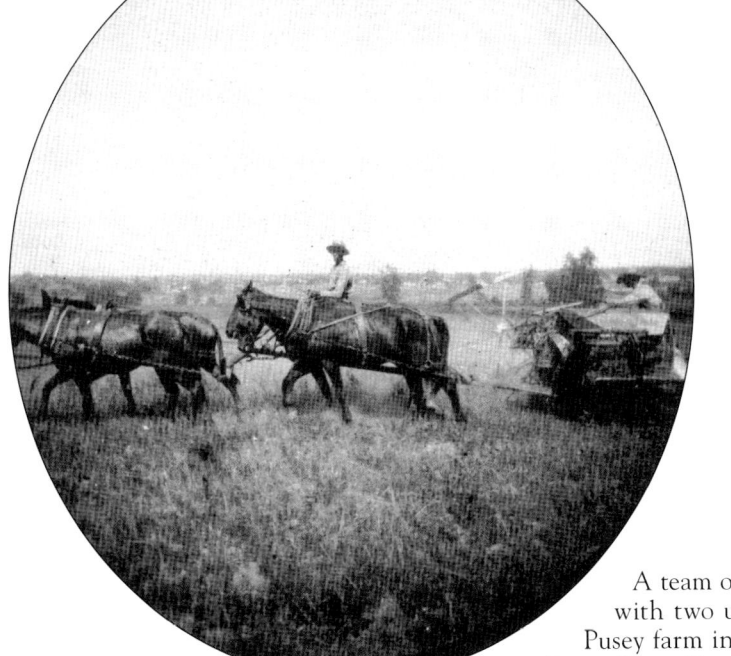

A team of mules moves something with two unidentified men on the Pusey farm in the 1890s. (Courtesy of Brown-Pusey House.)

An unidentified man and a horse and cart transport a stack of hay or wheat on the Pusey farm in the 1890s. (Courtesy of Brown-Pusey House.)

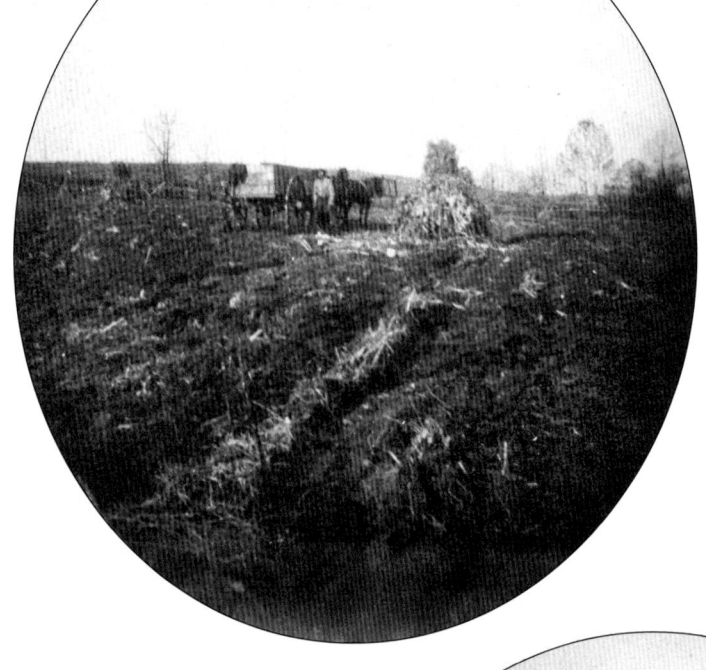

Pictured is a boy on a horse pulling wheat or hay on the Pusey farm in the 1890s. Hardware and groceries were bought at R. L. Wintersmith's store in Elizabethtown, where the old Marshall Jewelers store is today. Many items were bought in town due to its prosperity during the 1890s, as well as in the travels to Louisville and Nashville by train. (Courtesy of Brown-Pusey House.)

Pictured about 1922 are three Walters boys; from left to right are Howard (born 1921), Marshall (the eldest), and Louis "Bullseye" (born 1915). The Walters family is related to the Gaddie family. Paul McClure, a hermit, had hand-written, in calligraphy style, the book *Millerstown and Its People*, based on oral histories. (Courtesy of Michelle Walters.)

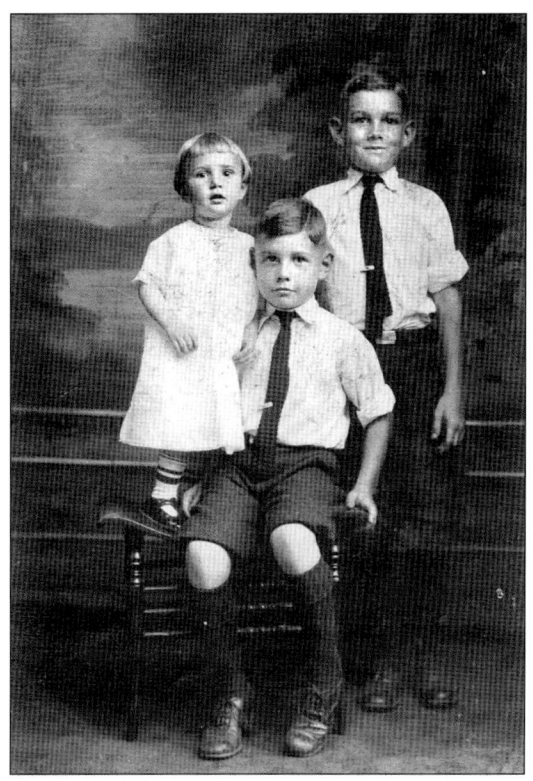

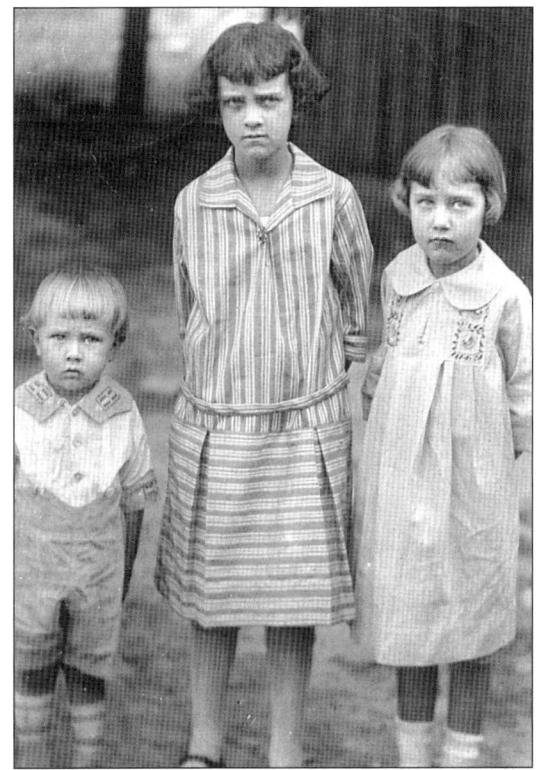

This photograph, taken in 1926, has one boy and two girls, children of the Gaddie family. From left to right are Blond (3), Edith (10), and Hartsell (9). The Gaddie family lived in Millerstown, a booming town in the late 19th and early 20th century. It is situated on the boundary of three counties: Hardin, Grayson, and Hart. The mother of the Gaddie children is a Lawler. The Lawler family came from Ireland. Annie Oldham, on the front cover, married Homer Lawler. (Courtesy of Steven Gaddie.)

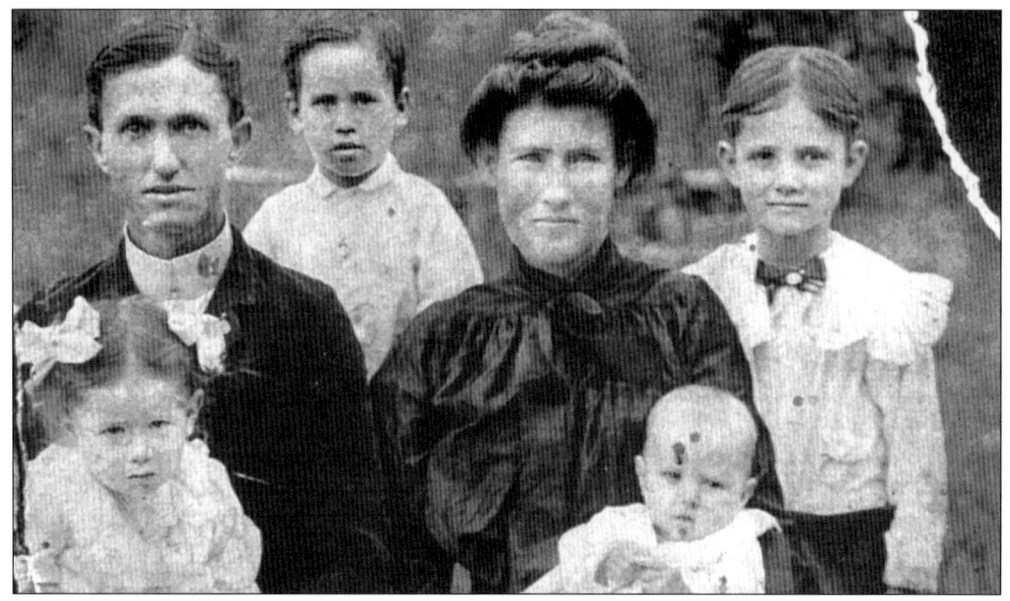

The paternal ancestors of the author are Ida Francis Oldham and Thomas Caswell, pictured as adults in this photograph. Their children were Van, Amy, Shirley, Dillard, Archie, Nettie, Bert, Roy, and Louis. The family lived in Millerstown, and the genealogy information can be found in the three counties. Thomas's father, John Caswell, served in the Union army and died in 1926. Ida's father, Samuel Oldham, lived in Hart County. (Courtesy of Carmel Powell and Meranda Caswell.)

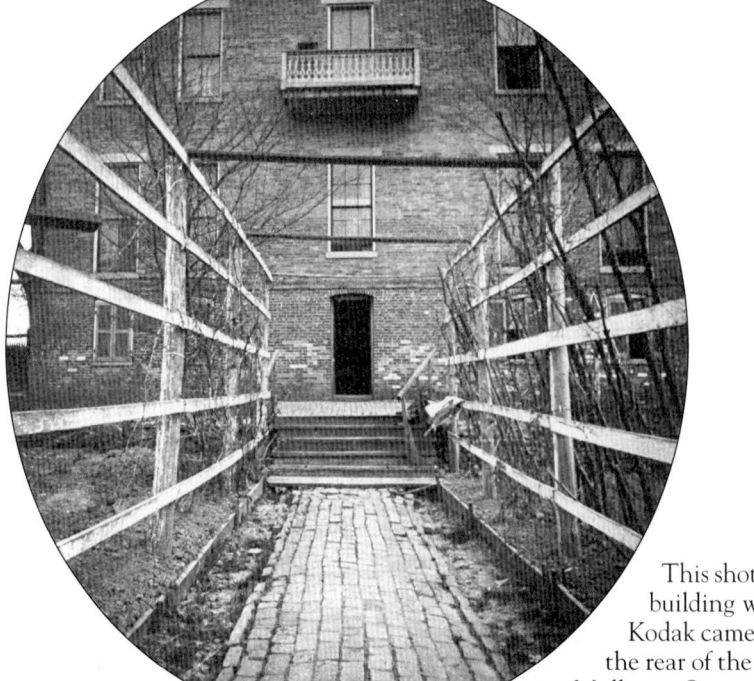

This shot of a walkway to a brick building was taken with the first Kodak camera. This may have been the rear of the Pusey House on North Mulberry Street. (Courtesy of Brown-Pusey House.)

Found in the Brown-Pusey House museum is this 1890 photograph, with the handwritten note that the water gate at the Pusey farm was the bridge to cross a creek. (Courtesy of Brown-Pusey House.)

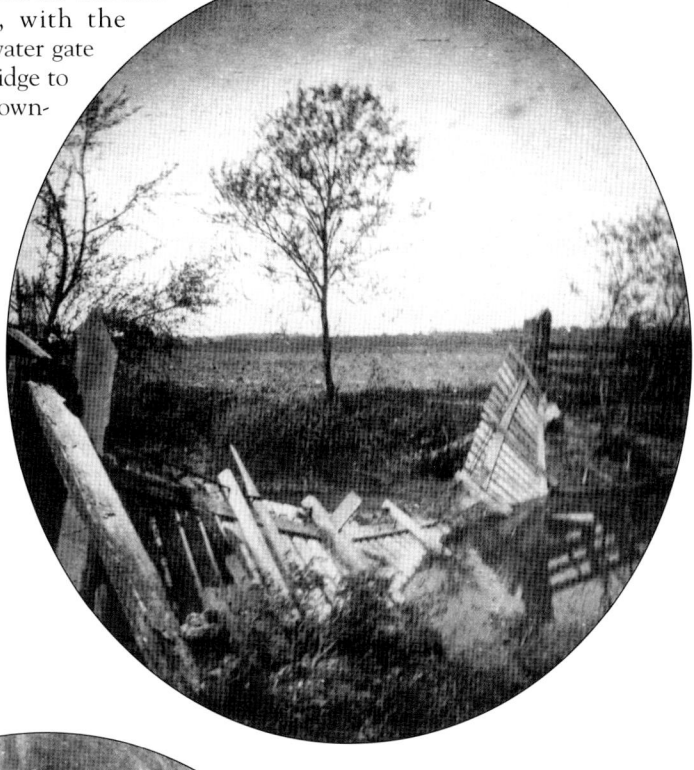

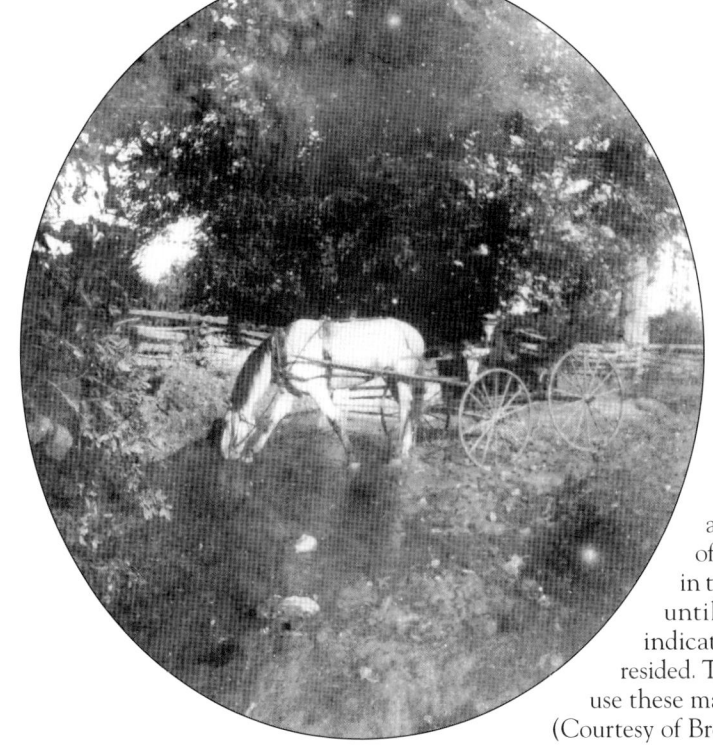

This horse attached to a buggy is drinking from a creek in the 1890s. Watercourses described in the 19th century were tributaries off of the main rivers. Rolling Fork River, Nob Creek, Clear Creek, Otter Creek, Valley Creek, and Middle Creek are examples of the names of the watercourses in the Hardin County tax records until 1860, which were used as indicators of where the landowner resided. The deed records continued to use these markers into the 20th century. (Courtesy of Brown-Pusey House.)

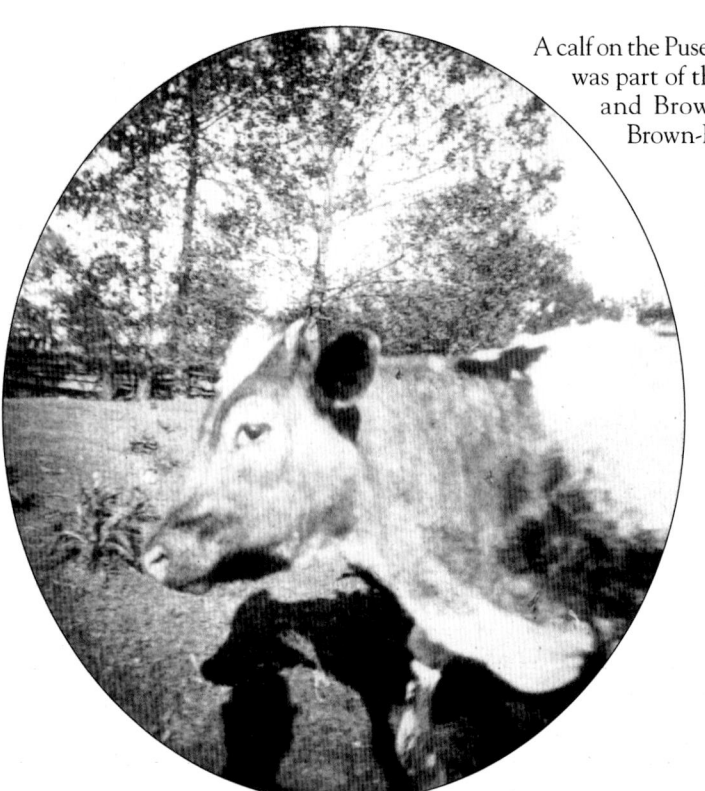

A calf on the Pusey farm in the 1890s, pictured, was part of the subsistence for the Pusey and Brown families. (Courtesy of Brown-Pusey House.)

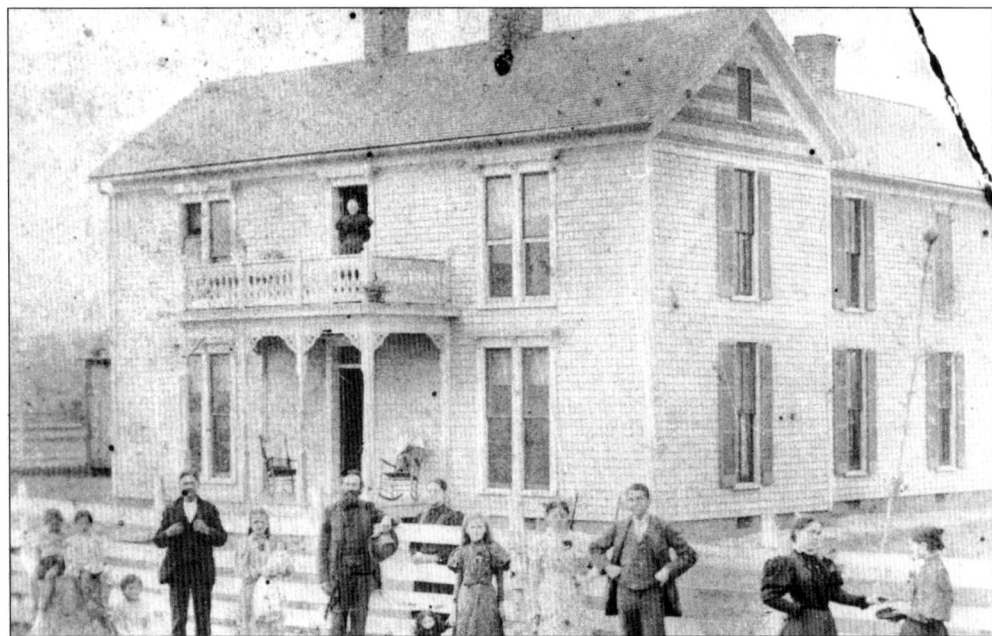

The largest gooseberry farm in the world was located near Stithton and was owned by H. O. Rahm. Crops provided over 10,000 gallons of berries, which were shipped to Louisville, Pittsburgh, Indianapolis, Memphis, New Orleans, Dallas, and many other places. The Ray House in Stithton, c. 1890, is pictured. (Courtesy of Matthew Rector and Billie Ray Alvey.)

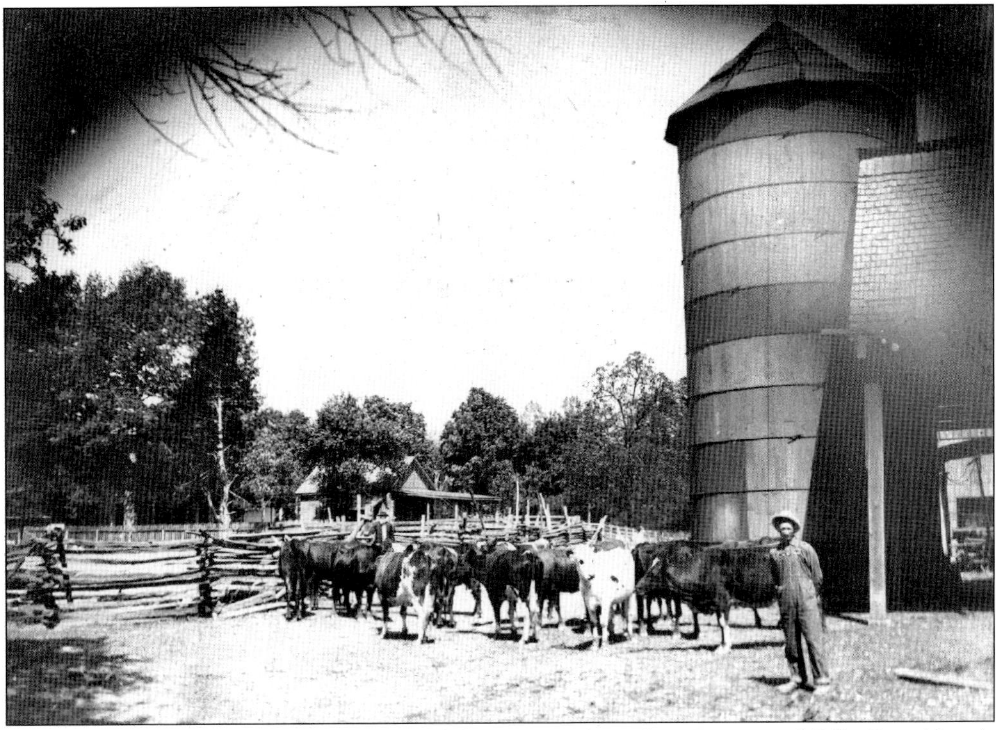

The Ray family farm in Stithton is pictured. (Courtesy of Matthew Rector and Billie Ray Alvey.)

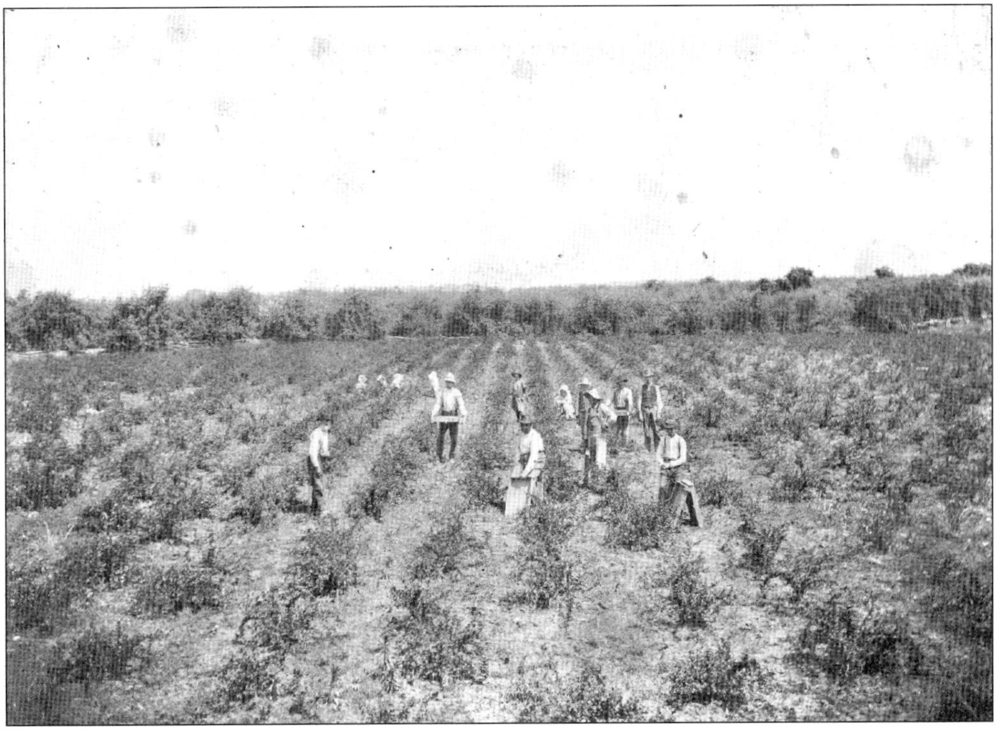

The Ray family farm in Stithton is pictured. (Courtesy of Matthew Rector and Billie Ray Alvey.)

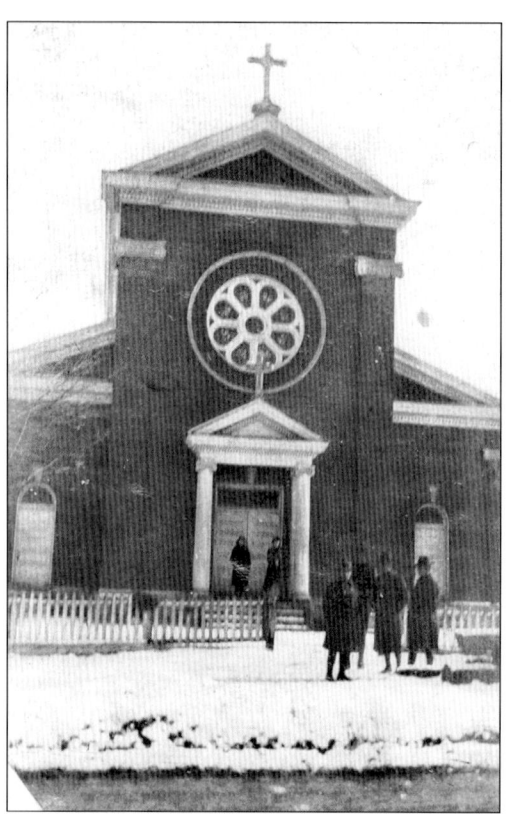

Stithton, as well as the following post offices, were discontinued by 1974: Howell's Springs, Lawsonville, Big Spring, Coombsville, Nolin, McMurtryton, Southland, Red Hill, Cofer, Otter Creek, Yagersville, Robertsville, Franklin Cross Roads, Buck Snort, Claiborne, Phillipsburg, Meeting Creek, White Mills, Dorret's Run, Long Grove, High Up, St. John, Hardin Springs, Tunnel Hill, Farleigh, Colesburg, Tip Top, Limp, New Fruit, Melrose, Nallton, Easy Gap, Cash, Sand Springs, Wigginton, Amity, Star Mills, Harcourt, Huber, Arch, Red Cloud, Warner, Cowley, Spurrier, Neff, Laurel Ridge, and Fairfarm. (Courtesy of Matthew Rector and Billie Ray Alvey.)

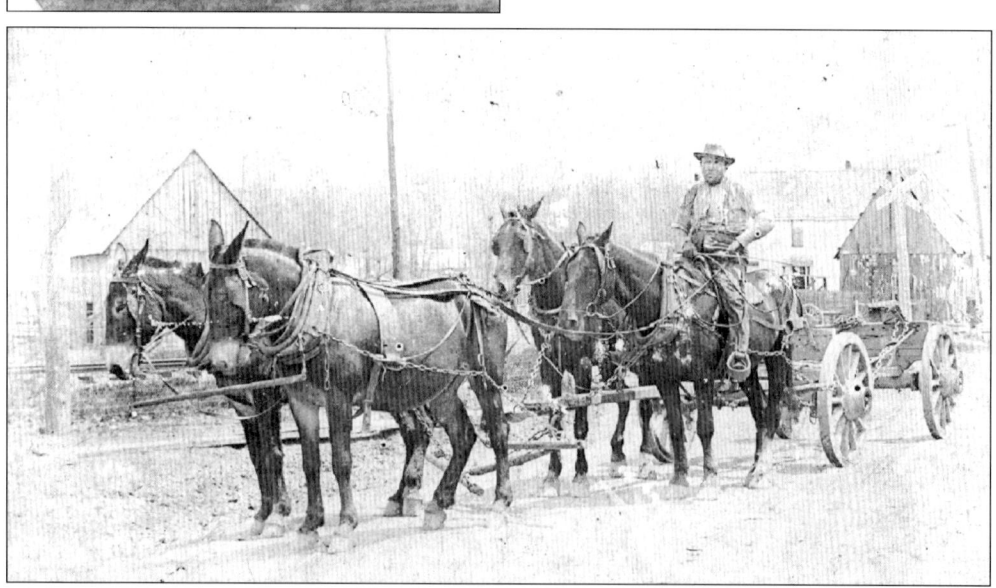

Stithton is just one of many communities and towns that have disappeared. Many of these communities today may have one farmhouse standing, a cemetery present, a ghost town, a dam, a sign, a grocery, or a hardware store. Fort Knox Military Reservation may have demolished the town of Stithton, but most of the history of this town has been well preserved in book form by Gary Kempf and several others. However many of the other communities go unspoken. (Courtesy of Matthew Rector and Billie Ray Alvey.)

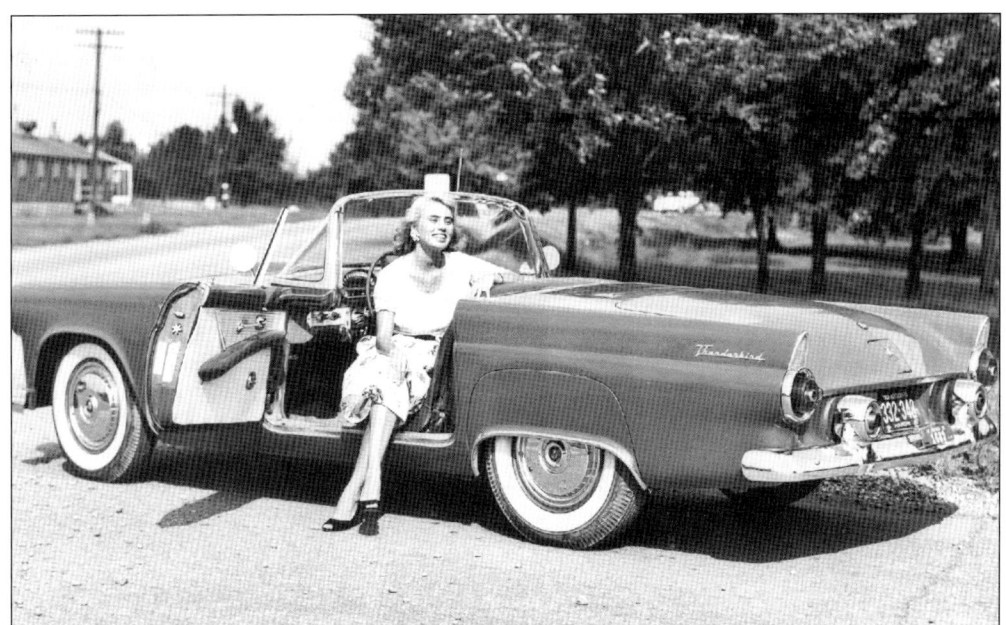

Laura Kille visited Fort Knox in 1955 after the Korean War. The railroad traffic in Hardin County began to decline and was replaced with the commerce and the temporary residence of the soldiers at Fort Knox. The Nolin and Ohio Rivers, U.S. 31 West, the L&N, and the Fort Knox Military Reservation have kept a steady commercial flow in Hardin County. (Courtesy of Matthew Rector.)

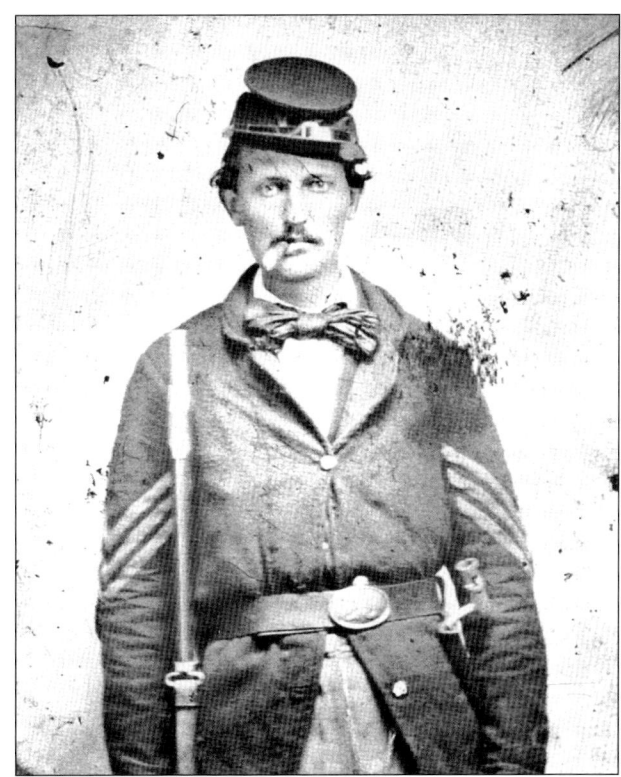

Pictured is Sgt. Charles Shane of the 28th Kentucky Infantry from the Civil War. In the 1880s, Captain Weller, an ex-Confederate soldier, was one of the 12 jurors that boarded at the Hill's Hotel for the trial of Will Showers, accused of the murder of his dear young wife. Captain William Franklin Bell, an ex-Confederate soldier who was part of the first national bank that was organized in Elizabethtown, married Mary F. Gray and then boarded at the Hill's Hotel after their marriage. (Courtesy of Matthew Rector and Richard Briggs.)

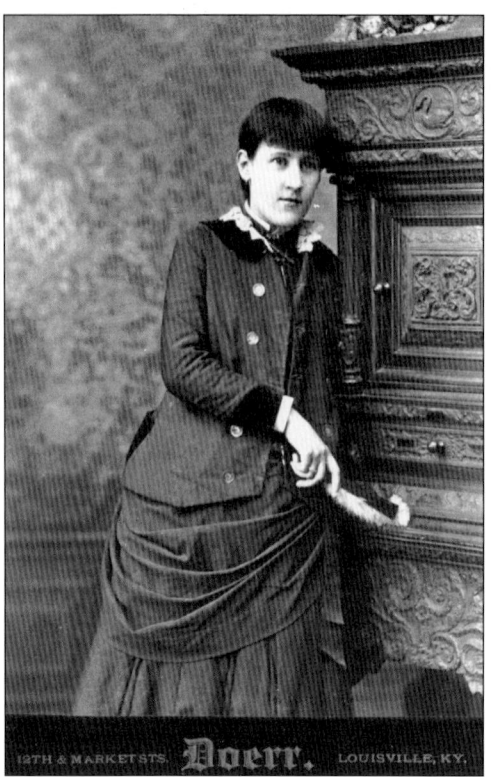

The lady pictured is Halbe Hall, but no other information is known. Many photographs in the Pusey Room Museum have unidentified names or unknown histories. This is the case around the world. Family members recognize the photographs for only a small time period. Visit your relatives and gather precious family memories and facts before they are gone forever. (Courtesy of Brown-Pusey House.)

This unidentified lady had her photograph taken in the 19th century. Many photographs are unidentified in a collection. Please take your photographs to a local archival facility to see if they can assist you in identifying the people or the surroundings. Be sure to explain where you discovered the photographs and what you found with these items. Bring your family heritage to life by scrapbooks, genealogy trees, memory boxes, calendars, or a quilt. (Courtesy of Brown-Pusey House.)

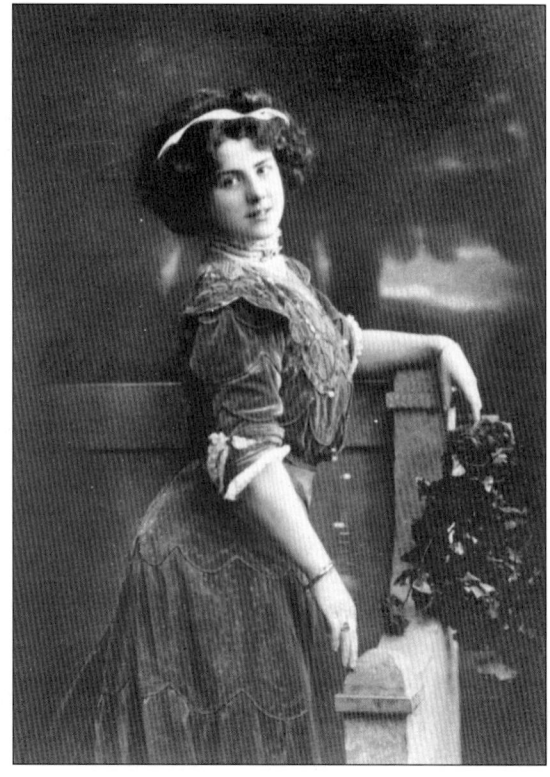